A Modern Plutarch

A MODERN
Plutarch

COMPARISONS OF THE MOST
INFLUENTIAL MODERN STATESMEN

Robert Lloyd George

Overlook Duckworth
New York • London

This edition first published in hardcover in the United States and the
United Kingdom in 2016 by Overlook Duckworth, Peter Mayer Publishers, Inc.

NEW YORK
141 Wooster Street
New York, NY 10012
www.overlookpress.com
For bulk and special sales, please contact sales@overlookny.com,
or write us at the above address

LONDON
30 Calvin Street
London E1 6NW
info@duckworth-publishers.co.uk
www.ducknet.co.uk

Copyright © 2016 by Robert Lloyd George
Maps by Roddy Murray

Cataloging-in-Publication Data is available from the Library of Congress
A catalogue record for this book is available from the British Library

Book design and typeformatting by Bernard Schleifer
Manufactured in the United States of America
ISBN US: 978-1-4683-1249-2
ISBN UK: 978-0-7156-5133-9

FIRST EDITION
1   3   5   7   9   10   8   6   4   2

For my ten children
Anglo-Americans all
Ricky, Alice, Julia, Alexander, Nicholas, Robert Owen,
David, Sophia, Elizabeth, and Isabella

Contents

We are the Greeks in this American Empire.

—HAROLD MACMILLAN

The world of man is best captured through the lives of the men who created history.   —PLUTARCH

Read no history, only biography, for that is life without theory.

—BENJAMIN DISRAELI

. . . whatsoever things are true, whatsoever things are honest, whatsoever things are just . . . whatsoever things are of good report; if there be any virtue, and if there be any praise, think on these things.   —PHILIPPIANS 4:8

━

Having determined to write the life of Alexander and of Julius Caesar, the multitude of the deeds to be treated is so great that I shall make no other preface than to entreat the reader in case I do not tell of all the famous actions of these men, nor even speak exhaustively at all in each particular case, but in epitome for the most part, *not to complain.* For it is not Histories I am writing, but Lives; and the most glorious deeds do not always reveal men's virtues and vices, indeed a small thing, a word or jest often makes a greater revelation of character than battles when thousands fall: so, just as painters get the likenesses in their portraits from the face and the expression of the eyes, wherein the character shows itself, but make very little account of the other parts of the body, so I must be permitted to devote myself rather to the signs of the soul in men, and thereby show the life, leaving to others to write the battles and other great things they did.

Lives of the Noble Greeks and Romans
compared by Plutarch

Preface

I WAS INSPIRED AT AN EARLY AGE BY VISITING THE SMALL AND MODEST museum in North Wales dedicated to the memory of my great-grandfather David Lloyd George, prime minister from 1916 until 1922. In the two-room stone cottage where he was raised by his uncle, the village cobbler Richard Lloyd, there is scant furniture: a table, some chairs, one bed. Over the fireplace, however, there is a portrait of Abraham Lincoln, taken from a newspaper of the time and framed. It presided over the boyhood of Lloyd George and inspired him, in turn, to qualify as a lawyer and then stand for his office, first as a member of Parliament, then in Cabinet and ultimately as prime minister. The story of Lincoln, who had risen from log cabin to White House was, I believe, one of the first instances of an American exemplar inspiring a British statesman.

Since 1976, when I first came to the United States, I have been fascinated by American history, particularly that of the Founding Fathers, about whom we know so little in Britain. In 1979 I was at the New York Society of Security Analysts, standing at the window looking over Trinity Churchyard with Robert O. Anderson, Chairman of Atlantic Richfield, who was the largest landowner in the United States at the time. He looked down into the churchyard and said, "There lies, I believe, the greatest of all the founding fathers." "Excuse me, sir, who?" I asked. "Alexander Hamilton." I knew scarcely anything about Hamilton at the time but have since read everything I can lay my hands on, and realized he was one of the great thinkers and decisive figures in the early years of the republic. That year I made my first visits to Mount Vernon, Monticello and Hyde Park. Later, when I traveled to California at the end of 1979 and came to the Getty Roman villa in Malibu, based on the Pompeiian original, I thought: This is AD 79 as well as 1979; Hollywood is Pompeii, and America is the Roman Empire; and I am a visiting Old World historian just as that early biographer, the Greek Plutarch, was in Rome.

I have written this book for several reasons: first, for my children, who have a dual Anglo-American heritage, so that they may read, in Matthew Arnold's words, "the best that has been said and done" by the outstanding statesmen of Britain and America in the past two hundred years. I hope that they will be inspired by the protagonists I have selected. As Plutarch demonstrated in his *Lives of the Noble Greeks and Romans*, there are lessons to be learned from the lives of great men and a purpose to be discerned in them. Secondly, I have tried to write sketches of some of the American figures who are less well known to my fellow countrymen in Britain, many of whom are as ignorant of American history and its titans as I was.

Over the last forty years, I have read extensively in the biographies and studies of the American and British figures whom I have chosen. Two themes in particular emerged in writing about the 1770s especially and the founding of the American Republic: one was slavery and the attitudes of various leaders towards the "peculiar institution." I have therefore included William Wilberforce, John Quincy Adams, Lord Mansfield, and John Marshall; but it also deeply involved Washington, Jefferson, Madison, Lincoln and Lee. The other theme is the French Revolution of 1789, as supporters as disparate as Jefferson and Fox on the one hand, and opponents like Burke, Hamilton and Pitt on the other, reacted to the Revolution and, subsequently, the Terror and Napoleonic dictatorship.

I have tried to highlight, by means of quotation and anecdote, the characters of leading men and women. I have drawn heavily on existing biographies and, where they are lacking, on general sources.

I am not trying to rewrite history or do original research. I am trying to create original comparisons of important figures in order to throw fresh light on their character and actions, as Plutarch did 2,000 years ago. The originality of this book lies not in the facts themselves but in the pairings, the parallels and comparisons that are based on Plutarch's ancient model. In the pairs that I have selected for these modern "parallel lives," I have tried to find common threads in figures who had the same professions or followed like paths or lived through similar times, especially those parallels which may illustrate some facet of their characters that may not have been highlighted before.

The body of the book is devoted to statesmen and generals, but I have also included thinkers and lawmakers. I had planned to compare Washington to Oliver Cromwell, but it was Wellington's descendant the ninth duke who persuaded me that his ancestor was a much better match. There are many other comparisons that I have considered and rejected and characters whom I would have liked to include – John Adams, Ulysses S. Grant and Eisenhower among a few presidents left out. Of course, it is somewhat of a parlor game, and many readers may disagree with my pairings. But that is part of the challenge and fun of this book – everyone will have a different view as to who are the most significant figures and with whom they might be compared.

I have approached history through the character and background of its greatest leaders. One of the most revealing aspects of their lives is, I believe, their home and family life. For this reason, I have appended to the book a short tour of the relevant birthplaces and museums in both the United States and the United Kingdom. In the U.S. in particular, to visit the places they came from – Washington's Mount Vernon, Jefferson's Monticello, and FDR's Hyde Park, to name but three – grants us insight into their family life, and illuminates our understanding of what they believed.

A Modern Plutarch

Introduction

A MODERN PLUTARCH TAKES ITS INSPIRATION FROM THE "FATHER of biography" Lucius Mestrius Plutarchus, known as Plutarch, who lived from about AD 42 to 120 in the Greek province of Boeotia. He visited Rome many times and may have lived there for several years. He was a tutor to the Roman emperor Trajan and respected as a professor and philosopher who wrote on the subject of morality. But his greatest work has always been considered to be the *Lives of the Noble Greeks and Romans*, in which he chose a pair of statesmen, one Greek, one Roman – founders, law-givers, soldiers, orators and even villains – wrote short biographies of each, and then compared the pair. His subjects lived in different eras and had different cultural backgrounds; but whatever greatness they achieved, the parallels he draws are based on small incidents that he believed revealed their true nature. What interested Plutarch (and, of course, inspired his subsequent reader William Shakespeare) were the tragic flaws in characters like Julius Caesar, Mark Antony or Coriolanus that, magnified by power, led to their downfall.

Before the modern era there was little interest in biography, though much in heroes, myths and legends. Our natural curiosity about individual personality was born of the Renaissance; the author whose influence nourished this new art of biography was Plutarch. Shakespeare's was an age of kings and philosophers, "Renaissance men" and powerful statesmen and courtiers, and it was to the *Lives* that writers like Shakespeare owed their most memorable classical characterizations: Julius Caesar, Coriolanus, Mark Antony, Brutus, Pompey, Cicero, Pericles and Timon.

When Plutarch wrote his *Lives*, he looked at imperial Rome from the position of a Greek philosopher living in a relatively obscure province of Northern Greece. Greece had been a galaxy of city-states, whereas Rome was always a unified power expanding outward like a force of nature. Greece had only briefly been a world power (in the aftermath of Alexander), but its influence stemmed from as far back as fifth-century-BC Athens: it was essentially a cultural influence rather than an imperial tradition.

It did not appear bold to the Romans to compare their statesmen with the ancient heroes of Greek history or legend – was not Roman art and literature saturated with Greek exemplars? Did they not use Greek as a fashionable literary and philosophical language? Like nineteenth-century Russians speaking French among themselves in society, they were conscious of a cultural inferiority despite the fact that they had conquered the entire Mediterranean world, including Greece. The only literary critics who may have bridled at Plutarch's consideration of Roman generals and orators as parallels to Pericles, Demosthenes and Alexander, were his fellow Greek philosophers. We have no evidence of this but we do know that Plutarch dedicated his *Lives* to a Roman patron (the consul Quintus Socius Senecio). Clearly Plutarch's task was in part to glorify the great Roman figures of the previous 200 years by comparing them with earlier Greek heroes.

Plutarch, though a moralist, is an honest historian. He never forces the parallels. The lives are written to stand on their own, and, where the comparisons have survived, they are brief. His plan may have included a whole series of Roman emperors, leading up to Trajan, his contemporary and patron. His surviving pairs are:

> the legendary founders Theseus and Romulus,
> the law-givers Solon and Publicola,
> the generals Pericles and Fabius,
> the great failures Alcibiades and Coriolanus,

the consuls Pelopidas and Marsellus,
the soldiers Cimon and Lysander,
the conquerors Alexander the Great and Julius Caesar,
the tribunes or demagogues Agis and Cleomines, and Tiberius
and Caius Gracchus,
the Greek orators Demosthenes and Cicero,
the libertines Demetrius and Mark Antony, and
the tyrannicides Dion and Brutus.

It is notable that the Greek lives are weightier, better researched and usually appear to benefit from the comparison. But the Roman lives, such as those of Antony, Coriolanus and Brutus, have proved more enduringly popular from Renaissance to modern times. Roman history is easier to assimilate and makes more popular drama. There are more rags-to-riches statesmen (e.g. Sulla, Marius), civil-war heroes (Caesar, Pompey), civil-rights leaders (the Gracchi, Brutus), dictators (Coriolanus), martyrs (Cicero) and libertines (Antony) – the entire cast of characters necessary, in fact, to illustrate the political history of a state, to teach lasting lessons about the dangers of tyranny or the excesses of democracy. Why else have Plutarch's *Lives* lasted so well? Apart from Shakespeare, they were an influence on Rousseau, the leading *philosophe* of the French Revolution, and, of course, Napoleon; each age can find in them reflections of its own political situations and protagonists. And most interestingly, Plutarch deeply influenced Madison, Hamilton, and Jay, the three authors of *The Federalist*, the anonymous 1787 essays that so deeply affected the making of the U.S. Constitution.

The lives of historical figures owe so much to their background and circumstances, to the times in which they lived and the national traditions that nourished their ideas, that any comparison between different nations and centuries must appear superficial or audacious. Britain and the United States are, however, somewhat unusual in the family of nations: apart from the self-conscious rhetoric of a "special relationship" between transatlantic "cousins," there is the underlying truth that their culture reflects a shared inheritance.

The more closely we examine the worlds of Greece and Rome, the more does the ancient model illuminate our modern equivalent of Britain and the United States. Perhaps like the Romans, "the unique experience of a built-in empire [makes] it especially difficult for Americans to understand the conditions of other less fortunate people, and for others to understand America as well." American presidents are today the popular figures once represented by Roman consuls and emperors. Not only do they have the power and prestige, they have demonstrated a similar range of virtues and vices, from the nobility of a Washington to the tragic fall of Nixon. Hence the interest in the smallest biographical details that stimulates our modern industry of writing "lives." Plutarch would not have been wholly amazed: he had an instinct about what was attractive to his readers and what was revealing about character; he understood the power of the anecdote, its insight into a great man's strengths or foibles.

The American Revolution began in as unpromising conditions as had the English Revolution. In 1640, the English Parliamentarians were reluctant to fight their king but they had an idea for which to fight, as did the Americans 136 years later. The men in Independence Hall, Philadelphia, in July 1776, were sober lawyers, farmers, clergymen – not in any accepted sense "revolutionaries." The enthusiasm of Jefferson, Franklin, and Adams was for liberty and some political ideas from the "age of reason" that would have surprised their puritan forebears.

Like the English Parliamentarians, this group of reluctant rebels is alive to us today because we understand and sympathize with their grievances. They had justice on their side and, more importantly, they won and so became the founders of much of our modern political thinking. Of course, individual freedom of political thought or expression also means the ability to influence the course of events by eloquence, force of character and action.

Ours is an age of both democratically elected politicians and dictators. The twentieth century saw the best and worst of them: Roosevelt and Churchill; Hitler and Stalin. But during the last few decades there has been a retreat from the cult of personality. The myths of leaders have been broken, their private faults and weaknesses exposed. The biographer today is subject to no holds barred, no restricted areas upon which he cannot freely trespass. Why, therefore, this continuing desire for strong leaders?

The character of a statesman assumes a particular importance in times of national crisis. The power of a modern American president does not alter the basic principle involved here: the reactions of a Pitt, a Lincoln or a Churchill to the challenges of war, and the character of the leadership that such men reveal in their actions, is the nub of the matter. This elusive "character" (what Tom Wolfe called "the right stuff") is the result of youthful formation and the individual's response to the political situation of his lifetime. (Power, of course, magnifies flaws as well as strengths of character.)

Tolstoy thought the individual was insignificant in the face of huge natural forces; that the mass movement of people mattered more than anything the generals did. He ridiculed the idea that Napoleon's cold could have affected the Battle of Borodino. Marx thought that economic forces shape the behavior of individuals. Neither was well placed to take account of entirely free individuals acting in the spontaneous or disinterested tradition of Britain or America.

Emerson said, "There is properly no history; only biography." I have certainly become increasingly convinced that the key to modern history is the influence of great personalities and, at turning points in history – in war and peace – the judgment that they brought to the great decisions required. What interests me are the questions of what inspired this man or woman to go into public life? What might be the turning point in his or her career? How did they overcome adversity? What created their determination to succeed? What made them great?

Although I met Macmillan, the only one of my subjects whom I had the opportunity to interview was Margaret Thatcher, and I confess I had some difficulty getting her to answer my questions. She died in 2013. I have since then taken the view that it is too soon to write about living statesmen; the verdict of history must wait until some time after their passing.

For the time being, I second Plutarch's introduction to his *Life of Timoleon*:

> When I first took up the writing of these *Lives*, I did it for the sake of others, but now I find I have grown fond of the task and continue it for my own pleasure. The reason is that it allows me to treat history as a mirror, with the help of which I can adorn my own life by imitating the virtues of the men whose actions I have described. It is as though I could talk with the subjects of my *Lives* and enjoy their company every day, since I receive each one in turn, welcome him as my guest, observe with admiration as Priam did of Achilles 'what was his stature, what his qualities' and select from his career those events which are the most important and the most inspiring to record. As Sophocles has written, 'What greater joy could you attain than this?' And what could do more to raise the standards by which we live?

In this book I have tried to emphasize in every chapter the importance of visiting the homes of the great historical figures whom I describe. The reader's imagination and his understanding of the human being behind the great historical name will be enlarged by actually moving around the rooms inside the boyhood home of the prime minister or president. Sometimes it is the small details, such as the cobbler's bench in my great grandfather's boyhood home at Llanystumdwy, where his uncle, working on a pair of shoes, used to jot down bible quotations and thoughts during the day; or at Hyde Park, New York, where FDR's wheelchair is still to be seen. It is interesting to reflect that even in the 1930s, very few people in America realized that their president was, in fact, crippled, because he was never seen in public or in photographs except standing up.

Washington's house at Mount Vernon near Washington, D.C., is a unique experience, emphasizing Washington's concern about the appearance of his house, and the grand squirearchial image which he wished to convey. (As well as the prominence and extent of the slave quarters behind the main house.)

So, too, Jefferson's Monticello enables one to come into personal contact with Jefferson's quirky, but original, genius. He has been described as a kind of "American Leonardo da Vinci." However many times one visits Monticello, one is always struck anew by some detail of the architecture or domestic arrangements, all of which were imagined by Thomas Jefferson himself.

Some of the other characters in this book, like Franklin, Hamilton, or the Virginians, Marshall, Madison, and Monroe, all aspired to the image created by Washington and Jefferson but lived in simpler and less imposing surroundings. This is even more true in the modern age when one travels to the Midwest to see Lincoln's simple square-framed house in Springfield, Illinois, or Harry Truman's home at Independence, Missouri.

I have also described some of the less well-known British homes and museums, such as William Wilberforce's house and The Museum of Slavery in South Yorkshire. In some cases there are no physical remains or homes to evoke the Plutarchian spirit, but we have added a detailed map of the USA and the UK to show all the possible homes that can be visited.

Just as Camp David became the retreat of the American presidents starting with Eisenhower (he named it in honor of his father and grandson, both named David), in 1921 Lord Lee of Fareham, an American who had become a naturalized British citizen in the First World War, donated his beautiful country home, Chequers, as a weekend retreat for the British prime minister in office. As it happened, the first one to benefit from this extraordinarily generous gift was David Lloyd George, who, unlike all his predecessors – most of whom were wealthy or aristocratic, with their own country houses – had no such home. It was, indeed, at the end of the First World War, a wonderful retreat from the pressures of 10 Downing Street and the stresses of London.

The Duke of Wellington   George Washington

CHAPTER 1

The Duke of Wellington and George Washington

❧

The Duke of Wellington

A battle is like a ball. Everybody sees something. Nobody sees everything.

An extraordinary affair. I gave them their orders and they wanted to stay and discuss them! [at his first cabinet meeting]

ARTHUR WESLEY – HIS BROTHER RICHARD WOULD LATER CHANGE the spelling to Wellesley – was born in County Meath, Ireland, on May 1, 1769, just over three months before the birth of Napoleon. He was the third of five surviving sons of the Earl of Mornington, a member of the Anglo-Irish ruling class. Wellesley always denied he was Irish, saying, "Sir, because a man is born in a stable it does not make him a horse." Richard Wellesley would describe their parents as "frivolous and careless personages" and, in fact, they were too busy frittering away the earl's inheritance to pay much attention to their sons, sending them off to public school – in Arthur's case, Eton – and then ignoring them.

By the time Arthur was eighteen, he had still not settled on a career. It is said that his mother spotted him at a London theater one night and confided to her companion, "I do believe there is my ugly boy, Arthur. What can I do with him?" She arranged a commission for him in the infantry. After short service in Ireland, Wellesley went to India. There his career really began, at the age of 27. He had saved his money, managed to purchase a colonelcy (until the Crimean War,

British officers could buy their commissions), and he thrived. He was not a typical British officer, who spent their days gaming, playing polo (although Wellesley was an excellent horseman), and drinking. Instead, the slim, austere young man – who might have been handsome except for what one historian has called "an astonishingly large and ugly proboscis" – read books on philosophy and military strategy and awaited his chance to distinguish himself in combat.

That chance came in 1799, as the British sought to conquer the state of Mysore. Leading the 33rd Indian Army Regiment, plus thousands of sepoys (native Indian troops), Wellesley captured Tipu, the fortress of the Sultan of Mysore, killed him, and seized treasure valued at over £1,100,000. The British government rewarded Wellesley by making him governor of Mysore and giving him £4,000 from Tipu's treasury. The young man was on his way.

Four years later, on September 23, 1803, on India's Deccan plateau, Wellesley's army of 7,000 expected to find 20,000 Marathi infantry, but instead found itself faced by the entire Marathi Army, numbering some 50,000 and accompanied by vastly more cavalry. Wellesley personally led the infantry charge against the Marathi guns, almost 100 of which were captured. In the words of one volunteer in the 78th, "I never saw a man so cool and collected."

Arthur Wellesley had arrived in India, still only thirty-six years old, with very little to show for himself. When he returned home, in 1805, it was as a major-general and a Knight of the Order of Bath, a figure of national renown in England. (At the same age, Napoleon had made himself the Emperor of France.) His first order of business was to marry the wealthy Kitty Pakenham, who had rejected his first marriage proposal in 1793. Conscious of his newfound prestige and reputation, Wellesley had proposed to her long-distance from India. To his dismay, she was no longer the young and glamorous London society girl he remembered, having aged quickly. Honor demanded that he go through with his proposal but theirs was an unhappy and distant marriage, the strains of which Wellesley relieved by seeking outside female companionship.

In May, 1808, there was a popular uprising in Spain against the French, which Wellesley argued could be turned to British advantage. In June, he was ordered to command a force assembling in Cork for an attack on the Peninsula. In July, Wellington's expeditionary force of 9,000 sailed for Portugal. On arrival he received word that 15,000 men under the command of Sir Hew Dalrymple, the Governor of Gibraltar, would join him. Wellesley decided to seek out the French before he lost his command to Dalrymple. On August 17th he got his wish when he encountered the French at Roliça and drove them back.

Once Wellington was appointed Marshal-General of Portugal, he used his position to mobilize every able-bodied male in the country for defense. He ordered all the inhabitants of the districts in the French army's path to fall back towards Lisbon and take their goods and cattle with them. Wellington's order showed an understanding of the weakness of the French, who sacrificed the weight of food and other supplies for speed. His order was also one of the few examples of scorched-earth warfare in nineteenth-century Europe, and it caused Napoleon to remark, "Only two men have the necessary ruthlessness to carry out an operation like that, myself and Wellington."

Wellington stormed Ciudad Rodrigo in January, 1812, and was appointed an earldom. By this point, the tide had turned in Spain, he was receiving reinforcements, and, more importantly, his men were confident of victory. While the French still greatly outnumbered the British on the Peninsula, they were broken up by its geography and the difficulties of finding forage for their soldiers.

By the spring, Wellington was in command of 100,000 soldiers, including 55,000 Britons, 31,000 Portuguese, and 21,000 Spaniards. He routed the French at the Battle of Vitoria in June, 1813, and in October he invaded France. In April, 1814, Napoleon abdicated.

After having been given the title the Duke of Wellington, he entered Paris on May 4th, and once returned to England he was showered with honors: the Commons voted him £400,000 for the purchase of an estate.

Following Napoleon's escape from Elba in March, 1815,

Wellington was placed in charge of the allied forces in the Netherlands. By May, he had 68,000 men in Belgium and was waiting for and additional 70,000 Prussian troops under the command of General Blucher, whose mission was to capture and execute Napoleon. In June, Napoleon moved north with the objective of capturing Brussels and preventing Blucher and Wellington linking up to form an army that would greatly outnumber the French. On June 16th, in a stunning victory, Napoleon defeated Blucher's forces at Ligny, driving them back.

On the morning of June 18th, near the Belgian village of Waterloo, the Allies and the French faced each other on a piece of farmland two miles wide and about two-thirds of a mile across. On the north side, drawn up along and behind a ridge, was the Army of the Netherlands, an Anglo-Belgian-Dutch force of 68,000 men (only 28,000 were British) led by the Duke of Wellington. On the other side was Napoleon Bonaparte with an army of just over 72,000, some of whom were from his Grand Army of the old days, but many of whom were old men or raw recruits.

Now, finally, Napoleon and Wellington were to face each other in combat. Wellington was 46 years old, Napoleon 45. Both had begun their military career young, had studied military history, and gained battlefield experience in India and Italy, respectively. The two rivals had, however, developed vastly differing command styles.

Wellington, who went into battle in a civilian grey frock coat, was always present on the front lines and accorded very little responsibility to staff officers. "There is nothing I dislike so much," he said, "as those extended operations which I cannot direct myself." Unable to delegate, Wellington was a constant presence at the forefront of the battlefield in the crossfire, leading to numerous horses being shot out from under him and at least one battle wound that left him bedridden for a week. "I began to feel as if God has his finger on me," he once said. However, his men loved him for sharing their dangers – they called him "Old Hookey" or "Old Nosey" for his outsized nose – and had supreme faith in him.

Napoleon, while certainly brave and not averse to personal risk in combat, was more of a theorist – he drew up his battle plans and expected his subordinates to carry them out. To many of his veterans, he was a god-like figure. But after twenty years of military success, he had become too arrogant to bother to study Wellington's command style, sneeringly calling him "the Sepoy General." As morning dawned on June 18th, the emperor, eating breakfast off a silver plate, said the battle would be *"facile comme manger le petit dejeuner"* (in other words, a picnic). His main concern appeared to be to capture Wellington.

Wellington despised Napoleon's speeches to his troops, something in which he (and British officers generally) never indulged, saying they were "false heroics," the "stuff of players." Wellington deployed his forces as he did best, namely in a defensive formation. Napoleon mounted a series of uncoordinated attacks in the center but Wellington's flanks held until the afternoon, when the arrival of the Prussians ensured the outcome of the day.

The Battle of Waterloo secured Wellington's reputation on the Continent and in November, 1815, he used his newfound political leverage to put the Bourbons back on the throne in France. He was given the post of master-general of the ordnance, which gave him a kind of "non-partisan" seat on the Cabinet, but it was inevitable that a man of his profile would come to wield political clout, and by 1824 he had emerged as a rival to foreign secretary Canning.

Given his military (rather than political) background and experience, Wellington was a natural authoritarian. In January, 1828, the King asked him to form an administration. After some high-profile resignations from the Cabinet, Wellington employed two of his old staff officers from the Peninsula (Sir George Murray and Sir Henry Hardinge). All of this strengthened impressions of a militaristic administration. In *A History of the English-Speaking Peoples*, Churchill wrote:

Wellington's military view of politics had led him to overawe his critics by a characteristic challenge to a duel. Lord Winchilsea had overstepped the bounds of decorum in an attack

upon the Prime Minister in the House of Lords, accusing
Wellington of dishonesty. A full-dress challenge followed ...
The Field-Marshal, now aged sixty, was almost nonchalant,
slow and deliberate in his movements. This was much more his
line than smoothing the susceptibilities of politicians, or, as he
once put it in a moment of complaint, "assuaging what gentlemen call their feelings." Turning to his second, who was also
his Secretary at War, he said, "Now then, Hardinge, look sharp
and step out the ground. I have no time to waste. Damn it!
don't stick him up so near the ditch. If I hit him he'll tumble
in." Neither party was wounded, and Winchilsea signed a
paper withdrawing his insinuations.

Wellington introduced a bill to emancipate the Catholics, and then
stoically endured all the abuse and scorn poured upon him. His influence was especially important in carrying the Catholic Relief Act
through the Lords; he could always be relied on to tell the Lords
bluntly and honestly when they had to fall in line.

The Whigs considered Wellington unspeakable – the recent introduction of the Metropolitan Police in London (really Peel's idea)
was held up as evidence Wellington intended to impose an authoritarian regime. On November 22nd, 1830, following a grave defeat in
the Commons, he retired from office and was succeeded by Lord Grey,
who introduced the Great Reform Bill. Wellington was widely regarded as an extreme reactionary and was a prominent opponent of
reform during the debates on the bill.

In subsequent years, Wellington preferred to remain out of office. When the Grey administration was dismissed in 1834, Wellington
took the role of head of the government only until Robert Peel could
return from Italy; in 1839, when the Melbourne Government fell for
about six weeks, young Queen Victoria wanted to send Wellington,
but he requested that she send for Peel.

When asked a question Wellington did not wish to answer, he
had a habit of saying, "Ha!" Gladstone, who heard this in 1836,

noted that "Ha!" was "a convenient *suspensive* expression." Asked for advice, he could be unforthcoming: "Sir, you are in a devilish awkward predicament, and must get out of it as best you can." His golden rule was: "There is only one line to be adopted in opposition to all tricks: that is the steady, straight line of duty, tempered by forbearance, levity, and good nature." He lived simply to the last. General Ayala, his valet who traveled back and forth to Vienna with him, said, "The two English phrases I got to hate most were 'early start tomorrow' and 'cold meat.'"

—

George Washington

The time is now at hand which must probably determine whether Americans are to be freemen or slaves. The fate of unborn millions will now depend, under God, on the courage and conduct of this army.   —address to the Continental Army before the Battle of Long Island, August 27th, 1776

My ardent desire is, and my aim has been, to comply strictly with all our engagements, foreign and domestic; but to keep the United States free from political connections with every other country, to see them independent of all and under the influence of none.   —letter to Patrick Henry, October 9, 1775

IN THE 1750s THERE WAS A COLD WAR BETWEEN BRITAIN AND FRANCE, which, like the Cold War of the 1950s between America and the Soviet Union, only flared into conflict on the frontiers, often with proxy participants. On the western frontier of the United States, beyond the Allegheny Mountains, there was a quiet and unreported struggle for control of the Ohio River Valley, which also involved Indian tribes and the colonial militia. Washington's military career began as a messenger for Virginia's governor Robert Dinwiddie. London ordered Dinwiddie to send a message to the French, demanding that they clear out of British territory or be forcibly ejected. Washington sought and won the assignment to deliver the message. Despite his inexperience, he was considered to be an expert of the western wilderness, where he had done some land surveying. He delivered the message, gathered the news that the French refusal to withdraw, and returned after three months. The foray generated public recognition and within a few months he was appointed lieutenant-colonel and second-in-command of Virginia's troops.

The future messenger was born on February 22nd, 1732, to Augustine and Mary Ball Washington. Though their eldest child, George had several older half-siblings from Augustine's previous marriage. At eleven, George's father died, and George went to Mount Vernon to live with his older half-brother Lawrence and his wife Anne Fairfax. Lawrence and Anne's father, William Fairfax, became George's teachers and role models. His ambition as a boy was to be an affluent country gentleman, and he was brought up in the same English fashion as his forebears were in Lincolnshire. Indeed, his great ambition as a young man had been to visit the mother country. He admired all things English, except the treatment of the American colonies, which he thought stupid and ignorant as well as immoral.

George's education gave him skills in land surveying and in July, 1749, at 17, he became the surveyor of Culpepper County. Though unusual for a 17-year-old to hold such a post, he probably got the job because of his close ties to the Fairfaxe family (the county lay within Lord Fairfax's ownership). In October, 1750, when he was only 18, George bought his first plantation and became a landowner.

By this time, Washington was a strong six foot three, very tall for his day. Lafayette said, "He had the largest pair of hands I have ever seen in a man." Already he stood out. To further his social prospects, George joined the Masonic Lodge in Fredericksburg. By 1753, he owned 2,500 acres, had achieved the title of Master Mason, and sought military involvement like his elder brother Lawrence.

In the spring of 1754, Washington and his regiment set out into the disputed territory. While waiting for the arrival of his superior,

Colonel Fry, Washington learned of the approach of a small enemy party. Washington and his men ambushed the intruders and killed or captured the majority, including Joseph de Jumonville. The surviving French claimed Jumonville had come on a diplomatic embassy and criticized the Virginians for attacking the ambassador and his retinue. Known as the Jumonville affair, French propagandists later used the event to blame the war on the British. However, global tensions would have erupted with or without the clash, and the incident brought Washington local praise and adulation.

Washington played a leading role in two expeditions into the wilderness where the British Red Coats found the conditions unfamiliar and hostile. Washington begged them to fight in the same way that the Indians fought, only to be ignored. The British General Braddock lost his life in an Indian ambush in which Washington was the only officer who survived. Washington had to lead his troops back on a long journey over the mountains to Virginia.

His early military experiences on the frontier were the crucial factor in making Washington "the indispensable man" to lead the revolutionary army. He won respect and admiration among the local community of Virginia but little recognition from the British, who refused to make him a regular officer. His resentment of the British may have begun at this time. He was also, of course, a Virginian plantation owner who lived in perpetual debt to his London-based factor and soon gave up growing tobacco in favor of growing wheat and corn for the local market.

After retiring from the military, in January, 1759, George married a wealthy widow and mother of two, Martha Dandridge Custis. This established Washington, who at last a large landowner, as a man of prominence in Virginian society, and he took his first seat in the Virginia Assembly on his 27th birthday, in February 1759. During his first four years in the House, he remained in the background, quietly learning about politics. Washington twice won re-election and, by the summer of 1774, had become a respected figure in Virginia politics as well as society. As one of Virginia's seven delegates to the First Continental Congress, Washington traveled to Philadelphia in the spring of 1775. With tensions building towards the War of Independence, Congress voted to raise companies of armed men, the "American Continental Army," and Washington was asked to head the committee to draw up regulations for it. On June 16th, Washington appeared before Congress in his uniform and accepted the supreme command of the newly formed American forces.

On the subject of pay, Washington said: "I beg leave to Assure the Congress that, as no pecuniary consideration could have tempted me to accept this arduous employment at the expense of my domestic ease and happiness, I do not wish to make any profit from it. I will keep an exact account of my expenses. Those, I doubt not, they will discharge, and that is all I desire." This is typical of the honest, modest, and public-spirited character that was to win him broad support and admiration both as a general and later, as president.

By refusing payment, the independently wealthy leader became the exemplar of a citizen-soldier. Because of discrimination against the provincials by the royally appointed regulars, Washington had suffered in his desire for promotion during the French and Indian War. As tensions mounted between Britain and the colonials, the military became a flashpoint for conflict. Washington also endeared himself to Congress and the public by adopting a deferential manner towards civilian authority. This helped dispel worries about a military dictatorship or his own possible ambitions.

Washington was conscious of his limited education, and this resulted in a diffidence that sweetened his use of power (Washington also cited this as the reason he never put his recollections of the Revolution on paper). It also forced him to learn from experience, an ability proven time and again by his growth as a military and later political leader. However, he constantly supplemented his practical experience with reading. He felt "a knowledge of books is the basis upon which other knowledge is built." He liked to collect and read books, pamphlets, periodicals, and other publications to bolster his knowledge of farming, history, society, literature, and politics.

At the time of the Revolution, he knew more about America than all but a handful of his fellow revolutionaries – and had an overwhelming sense of the potentialities of the country. To Washington, the interior, and especially the Mississippi Valley, the largest river system with the best agricultural land in the world, was America's future. He was, in a sense, the first believer in Manifest Destiny.

The Revolutionary War made Washington's fame, but these achievements arrived after a long, tortuous journey through disappointment, failure, and defeat. He was always outnumbered and fought a war of attrition. As a general, he was primarily a strategist rather than a battle commander. (Fabius, rather than Caesar. And he also laid down his sword to return to his plough.)

In September, 1783, Congress ratified the peace treaty in which Britain recognized the independence of the United States. By Christmas, Washington had disbanded the army, resigned his commission and returned home to Mount Vernon.

He threw himself into domestic tasks, attending to his plantation, family, and local affairs. He was always looking west and trying to acquire land in the wilderness, up to the Blue Mountains and beyond. In time, he became one of the largest landowners in Virginia, and by his exertions as a farmer-landowner, one of the richest men in America (his will shows him owning 96 square miles). Washington was a soldier and a general but also a squire and a plantation owner; one used to having his commands obeyed, but beneath it all a modest patriot.

Though he remained far from the center of national activity, he stayed in touch. When Shay's rebellion occurred in 1786, Washington feared the nation he had fought hard to secure would self-destruct. The crisis gave way to a constitutional convention to define and strengthen the disorganized government of the young Republic, and Washington reluctantly agreed to accept a position on Virginia's delegation to the Constitutional Convention in Philadelphia. At the end of the war, he had declared his public service officially over, and he feared what people might think of his reentering public affairs. However, after receiving encouragement from his friends, Washington left for Philadelphia, and on the opening day, May 25, 1787, he was unanimously elected president of the convention. The draft of a new constitution was signed in September, and the convention adjourned. In February, 1789, the Electoral College met for the first time and unanimously voted for Washington as the first president of the United States.

Washington, facing the daunting prospect of becoming the new nation's leader, established important precedents and set the tone and character of the high office. One of his challenges was how to act towards the public, how to interact with other branches of government, and even what was proper conduct towards old friends. He decided to set aside two times a week to receive the steady stream of people wishing to speak to him: a levee only for men held every Tuesday from 3 to 4 p.m., and his wife Martha's weekly tea party for both men and women on Friday evenings. To gather more information on the public's concerns, he set out on a tour of New England in October, 1789, and made a similar trip through the south two years later. He determined the role of his "Cabinet," a term borrowed from the British. It comprised Secretary of War, Henry Knox; Attorney General, Edmund Randolph; Secretary of State, Thomas Jefferson; and Secretary of the Treasury, Alexander Hamilton. He relied on Cabinet meetings to make important decisions. Washington especially valued the presence of what were developing into opposing political views in Jefferson and Hamilton. These discussions gave Washington a sense of the public's reaction to various policy decisions. Jefferson noted: "His temper was naturally irritable and high toned; but reflection and resolution had obtained a firm and habitual ascendancy over it. If ever, however, it broke its bonds, he was most tremendous in wrath."

Washington's self-control is remarked upon by a number of biographers. His diary contains the basic daily actions that filled his day, such as the weather, where he went, whom he saw, how he amused himself, illnesses, and death. He also filled his diary with details of his farming operations. But the man who cultivated self-control never spoke freely or emotionally in its pages. When he did, he wrote in cipher, using single letters to indicate happenings and emotions that remain mysterious secrets.

Washington relocated the capital to his beloved home state of Virginia. As an experienced land surveyor he chose the exact location of the new city and took an active role in planning its development. Though he hoped not to serve a second term, the Electoral College unanimously elected him again in 1793.

Washington's last public appearance was his eighth annual address, delivered on December 7, 1796, three months before the official end of a turbulent term. He welcomed retirement, yet he was soon recalled from the quiet pleasures of Mount Vernon. The US found itself in a quasi-war with France, and President John Adams nominated Washington Commander-in-Chief. Washington accepted the call of duty, on the condition that he could select his own staff, and set out from Mount Vernon on November 5, 1798. Tensions with France soon subsided thanks to French defeats in the European theater, and he returned home. In December, 1799, Washington complained of a sore throat, and after several days of unsuccessful bleedings and other medical ministrations, he died on December 14th at the age of 67. His will liberated his slaves and directed that all of them be freed after his wife's death. He had said, "I never mean, unless some particular circumstances should compel me to do it, to possess another slave by purchase, it being among my first wishes to see some plan adopted by which slavery in this country may be abolished by law." He was buried in his family vault at Mount Vernon.

Washington was the man who led America to victory. As its first president, he was the definitive founder of the United States, considered the indispensable man. He made the nation that emerged law-abiding, stable, and prosperous, as well as free.

COMPARISON OF THE DUKE OF WELLINGTON WITH GEORGE WASHINGTON

"I have always felt the highest respect for the character of General Washington," wrote the Duke of Wellington to Edward Everett, the American Minister. Wellington loved the story of Washington riding through a small town and overhearing a seven-year-old girl exclaim, "Why, he is only a man!" The General swept off his hat, bowed, and said, "Yes, miss, that's all I am."

Though Washington was an early, ambitious starter, while Wellington rose more gradually, both challenged orders to get ahead (Wellington at Rolica, Washington in the Jumonville affair). Both were able to use family connections for advancement. (Charges of nepotism dogged Wellington's early commissions and military career.) Both took pleasure in the company of clever women.

Wellington was one of the greatest soldiers Britain has ever produced and was certainly more comfortable as a soldier than a politician. Even as a politician he tended to command rather than persuade. Washington, the citizen-soldier, was a more limited battle commander, but he was lucky and successful. Both eventually entered the political world, and it was their military success that led them there. They accepted their jobs because of their sense of duty but were disinclined to re-enter politics once they had left.

Though not men of great eloquence, each man gave the impression of strength and leadership. Wellington had no desire for popularity, but nevertheless his policies proved enlightened. Lord Rosebery said of him: "He was willing to press any measure that might be considered necessary in the public interests without reference to his opinions." He pressed on, for instance, with Catholic emancipation, a cause of which he personally disapproved.

To many people, Napoleon is still seen as a hero and a genius, the author of the Code Napoleon – the legal system which still governs France and many other countries in Europe. But the truth that history tells us is that Napoleon, like Hitler after him, was in the end an egomaniac and a dictator who sacrificed millions of lives in his quest for glory and to expand his empire. Wellington, like Washington, was "the indispensable man" without whom the British army and its allies could never have defeated the resurgent French dictator. When Washington died in 1799, his large acreage of Western lands alone made him almost the richest man in America, and he had a tenacious proprietorial instinct. Yet, being a surveyor of western lands as a young man, he always saw the potential for land development in Virginia and beyond. Washington was compared to Cincinnatus, the Roman farmer turned general, who reluctantly led his men to victory and then went back to the plough. (The Society of the Cincinnati is still an influential group in the USA.)

To this day, a portrait of Washington hangs at Stratfield Saye, the home of the Wellesleys. The present Duke has said that his ancestor had a great admiration for the first US President, who was, in many ways, a man like himself, a country squire, gruff, and taciturn, but with a strong sense of duty and patriotism.

William Penn

Brigham Young

CHAPTER 2

William Penn and Brigham Young

William Penn

I take history then to represent to us, as in a glass, the whole world at one view, or as if the dead were returned, to report to us the actions done in their time; it is a sort of pre-existence, making us to have always lived, or to have lived and had knowledge before we were born. For, by story, we at once see all ages together in their customs, governments, policies and declensions; a most edifying and profitable scene of life, to be the heirs of so much knowledge and experience, as this mighty view affords us.

—Penn in the foreword to *Memorials of the English Affairs* by Sir Bulstrode Whitelocke, 1709

IN 1682, WILLIAM PENN WAS GIVEN A VAST LAND GRANT BY KING James II that was to become Pennsylvania. What was unique and admirable about him – apart from the tenacity of his Quaker beliefs, for which he was imprisoned more than once – was the idealism and philanthropy he applied to his development of Philadelphia and the surrounding colony. Compared to the Puritans in Massachusetts or Rhode Island, he was more tolerant of different beliefs and has been described as the "first great hero of American liberty."

In the late 1600s when Protestants persecuted Catholics, Catholics persecuted Protestants, and both persecuted Quakers and Jews, Penn established an American sanctuary that protected freedom of conscience. In almost every other settlement, English colonists stole land from the Indians, but Penn traveled unarmed among the Indian tribes in Pennsylvania and negotiated peaceful purchases of land. He insisted that women deserved equal rights, and he established a written constitution in Pennsylvania that limited the power of government, provided a humane penal code, and guaranteed many fundamental liberties. The French philosopher Voltaire said, "William Penn might, with reason, boast of having brought down upon earth the golden age which never had any real existence but in his dominions."

Penn was born in 1644 to Admiral Sir William Penn and Margaret Jasper. He was a handsome young man and enjoyed horse racing and running. He grew up on an Irish estate during the Commonwealth of Cromwell and later attended Oxford University. When Penn was about 15, he met a Quaker missionary called Thomas Loe whose discourses on the "Inner Light" made a deep impression on him. Penn later recalled that "the Lord visited me and gave me divine impressions of himself."

Because of his father's position, young Penn was a Cavalier while an Oxford undergraduate at the time of the 1660 Restoration, but his sympathies lay with the Quakers. At Oxford he supported Dean Owen, who was sent down for his free-thinking views. Penn himself was fined by the university, and the Admiral sent him to Paris to "improve his manners." There, Penn was drawn to the French Protestant theologian Amyraut, who taught him religious tolerance. Although Penn developed a taste for fine clothes in France and was usually much better dressed than other Quakers, nothing would change his inner beliefs.

He studied law and then became his father's secretary in the Navy, often relaying messages between the King and the Admiral. The young Penn briefly became a soldier in 1666, when he was involved in suppressing an Irish rebellion, but his military career did not last long (nor did it agree with his Quaker convictions).

The Plague raged through London in 1665, and the Great Fire burned most of the city in 1666. These catastrophes confirmed Penn's deep sense of the vanity of the world, and he began to attend Quaker meetings again. At the age of 22, he publicly declared himself a member and joined the Society of Friends (Quakers) and was soon arrested (Anglicanism was the only religion accepted in England at the time). He pleaded that, unlike the Puritans, the Quakers had no political agenda, but was released from jail only because of his father's influence. The Admiral was distressed by his son's religious views, which made it difficult for him to win favor at Court. He felt he had no choice but to order his son out of the house and cut him off. Penn went to live with Quaker families, strict Christians who refused to bow or take off their hats to social superiors, believing all men equal under God – a belief at odds with the idea of monarchy and English society. They were called heretics because of these principles and their failure to pay tithes. They also refused to swear oaths of loyalty to the King, following the gospel of Matthew, Chapter 5, where Jesus said, "do not swear . . ."

Penn became a close friend of George Fox, the founder of the Society of Friends, whose movement had started in the 1650s. Fox had effectively abolished the Church's authority over his congregation, thus extending the rights of the individual. Penn later wrote an introduction to the journal of George Fox and became the leading defender of Quakerism. Following the publication of his pamphlet *Truth Exalted* in 1668, Penn was imprisoned in the Tower of London and charged with blasphemy. He was placed in solitary confinement and threatened with a life sentence. He responded, "My prison shall be my grave before I will budge a jot. I owe my conscience to no mortal man." He was released after eight months' imprisonment but showed no remorse.

Effectively exiled from English society, he was sent down from Oxford for being a Quaker, and arrested several more times. In 1670, he was accused of preaching in the street. During the trial, the judge directed the jury to come to a verdict without hearing the defense, but despite this, the jury returned with a verdict of "not guilty." They were sent to a jail cell for several nights to review their decision, but ultimately, they refused to change it. This was a groundbreaking case in which the members of the jury managed to win the right for all

English juries to be free from the control of judges. It was also an important influence on American jurisprudence, in particular the use of *habeas corpus* to free those detained unlawfully.

Penn's father died in 1671, but he had forgiven his son and come to respect his integrity and courage, telling him, "let nothing in this world tempt you to wrong your conscience." Before he died, the Admiral wrote to the Duke of York, the future James II, who promised to protect the young Penn and make him a royal counselor in recognition of his father's service to the crown.

In 1672, William Penn married and continued his Quaker missionary work in Holland and Germany. At that time, some Quakers had already moved to North America, and, in 1677, Penn purchased the colony of West Jersey (part of New Jersey). Penn pressed the King to extend the region of Quaker settlement, and, in 1680, the King granted a charter that made Penn the largest private landowner in the world with over 45,000 square miles of land south of New Jersey and north of Maryland. In return, one-fifth of all gold and silver mined in the province (not that there were mines) was to be remitted to the King, and the Crown would be absolved of a debt to Admiral Penn of £16,000. Penn first called the area New Wales, and then Sylvania – meaning the wooded country – which Charles II changed to Pennsylvania in honor of Admiral Penn. On March 4th, 1681, the King signed the charter; and the next day Penn jubilantly wrote, "It is a clear and just thing and my God who has given it to me through many difficulties will, I believe, bless and make it the seed of a nation."

Penn established the frame of government for the Pennsylvania colony, which granted absolute freedom of worship, as well as all of the traditional rights of Englishmen. He drafted a charter of liberties, including free and fair trial by jury, freedom of religion, freedom from unjust imprisonment, and free elections. The government would protect private property, free enterprise, and a free press. Whereas the 1680 English penal code specified the death penalty for 200 offenses, Penn reduced it to just two: murder and treason. He also insisted on low taxes and suspended all taxes for the first year (he had some difficulty collecting rent and taxes after that). He called it his "holy experiment" but also hoped to make it a profitable venture for his family without exploiting either the natives or the immigrants. "I would not abuse His love nor act unworthy of His providence and so defile what came to me clean."

Penn sailed to America on the ship Welcome, arriving on November 8th, 1682, and founding Philadelphia, the City of Brotherly Love, between the Delaware and Schuylkill rivers. Initially, he served as governor himself, and within six months he had parceled out 300,000 acres to over 250 prospective settlers, mostly wealthy London Quakers. He also attracted other persecuted minorities, including Huguenots, Mennonites, Amish, Catholics, Lutherans, and Jews from England, Wales, France, Holland, Germany and Scandinavia.

Penn returned to England in 1684 to see his family and resolve a territorial dispute with Lord Baltimore on the borders of Maryland. After 1688, with the accession of King William of Orange, Penn's situation at court deteriorated. His Stuart connections were cut off, his estate was seized, and he was arrested for treason. Penn became a fugitive for four years. His wife also died in 1694. He was, in fact, an unsuccessful businessman, and never earned enough from the colony to offset the costs of administration—which he paid out of his personal capital.

There were problems with the colony as well. He had delegated much of the administration to his fellow Quaker Phillip Ford, who embezzled substantial sums from Penn's estate and managed to fool him into transferring ownership of Pennsylvania to Ford – Penn had a careless habit of signing documents without reading them. This dispute went on until 1708, when the Lord Chancellor ruled that the equity of redemption still remained to William Penn and his heirs. Penn had returned to America for another visit in 1699 and stayed for two years, building Pennsbury Manor outside Philadelphia, and fathering an American-born son. In 1696, at the age of 50, he had married Hannah Callowhill, who was 23 at the time of their wedding. They had eight children in 12 years. Of Penn's 15 children, only seven survived to adulthood, a typical average for the time, and of those, only two appear to have had offspring. The family maintained ownership of Pennsylvania until the American Revolution.

Penn returned to England in 1701. He had hoped to have his eldest son, William, Jr., succeed him as governor of Pennsylvania, but William had led a dissolute life and had massive gambling debts as a result. Penn might have paid his son's debts had he not sunk over £30,000 into his American lands and received almost no return on investment. He had also made many generous loans that were never repaid. At the age of 62, Penn landed in debtor's prison. A wave of public sympathy and protest eventually reduced his punishment to house arrest. On his second attempt, in 1712, to sell Pennsylvania back to the Crown, he suffered a stroke, which left him unable to speak. He died penniless in 1718 and is buried in the cemetery of Jordan's Quaker Meeting House at Chalfont St. Giles in Buckinghamshire.

Though he did not achieve monetary success, Penn's ideals live on in the religious freedom now enjoyed all across the United States. He inspired Benjamin Franklin, Thomas Paine, and Thomas Jefferson, and consequently the American Constitution, which was drafted in Philadelphia. He is, therefore, one of the real fathers of modern American democracy.

Brigham Young

We shall need no commerce with the nations. I am determined to cut every thread of this kind and live free and independent, untrammeled by any of their detestable customs and practices.

—BRIGHAM YOUNG

A PIONEER OF THE AMERICAN WEST, BRIGHAM YOUNG BECAME the forceful, sometimes ruthless, leader of the Mormon Church. He also effectively founded and organized the settlement of Salt Lake City in the state of Utah in the 1850s.

The origin of the Mormons is a controversial topic. Joseph Smith

(1805–44) claimed, as a young man, to have been visited by the angel Moroni and given an account of the pre-Columbian history of North America. Moroni told Smith that Smith was the prophet of the Lord destined to redeem the world. He led the prophet to certain sheets of solid gold buried in a hillside near Palmyra, New York, on which were inscribed the Book of Mormon. Mormon, Moroni's father, had written in ancient Egyptian, but fortunately Smith, who had had only a minimal education, was granted angelic assistance to translate the ancient Egyptian into quasi-biblical English. The book was published in 1830, and Smith began organizing the Church of Jesus Christ of the Latter Day Saints, known to the rest of the world as the Mormons. Brigham Young was among his first converts and became the "Lion of the Lord," leader of the 12 Apostles. They introduced the practice of polygamy and adapted the new creed to the frontier society in which it had been born.

Mormons were extremely unpopular in New England and, subsequently, in Missouri, where they moved in the 1840s. This unpopularity stemmed not only from their financial success, but also because Mormons renounced their political rights and freedoms to the prophet, who told them how to vote. Their clashes with the "Gentiles" became increasingly violent and, in 1844, Joseph Smith was lynched in Missouri.

With great executive ability and an indomitable will, Brigham Young began to organize the journey of 16,000 saints to the safe refuge in the west that had been prophesied. They crossed the Mississippi River in the winter of 1846. Many died on the road, but Young ensured that they had supplies to survive the trek. When they reached Salt Lake City in July, 1847, he organized the town plan and irrigation system for about 5,000 "saints."

Joseph Smith had communed with God and his angels, but Young was more concerned with economic advantage. He ruled that rivers or timber belonged to all the people and would no longer be privately owned. Mormon families were organized into groups and required to contribute labor in proportion to the amount of land they wanted to water; the use of timber was regulated on the same principle. It was the most successful cooperative undertaking in the western states, managed with almost no outside capital.

Brigham Young was an unattractive character in many ways. As the prophet and governor of the Utah territory, he had authority similar to a big-city boss. He had an instinct for power and knew the surest means of getting it, wielding it, and cutting down rivals with it.

Despite their relocation, Mormons also continued to suffer from the aggression of the "Gentiles" and defended themselves by violent means. Young's use of violence was widespread; the most notorious episode was the Mountain Meadows Massacre of 1858, when a party of Mormons – commanded by one of Young's closest colleagues – slaughtered 120 Gentile men.

The population of Salt Lake City grew steadily from 11,000 in 1850 to 87,000 in 1870. The principal of stewardship on behalf of the kingdom of God – the fundamental Mormon tenet – made the practice of cooperation easy; the pursuit of prosperity was sanctioned by the duty to make the land fruitful; plain living was emphasized and alcohol, tea, and coffee were forbidden.

Young had organized a battalion of soldiers to participate in the US–Mexican War of 1848. But during the Civil War, Mormons, still led by Young, remained neutral, although they supported the idea of slavery. The divisive issue that separated Mormons from the rest of the country was polygamy. Brigham Young had 55 wives and 56 children.

Mormonism is one of the most effective Evangelical branches of Christianity today. It has spread and grown wealthy. Mitt Romney's candidacy for president in 2012 and the appointment of Jon Huntsman as US Ambassador to China demonstrate that the Church of Latter Day Saints is still a force to be reckoned with.

THE COMPARISON OF WILLIAM PENN
WITH BRIGHAM YOUNG

Penn and Young founded states and designed capital cities; they were both religious, Penn more sincerely so, apparently. In their states, both men sought to make a haven for their persecuted branch of Christianity. Penn was granted land for this purpose, while Young trekked west and staked his claim. Young was an outstanding organizer. Penn was more of an idealist.

One might say that Englishmen secured the early states on the eastern seaboard, and that homegrown Americans conquered the west. Today, Pennsylvania and Utah represent two extremes of the American Christian tradition.

William Pitt the Elder   Benjamin Franklin

CHAPTER 3

William Pitt the Elder, Earl of Chatham and Benjamin Franklin

William Pitt the Elder, Earl of Chatham

If you are in Parliament, show yourself on all occasions a good Englishman, and a faithful servant to your country. If you aspire to fame in the House, you must make yourself master of its precedents and orders ... Avoid faction, and never enter the House prepossessed; but attend diligently to the debate, and vote according to your conscience, and not for any sinister end whatever. I had rather see any child of mine want, than have him get his bread by voting in the House of Commons.

I am sure I can save this country, and nobody else can.

Unlimited power is apt to corrupt the minds of those who possess it.

THE BRITISH EMPIRE BEGAN WITH BUCCANEERS, NONE MORE audacious than Thomas "Diamond" Pitt, grandfather of Pitt the Elder. Thomas made his fortune in India in 1680 and acquired the most famous diamond on the subcontinent for £25,000. He later sold it to the French Dauphin for four times his cost. He achieved respectability as Governor of Madras and then returned to England, to the "rotten borough" of old Sarum, near Salisbury, where he bought a country estate and control of its parliamentary seat. It was for this constituency his grandson William entered parliament in 1735.

Thomas Pitt's temperament was volcanic. A brooding, solitary man, he dominated those around him with his personality. The stories he told his grandson William were meant to show how he had won his fortune by taking risks and violent, domineering action. Many of the traits that made his grandfather such a difficult but effective leader were evident in the career and personality of William.

William Pitt was born on November 15th, 1708, the second son of Robert Pitt, and while well brought-up, had few immediate prospects. Educated at Eton, he grew to hate the place, and refused to send his own children there. He attended Oxford in 1727, but left after a year, perhaps because he had already begun to suffer from the ailment – described at the time as "gout" or "lowness" – that was to afflict him all his life.

Between 1728 and 1730, Pitt attended the University of Utrecht. In 1731, a friend from Eton, George Lyttelton, introduced him to his uncle Richard Temple, the Viscount Cobham, a soldier who commissioned Pitt as a "cornet" in the cavalry regiment. Between 1731 and 1734, Pitt spent his time either in military camps or traveling the Continent, including France and Switzerland. In 1734, his older brother Thomas sent William to represent the family pocket borough of Old Sarum (Salisbury). In May, 1737, he lost his post in his regiment as a result of his opposition to the Prince of Wales. (Although in July the Prince of Wales made Pitt groom of his bedchamber, a post that paid £400 a year.)

Pitt sought to frustrate Prime Minister Robert Walpole, and helped bring him down in November, 1742, by which time he was well known for his eloquence and his willingness to annoy the king. In 1743, Sarah Duchess of Marlborough bequeathed £10,000 to Pitt, "on account of his merit, in the noble defence he has made for the support of the laws of England, and to prevent the ruin of his country."

Between 1744 and 1745, as ministry succeeded ministry, Pitt's future remained unstable. He deserved to be in office, and he desired it, but the King would not grant him a position. Matters did not improve when the Prince of Wales made peace with his father; Pitt resigned his household post with the Prince of Wales in 1745.

The following year, Pitt was made joint vice-treasurer of Ireland and became paymaster-general (neither of these posts required attendance on the King). It was here that Pitt began to be seen as a competent and honest administrator: the paymaster was generally delegated £100,000 by advance, for instance, which by custom was subscribed to a government security, a practice that returned £3,000 or more per annum to the lucky individual, but which left the army without funds (these being invested) when there was an emergency. Pitt scorned that practice and instead placed the money in a bank account. Another common practice was to skim half a percent or more off the top of subsidies that were paid by the Crown to other states, but Pitt refused to follow suit. One of his administrative reforms was to relieve the Chelsea Pensioners from moneylenders by paying them in advance rather than in arrears. Pitt applied himself to the drudgery of administration, and this ideal – of an honest and stable bureaucratic government serving the people – was quite a novel idea in the mid-eighteenth century.

In 1754 Pitt fell in love with Lady Hester Grenville, whose family was politically influential. He was 48, she was 34. They married on November 16th and produced five children.

During 1755, relations between Britain and France and Pitt called for war in America. He was immediately isolated in Parliament. Yet he was not isolated from the people: in the summer of 1756, the public was furious when Minorca was lost to the French. Pitt became Secretary of State in December, and planned to reinforce the American colonies and send ships to aid the East India Company.

Pitt's extra-European policy began to pay dividends. In 1758, Louisburg (commanding the St Lawrence) was won; Senegal and Gorée on the West African coast were also won; Quebec and Guadeloupe fell in 1759, and Martinique in 1762. These successes were facilitated by naval victories in 1759 that thwarted the French threat of invasion and established British naval supremacy. In India, the

East India Company won dominance in Bengal, the first time the Company had enjoyed a stable and secure position in India. Of all the creators of the British Empire none had the same far-sighted world strategy as Pitt. His grandfather's knowledge of India may well have played a part. He knew that India was the greatest source of wealth among Britain's overseas possessions. But he also understood the enormous potential and the future political complexity that lay in North America.

Pitt took personal charge of operations in America, moved offensive operations to the African coast and the West Indies, and was generous in his aid to the East India Company. He managed events down to the smallest detail, though he also left ample room for maneuvers on the ground to adapt when necessary.

The "Seven Years War" (or the "French and Indian Wars" as they are known in America) of 1756–63 saw the high point of Pitt's strategy with the great victories of Plassey and Quebec, securing both India and Canada for the British. Pitt, however, had no grand design. He wanted to settle matters with the French in North America; he wanted to preserve Britain's position in Europe. Pitt was also favored by systemic factors, such as an expanding population in Great Britain, and a robust fiscal system. But while every statesman responds to events, Pitt molded the national destiny to his will and his imperial vision. His drive and energy served him as well as his eloquence; he understood the nature of British interests and power better than anyone else. It was Pitt who wanted to drive France to the wall, understanding that this alone could bring Britain lasting security.

In 1761 Pitt demanded that Britain strike at Spain's annual treasure fleet from America. When this demand was denied, and Spain declared war after her treasure fleet had arrived, he resigned in disgust.

After some years of illness and political isolation, in January, 1766, Pitt returned to the Commons, and spoke forcefully against the Stamp Act in one of his legendary speeches. He condemned the

Act, not on grounds of expedience, but because the Commons did not represent North America, elucidating an enduring principle of liberty and government that is still cherished in the United States. Pitt's intervention also served as an advertisement that he was once again a force to be reckoned with on the political scene. On July 7th, the king offered Pitt an earldom (of Chatham) and Pitt became Lord Privy Seal.

Pitt's peerage dealt his reputation a severe blow, and later, in 1945, Churchill refused a Dukedom for the same reason. It caused him to be absent from the House, which had been the rock of his power. But he possessed what he had never held before: the confidence of a king. In 1768, Pitt finally resigned, his reputation almost destroyed. In the years that followed, Pitt rarely spoke in the Lords, and when he did, he generally supported Parliamentary prerogative and spoke against both Crown and any situation that might favor the Crown with power.

Between 1775 and 1777, as the Revolutionary War began, Pitt was incapacitated. When he returned to public life, he announced simply that the conquest of America was impossible. "If you conquer them, what then?" he enquired. "You cannot make them wear your cloth."

By this point Pitt was old and sick and in despair. On April 7th, 1778, he traveled to the Lords to defend his views. Listeners were unsure what those views were, and he did little to enlighten them. An attendee, Lord Temple, said: "You have forgot to mention what we have been talking about." To which Pitt replied, "I will do it by and by." Yet when he sought to rise, after trying two or three times, he fell in a sudden fit and was carried out unconscious.

Pitt died on May 11th, 1778. He was laid in Westminster Abbey, his monument ever afterwards bidding "England be of good cheer, and to hurl defiance at her foes."

His greatness lay in his ability to balance his dominant desire – to make Britain the leading world power – and his understanding of the independent spirit of the American colonists. Though in 1755, he had called for war in America, by 1766 he would defend Americans in the House of Commons against the petty taxes imposed by North, Townsend, and Rockingham. Pitt alone had the vision to see beyond budget requirements and political in-fighting to understand the great historical issue facing British statesmen – how to allow for the spirit of political liberty and independence that the Americans felt no less than their British cousins.

———

Benjamin Franklin

There never was a good war, or a bad peace.

I would rather have it said, *He lived usefully*, than, *He died rich*.

What renders Franklin so outstanding a figure in history is that he was the first man to envisage the US as a world power.

—HAROLD NICOLSON

ONE NOVEMBER DAY IN 1765, THE HOUSE OF COMMONS convened a special committee to discuss the affairs of the American colonies and, in particular, whether to repeal the unpopular Stamp Act. The principal expert witness called by the committee was a stout but distinguished-looking gentleman in his late fifties named Benjamin Franklin.

The recent French and Indian War had established British dominance of North America over the French. It had benefited the colonies by settling the western frontier. The British ruling elite regarded the American colonists as ungrateful upstarts who had not had to bear its cost. However, Franklin impressed the committee with his masterful answers to their searching and sometimes hostile questions.

Franklin had played his own part in this shift in global leadership by influencing opinion not only in the colonies but, more importantly, in London, in favor of British intervention. Under the inspired leadership of William Pitt the Elder, Britain had experienced the "year of victories" in 1759, when it defeated the French at Quebec to establish its dominance in Canada; India had already been subdued through the victory of Robert Clive at Plassey in 1757. In a triumphant mood, the British government had imposed new taxes on the colonies to pay for its military expeditions.

This is how Benjamin Franklin responded to the committee's questions:

Q. What was the temper of America towards Great Britain before the year 1763?

A. The best in the world. They submitted willingly to the government of the Crown, and paid, in all their courts, obedience to acts of Parliament. Numerous as the people are in the several provinces, they cost you nothing in forts, citadels, garrisons, or armies to keep them in subjection. They were governed by this country at the expense only of a little pen, ink, and paper. They were led by a thread. They had not only a respect but an affection for Great Britain; for its laws, its customs and manners, and even a fondness for its fashions, that greatly increased the commerce. Natives of Britain were always treated with particular regard; to be an Old England man was, of itself, a character of some respect and gave a kind of rank among them.

Q. And what is their temper now?

A. Oh, very much altered . . .

Then a question from a friend, to which Franklin's answer was as near a speech as he ever made.

Q. But if the legislature should think fit to ascertain its right to lay taxes, by an act laying a small tax contrary to their opinion, would they submit to pay the tax?

A. The proceedings of the people in America have been considered too much together. The proceedings of the assemblies have been very different from those of the mobs, and should be distinguished, as having no connection with each other. The assemblies have only peaceably resolved what they take to be their rights; they have taken no measures for opposition by force; they have not built a fort, raised a man, or provided a grain of ammunition, in order to such opposition. The ringleaders of riots they think ought to be punished; they would punish them themselves if they could . . . But as to an internal tax, how small so ever, laid by the legislature here on the people there, while they have no representatives in this legislature, I think it will never be submitted to. They will oppose it to the last. They do not consider it at all necessary for you to raise money on them by your taxes; because they are, and always have been, ready to raise money by taxes among themselves and to grant large sums, equal to their abilities, upon requisition from the Crown . . . America has been greatly misrepresented and abused here, in papers and pamphlets and speeches, as ungrateful and unreasonable and unjust; in having put this nation to immense expense for their defense and refusing to bear any part of that expense. The colonies raised, paid, and clothed near 25,000 men during the last war; a number equal to those sent from Britain, and far beyond their proportion; they went deeply into debt in doing this, and all their taxes and estates are mortgaged for many years to come for discharging that debt. Government here was at that time very sensible of this. The colonies were recommended to Parliament. Every year the king sent down to this House a written message to this purpose: that His Majesty, being highly sensible of the zeal and vigor with which his faithful subjects in North America had exerted themselves in defense of His Majesty's just rights and possessions, recommended it to this House to take the same into consideration and enable him to give them a proper compensation. You will find those messages on your own journals every year of the war to the very last; and you did accordingly give £200,000 annually to the Crown, to be distributed in such compensation to the colonies.

This is the strongest of all proofs that the colonies, far from being unwilling to bear a share in the burden, did exceed their proportion; for if they had done less, or had only equaled their proportion, there would have been no room or reason for compensation. Indeed, the sums reimbursed them were by no means adequate to the expense they incurred beyond their proportion; but they never murmured at that; they esteemed their sovereign's approbation of their zeal and fidelity, and the approbation of this House, far beyond any other kind of compensation.

Benjamin Franklin was born in Boston on January 17th, 1706, the tenth son of Josiah Franklin, a tallow chandler. By the age of ten, Benjamin was working full-time in his father's candle and soap shop. However, Benjamin had no desire to follow in his father's footsteps and in 1716 he began an apprenticeship with a printer alongside his older brother James. James put his brother to work publishing the *New England Courant* newspaper. In 1722, Franklin's first Silence Dogood essay appeared on the front-page. Anonymously submitted, his essays featured the voice of a prudish widowed woman from a rural area. With literary dexterity impressive for a sixteen-year-old city boy, Franklin wrote fourteen Dogood essays between April and October, featuring a quintessentially American humor of wry, homespun folksy tales and social commentary.

In October, 1729, Franklin became the publisher of the *Pennsylvania Gazette*. By early 1730, he had started to build an empire by sending his workers to set up shops in other locations, from Charleston to Hartford, providing presses and some content. He took care to "not only be in reality industrious and frugal, but to avoid all appearances to the contrary." He dressed plainly, never went out for idle diversion, and tried to show he was "not above" his business: for instance, he sometimes brought home the printing paper he purchased "thro' the streets on a wheelbarrow" rather than hiring someone to do the couriering. This image paid off; merchants used his services and his business thrived.

In September, 1730, Franklin married Deborah Read in a subdued common-law arrangement; it appears to have been a practically oriented partnership, though genuine affection grew out of their camaraderie and good-humored kinship. Around the time of the marriage, Franklin's illegitimate son (to a still-unknown mother), William, was born, and in October, 1732, Deborah gave birth to a son. That same year, Franklin began publishing his famous *Poor Richard's Almanack*. In the twenty-five-year run, the almanac served as America's first great humor classic, featuring vivid characters, homespun wisdom, and more folk humor. Selling 10,000 copies per year, *Poor Richard* made Franklin rich.

Franklin became postmaster of Philadelphia in 1737, an appointment that ensured an understanding of the colonies as a unit; he came to an early appreciation of the power and utility of unified colonies. He continued to involve himself in political issues, and formed a voluntary military force to help protect Pennsylvania from threats posed by Indians and their French allies.

Franklin began his political career in 1751 when he became a representative to the Pennsylvania Assembly, where he had clerked since 1736. This career would last 37 years, until his retirement as the president of Pennsylvania's Executive Council.

In 1749, Franklin had noticed similarities between electric sparks and lightning. This had been observed by others before, but no one had ever proposed a method for testing the connection. In 1752, Franklin came up with an experiment: he used a silk kite with a sharp wire protruding from its top and a key attached near the base of a wet string to draw charge from the sky. Assisted by his son William (now 21), he managed to collect some charge in a Leyden jar, which validated similarities between lightning and electricity.

Franklin was elected to the Second Continental Congress in 1775. At 69 he was its oldest member. He chaired a committee tasked with replacing the British-run postal system and eventually became America's new Postmaster General, donating his salary to the care of wounded soldiers. He helped establish a system of paper currency, collected munitions, dealt with Indians, and promoted trade with Britain's enemies. He also served as president of Pennsylvania's defense committee and oversaw construction of underwater obstructions to prevent warships from navigating the Delaware River.

The seventy-year-old Franklin traveled to Quebec to inspect General Arnold's military situation. During this rough trip in 1776, he picked up a soft, marten fur cap that contributed to Franklin's image as a simple, frontier sage, and later became famous when he wore it in France. He served on the committee that would write the Declaration of Independence during the summer of 1776. That same year, he was chosen to go to Paris to persuade the French to aid the Americans in their fight against the British.

When Franklin arrived in France, he discovered he was primarily known there as a scientist and philosopher. Medallions, snuff boxes, and signet rings bore his likeness. He set up a printing press near his quarters to issue pamphlets in support of the American cause. In December, 1777, thanks to an American victory at the Battle of Saratoga and Franklin's persuasiveness, the French agreed to full recognition of American independence, which would allow for treaties of trade and alliance. On February 5th, 1778, the two countries signed a treaty which was made official by Louis XVI when he received the three American commissioners at Versailles on March 20th. Representing American simplicity, Franklin dressed in a plain brown suit with his spectacles but without a sword or wig.

In September, Congress decided that only one commissioner was needed instead of three and, in a 12–1 vote, chose to keep Franklin as the sole minister in France. He succeeded in securing a loan of over $100 million ($2 billion today) from France. This accomplished, in March of 1781 he offered to resign from Congress, who instead appointed him as one of five commissioners to negotiate peace with Britain.

In October, the British general Cornwallis surrendered at Yorktown and the Revolutionary War was effectively over. Franklin promised the French he wouldn't negotiate a separate agreement with Britain but would only bargain. In 1783 he won better terms than expected from Britain in the Treaty of Paris, which set America's western border at the Mississippi.

Franklin accepted the presidency of the Pennsylvania Society for Promoting the Abolition of Slavery in 1787. Three year later, he presented a formal abolition petition to Congress, which was loudly denounced.

Franklin died on April 17th, 1790, at the age of 84. Polymath and Founding Father, he has been called "the First American."

THE COMPARISON OF WILLIAM PITT THE ELDER, EARL OF CHATHAM WITH BENJAMIN FRANKLIN

Chatham and Franklin were almost exact contemporaries, Franklin being only two years older than Chatham. The two had discussed American independence during Franklin's visit to London in 1766. In 1774 Chatham, though ill and out of government, had re-engaged in public affairs as an opponent of Lord North's policy of colonial oppression. Chatham met with Franklin again and professed support for colonial opposition to British taxation. Franklin and Chatham continued back-channel talks, devising a plan that Chatham presented to the House of Lords on February 1st, 1775. It was received with contempt. Franklin commented that Chatham was the only Englishman who understood the legitimate grievances of the Americans.

Both men were negotiators; but, though eloquent, Chatham seemed to end up alienating his allies. Franklin, on the other hand, though a man of few words, was generally popular; perhaps this was because he was an apostle of compromise, who specialized in finding common ground.

Chatham was motivated by patriotism and a desire for glory but had little or no interest in leading a political party or in administration. He stood above the Whig and Tory factions in the mid-eighteenth century and owed his position to his integrity and his popularity in England as a whole. He said, "If you are in Parliament, show yourself on all occasions a good Englishman and a faithful servant to your country ... Avoid faction, and never enter the House prepossessed; but attend diligently to the debate, and vote according to your conscience . . ."

Both men were patriots who belonged to no party or faction, and they've had a lasting influence: Chatham's expansion of the British Empire, which was realized in his time as Prime Minister in Canada and India; and Franklin in his practical steps towards making the United States a new and independent nation, first by a military alliance with the French, and then by negotiating the treaty that would secure peace with Britain.

William Pitt the Younger   Alexander Hamilton

CHAPTER 4

William Pitt the Younger and Alexander Hamilton

———

William Pitt the Younger

We must recollect what it is we have at stake, what it is we have to contend for. It is for our PROPERTY, it is for our LIBERTY, it is for our INDEPENDENCE, nay, for our existence as a Nation: it is for our CHARACTER, it is for our very NAME as Englishmen, it is for everything dear and valuable to man on this side of the grave.

—*on resumption of war with Napoleon in 1803*

He was a truly kind-hearted fellow. His feelings were so tender, that he could not endure to hear of an act of cruelty, yet in matters of principle his firmness of purpose was inflexible and his courage undaunted. There was in him a moral elevation and greatness of soul which raised him far above the level of most of his adherents. He truly loved his country, and sought its good. I feel sure his love for it was such that he would readily have consented any day to die for it, even though he were aware that it would never be known that he had made such a sacrifice. I never saw a man more entirely free from vanity.

—WILLIAM WILBERFORCE on Pitt the Younger

WILLIAM PITT THE YOUNGER BECAME PRIME MINISTER AT the age of 24 and is still the youngest man to have achieved Britain's highest office.

He was born on May 28th, 1759, the second son of Pitt the Elder. Often in poor health, he was educated at home by his father, who trained him in politics and debate. Pitt modeled his opinions on his father's politics, both in his conduct (his desire to remain independent of faction, his scrupulous sense of duty) and in his legislative concerns.

At the age of 14, Pitt was admitted to Cambridge University (in those days, it was not uncommon for an undergraduate to matriculate so young). His delicate health meant he was often at the college during the vacations, so he fraternized more with the dons than he did with his fellow undergraduates. Publicly he was cold, reserved, and standoffish; in private, however, he was witty, light-hearted, and boyish.

Pitt the Elder died in May, 1778, and Pitt left Cambridge to settle his father's affairs. He had relatively little money. Between 1779 and 1780, he practiced as a barrister, but when Lord North dissolved Parliament in September, 1780, Pitt canvassed for a seat in Cambridge. Although he was at the bottom of the poll, he was noticed by the Duke of Rutland, who procured him the Westmorland borough of Appleby.

Pitt took his seat in the new Parliament in January, 1781, and attached himself to his father's old friend and confidant, the second Earl of Shelburne. He participated in the opposition to the North government and made his maiden speech on February 26th, 1781. Although his speech was unprepared, he impressed Burke, Fox, and North by his manner and eloquence. As Burke said: "Not merely a chip off the old block; but the old block itself."

On March 20th, 1782, the North government resigned, and Rockingham formed a ministry alongside Shelburne and Fox. On July

1st, Rockingham died and Shelburne became premier; Fox and Cavendish resigned, so on July 10th, at the age of 23, Pitt was appointed Chancellor of the Exchequer.

At the beginning of 1783, Fox and North united to campaign against peace with the US, Spain, and France as Shelburne had argued. George III, who could not stand Fox, offered the premiership to Pitt, who declined. Consequently, a Fox–North coalition took power.

The new session provided Pitt – who had lost his position as chancellor and joined the opposition – the opportunity he had been waiting for. Late in 1783, Fox introduced his East India Bill (which proposed placing the struggling British East India Company more firmly under Parliamentary control, at the expense of the Crown). As Pitt wrote to Lord Rutland: "The bill which Fox has brought in relative to India . . . is, I really think, the boldest and most unconstitutional measure ever attempted, transferring at one stroke, in spite of all characters and compacts, the immense patronage and influence of the East to Charles Fox, in or out of office . . ." The King sought Pitt's views. Pitt advised George III to use his influence to have the bill thrown out in Lords and to bring down the Fox–North alliance.

Pitt formed an administration that few expected to last for more than six months. Fox dedicated himself to destroying the Pitt ministry, but although Pitt's conduct drove Fox and the Foxites wild with rage, he managed to combine spirited commitment to the country with his capacity to get the job done. Consequently, his administration was to last for 17 years.

The most troubling business before the twenty-four-year-old premier was national debt. In 1784, this stood at £243 million, and interest payments absorbed roughly one-third of all government expenditure (£8.5 million of £24 million). Pitt needed to raise revenue or reduce costs, and the majority of his time was spent debating with his advisors about how best to achieve financial stability. (What makes Pitt's financial acumen seem strange, however, is his complete lack of regard for his own finances, which, despite an income of roughly

£10,000 per annum and a rent-free house in London – Number 10, Downing Street – were ruinous. The question of where Pitt's money went – he didn't have a racing stable, nor a library or private collection, a wife or children, and he rarely gambled – is one of the mysteries of his life.)

Pitt's greatest successes continued in the realm of government finance. When George III asked for help paying his debts, Pitt moved the Civil List under the scope of the Consolidation Act, which extended Parliamentary authority over royal expenditures. He also suppressed sinecures in the customs and excise, which he developed into an efficient and able service. In 1787, Pitt suggested to his friend Wilberforce that he should make the abolition of the slave trade his issue, and he supported him thereafter, both in the Commons and as head of the government.

A regency crisis began in 1788 when George III suffered from a mental breakdown. The crisis was a threat to Pitt's political career; the Prince of Wales, the next in the line of succession, was a Foxite and would seek to replace Pitt with Fox. In December, Pitt established parliamentary committees to examine medical reports and the constitutional precedents, securing agreement in both houses that Parliament was by right entitled to provide for the regency. In 1789, with the agreement of all factions, he allowed a restricted regency power to be given to the Prince of Wales.

Pitt also kept the overburdened Exchequer from collapsing when France declared war in 1793. In doing so he helped lay the basis for a fundamentally different kind of centrally regulated, paper-based monetary system. Gold payments were suspended during the Napoleonic War, and they would be again in August 1914 by David Lloyd George.

Through 1798, Pitt searched for means of recovering Britain's naval mastery. Exemptions from naval service for men engaged in river and sea trade were suspended. This provoked a duel between Pitt and George Tierney, who accused Pitt of making demands hostile to the freedom of the country; Pitt replied that Tierney was obstructing the defense of his country. They fought on May 27th on Putney Heath, with pistols at 12 paces. Both men missed and agreed not to seek further satisfaction. But Pitt's health was poor, and he was unable to return to the Commons before it rose on June 29th.

Martial law had been declared in Ireland in 1797, against a backdrop of insurrections on both sides of the religious divide, Catholic and Protestant. In 1798, Pitt began to lay the groundwork for union with Ireland, thinking this might be the best way to pacify the island and bring it back within the boundaries of imperial politics.

Between 1798 and 1799, Pitt took an even more drastic financial measure to keep the country in the war: the introduction of a graduated income tax, with the burden of declaring income for tax purposes passing from the revenue officers to the taxpayer. Evasion remained a major problem. Pitt was forced to borrow heavily, but despite this his innovation did much to keep the country afloat.

The Act of Union with Ireland came into effect on January 1st, 1801; Pitt insisted that Catholic emancipation must follow but the King announced he would consider any supporter of emancipation a personal enemy. Pitt wrote to the King expressing his beliefs about emancipation; the King refused to discuss the issue, but he hoped Pitt would remain in his position. Pitt drafted a letter of resignation, which was accepted, on condition he stay to introduce the budget. Addington formed a ministry, and Pitt returned the seals of office – he had held them for almost two decades.

Many wondered why Pitt chose to resign on the issue of Catholic emancipation. Perhaps he was simply worn out. After 1793, he suffered attacks of "gout," and in September, 1797, was laid low by splitting headaches. There is evidence to suggest he suffered a nervous breakdown towards the end of 1800. Bouts of illness became more frequent after 1802, and he may have developed an ulcer. Already a shy man, Pitt had been increasingly withdrawn after 1795 and barely saw his own supporters.

In 1803, Pitt gave a resounding oration supporting the Defense

Act amendment. For some time he refrained from politics, but in 1804 he began to attack the government, until Addington resigned. Pitt took office on May 10th.

Despite Nelson's victory at Trafalgar in 1805, Napoleon entered Vienna, and crushed the Austrians and Russians at Austerlitz. Pitt was taking the Bath waters and in a poor state of health at the time, and news of the defeat brought on a total collapse. He died of exhaustion at his villa on Putney Heath on January 23rd, 1806, at the age of 46, his last words reportedly "How I leave my country!"

The Commons arranged for a lying-in-state funeral at public expense and, despite misgivings as to how his debts had accumulated, agreed to pay them (which came to approximately £40,000). On February 22nd, Pitt joined his parents in the crypt at Westminster Abbey.

—

Alexander Hamilton

For my own part, I sincerely esteem it a system which without the finger of God, never could have been suggested and agreed upon by such a diversity of interests.
—Statement after the Constitutional Convention (1787)

AN ILLEGITIMATE CHILD OF A SCOTTISH SEA CAPTAIN AND RAISED on Nevis in the West Indies, Alexander Hamilton is an unlikely hero. He died in a duel before he was 47. His philosophy and outlook were, if anything, at odds with the new spirit of democracy in the American colonies of the 1780s. He was an admirer of strong government, aristocracy, perhaps even monarchy. In George Washington he saw the principles of strong leadership and moral stature embodied in a leader to whom he was always passionately loyal. He fought with Washington in the War of Independence and served him when he became president.

Hamilton was, in effect, the first "prime minister" of the United

States. He believed in strong central government, not democracy, not states' rights, not even the Bill of Rights as proposed by Jefferson. He saw the need for the young republic to have a good credit rating, a strong currency, and a decisive executive with strong powers. He envisioned Washington as president for life, and there were rumours in the 1790s that he had suggested to Washington that he should be crowned king.

Hamilton's most important work was in reorganizing the finances of the nascent republic. In the *Federalist* papers, he expresses his views on the proposed political constitution of the US. Although he wrote the *Federalist* in collaboration with John Jay and James Madison, it is his hand that had the strongest influence (out of 150 essays or letters, Hamilton wrote the most by far). In the essays that Hamilton contributed to, he uses his knowledge of Roman history to show the dangers of both dictatorship and of anarchy resulting from unbridled democracy. He saw himself as a Roman consul, maintaining the integrity and order of the republic against the threat of chaos and dissent from the different states and new political parties. He did not trust the voice of the people, as Jefferson did. He failed to understand the enormous impetus of the new democratic movement that was to grow from the seeds of Jefferson's experiments in Virginia to the full-grown national flower of Jacksonian democracy in the 1830s.

His vision of a strong central government did not prevail; moderates such as James Madison and George Mason won the day, and within 20 years, Jefferson would become president (1801–09). Andrew Jackson would come to power in 1829, and it was Jeffersonian democracy that came to dominate the American political system. The balance of power between the legislative and executive branches that had been so carefully designed by the founding fathers was sufficient to prevent dictatorship and other political excesses, but it left a legacy of indecisive government. It made it difficult for any president to push his legislation through Congress. This problem persists to this day.

Alexander Hamilton was born on January 11th, 1755, to Rachel and James Hamilton. The couple lived together in a common-law marriage, unable to make their union official because, according to the Danish law that governed Rachel's previous marriage on St. Croix, Rachel could not remarry. James had grown up in a medieval Scottish castle named the Grange, and moved to the Caribbean as a merchant. He was largely unable to support his family – Rachel and their two sons: James, born in 1753, and Alexander, born in 1755 – so, in 1765, Rachel took her children back to St. Croix. Alexander never saw his father again. Rachel set up a store and Alexander helped her as a part-time clerk. She died shortly thereafter, in 1768, of yellow fever, leaving her two sons penniless.

Alexander went to live with the family of a friend and worked at the Christiansted office of the New York-based import-export house of Beckman & Cruger. When Cruger became sick and left the business in the hands of sixteen-year-old Hamilton, Alexander learned to take on a commanding air in order to assert himself towards older, more established individuals. The cocky youth managed Cruger's interests from October, 1771, through March, 1772, and greatly improved the business.

During this time, Hamilton befriended clergyman Reverend Hugh Knox and underwent a religious conversion. The awakened doctrine countered the Puritan idea of predestination and instead placed man's fate in his own hands. It appealed to the impoverished Hamilton because it made each individual responsible for his own actions. Impressed by Hamilton, Knox raised money to send him to New York for an education; Hamilton left St. Croix for New York in early October, 1772, and never saw his brother, Knox, or the Caribbean again.

Hamilton remembered his father with affection. As a child, he had listened to James's stories about his Scottish upbringing, complete with castle and aristocracy. Though descended from honorable clans, Alexander's status as a bastard denied him an aristocratic heritage.

His father's stories and his humble upbringing engendered a deep-seated desire for social position and prestige. While being educated for a year at Elizabethtown Academy in New York, Hamilton made friends with Northern aristocrats. These relationships only piqued his desire for prestige.

Over the next years at King's College in New York, Hamilton found himself in the minority position of radical revolutionary, pushing for a break from English rule. In 1774, at the age of 20, after the First Continental Congress when delegates from the North American colonies met to discuss relations with Britain, he published his first pamphlet, *A Full Vindication of the Measures of Congress*. He joined the volunteer corps of Major Edward Flemming soon after, attending drill sessions and studying gunnery.

Tensions mounted. In May, 1775, Hamilton was woken in his King's College dorm by shouting and yelling for the "damned Tory" – the Loyalist Reverend Myles Cooper, president of the college. Hamilton pulled on his military jacket, called for another student to wake the president, and ran to address the mob. The thin young Hamilton blocked their path, and while he spoke to them, Cooper fled the college. Throughout his life, Hamilton would continue to display contempt for mob violence.

On the night of August 23rd, 1775, Flemming's troops received the order to seize the cannons that lined the Grand Battery beneath Fort George. As Hamilton and the militiamen struggled to remove them, a British warship in New York harbor fired on them. Hamilton encouraged his comrades-in-arms and they successfully escaped with 21 of the Battery's 24 guns. In January, 1776, the New York Provincial Congress ordered that an artillery company should be raised, and Hamilton was appointed the commander.

When the Continental forces retreated towards Princeton in late 1776, Hamilton's artillery helped cover the escape. Soon after, he participated in Washington's surprise attack on the Hessians at Trenton and fought in the Battle of Princeton in January, 1777. That month, Washington invited Hamilton to join his headquarters staff as an aide-de-camp. Hamilton agreed and in March was assigned to deal with the treatment of prisoners of war.

Though serving as Washington's aide-de-camp meant responsibility and hard work, there were opportunities for rest and recreation. Martha Washington regularly hosted social events, and Hamilton threw as much passion and energy into socializing as into every other pursuit in his life. Fellow officers nicknamed him "the Little Lion" for his zeal, and Martha Washington named a tomcat that constantly pursued female cats "Hamilton."

Whatever his reputation, in his first leave since the beginning of the war, Hamilton traveled to Albany in 1780 to marry Elizabeth Schuyler at the Schuyler mansion, The Pastures. With the marriage, Hamilton had finally joined the ranks of the American aristocratic elite.

After the war, the New York legislature appointed Hamilton as one of its four-man congressional delegation and in 1782 he took his seat in Congress. During Hamilton's time there, he repeatedly experienced the frustrations of a weak Congress. In 1783, he began a regular correspondence with Washington, who was living at Mount Vernon. They shared similar views on the importance of a stronger national government and union.

On June 18th, during the Constitutional Convention, Hamilton took the floor for six hours, criticizing state governments, advocating a strong central government, and providing details of his own plans for government reorganization. These included a two-house supreme legislative power – one with three-year terms, the other with lifetime appointments – an executive chosen for life with veto powers, and judges chosen by the people.

Once the Constitution was drafted, the real work to gather public support began. Hamilton, James Madison, and John Jay agreed to write a series of essays that would be published in New York newspapers.

After being elected first President of the United States, Washington signed a bill that established the Treasury Department and nominated Hamilton as the first Secretary of the Treasury. Hamilton presided over the largest federal department, with 500 employees, mostly customs collectors. Washington's first command to Hamilton was to design a new federal financial system. In 1790, Hamilton presented his 20,000-word "Report on the National Credit" to Congress. Arguments raged, and a north-south split emerged as the still-indebted north favored assumption and the solvent south opposed. Hamilton's plan stalled until the "dinner-table bargain" of June 20th, 1790, when Thomas Jefferson invited Hamilton, Madison, and congressmen from Maryland and Pennsylvania to hammer out a compromise that led to the congressional approval of Hamilton's plan.

Once the plan passed, Hamilton threw his energies into the second part of the plan: the establishment of a National Bank. Hamilton then founded a US mint. In 1791, he submitted his "Report on Manufactures," which advocated making manufacturing the main focus of the American economy. He understood the necessity of protecting the infant industries of the United States against foreign competition.

Hamilton resigned in 1795, and returned to New York. Although out of office, he continued to advise Washington. When, in 1798, the second president of the US, John Adams, appointed Washington commander-in-chief of an expanded army during the Quasi-War with France, Washington demanded Hamilton serve as his second-in-command.

Hamilton had written in support of Jefferson against Burr during the 1800 election, and in 1804 denounced Burr in writing and in person. After an exchange of hostile letters, they fought a duel on the morning of July 11th. The following day Hamilton died from the bullet wound he had received. He was not yet 50.

THE COMPARISON OF WILLIAM PITT THE YOUNGER WITH ALEXANDER HAMILTON

The shadow of a father lay over the careers of both William Pitt and Alexander Hamilton. In Pitt's case it was the great Chatham, whose foresight established the British empire in Canada and India, and whose inspiration enabled his son to enter Parliament at a young age.

Hamilton's relationship to his father is more complex. Alexander was haunted by the idea of his penniless father wandering the Caribbean and sent him thousands of dollars that supported him in old age. He also had an adopted father, George Washington, whom he served under, in peace and war, as aide-de-camp. He received the general's praise for his courageous action at the capture of Yorktown. He later became the first president's Secretary of the Treasury, laying the foundations of the American financial system.

Both Pitt and Hamilton were influenced by the new ideas circulating in the 1780s, a decade of tremendous change that saw the birth of the American Constitution, the French Revolution, and the first attempt in England at parliamentary reform. Both men were also influenced by their reading of Adam Smith's *The Wealth of Nations*, first published in the 1760s, which rapidly became the ideological basis of free-trade legislation.

Pitt's first actions when he became Prime Minister in 1784 were to balance the budget, fund the national debt, and reduce customs duties (for example, lower tea tariffs from 119% to 12%). During the following decade, Alexander Hamilton planned the Bank of the United States – which was the germ of the idea that became the Federal Reserve System – and attempted to resolve the debt problem of the nascent republic.

Hamilton's belief in a strong federal administration owes much to his admiration for the British Constitution. Like Pitt the Younger, Hamilton viewed political ideas of the 1780s and 1790s in terms of the ancient Roman republic. America was threatened by dissent and rebellion from within and invasion from without, just as England was threatened by the revolutionary ideals of the Jacobin Rebellion in France.

In fact, Pitt and Hamilton were rather unlike their fathers. They weren't military heroes; they weren't national idols of unwavering integrity who stood above political scruples. They were both brilliant, mercurial, and youthful political geniuses.

Although Pitt held power for 17 years as prime minister, it is possible that his influence was no greater than that of Hamilton, whose tenure as American "Prime Minister" lasted only five years. Nonetheless, his ideas were of seminal importance.

Perhaps the most important similarity between Pitt and Hamilton is that both were great administrators. It isn't one of history's greatest terms of praise, but it's a role that is as significant in influencing events as that of a military hero.

Edmund Burke

Thomas Paine

CHAPTER 5

Edmund Burke and Thomas Paine

—

Edmund Burke

Great men are the guide posts and landmarks in the state.

Young men, there in America, which at this day serves for little more than to amuse you with stories of savage men, and uncouth manners; yet shall, before you taste of death, show itself equal to the whole of that commerce which now attracts the envy of the world.

My hold of the colonies is in the close affection, which grows from common names, from kindred blood, from similar privileges, and equal protection. These are ties which, though light as air, are as strong as links of iron.

EDMUND BURKE WAS BORN IN 1729 IN IRELAND. THE SON OF A solicitor, he was educated at Trinity College in Dublin, and moved to London at the age of 21 to study law at the Middle Temple.

In 1756 Burke published *Vindication of Natural Society*. This was followed, in 1757, by *A Philosophical Inquiry into the Origin of Our Ideas of the Sublime and the Beautiful*, which established him among European philosophers. In the same year Burke created the *Annual Register*, a survey of world affairs, which he continued to edit for 30 years. He also married Jane Nugent and became friends with a number of distinguished writers and critics, such as Doctor Johnson, Oliver Goldsmith, Sir Joshua Reynolds, and the actor David Garrick.

In 1765, Burke was appointed secretary to the Marquis of Rockingham, leader of one of the Whig groups in Parliament, and entered the House of Commons that same year. He worked to unify Whigs around Rockingham, and took an active part in the constitutional controversy of George III's reign (whether King or Parliament controlled the Executive). The King sought to assert a more active role for the crown without infringing upon the Revolutionary settlement of 1689. Burke published his pamphlet *Thoughts on the Cause of the Present Discontents* in 1770, which argued that George's action were against not the letter, but the spirit, of the Constitution; choosing ministers on personal grounds was favoritism, therefore the election should determine the selection of ministers.

In 1774, Burke was elected Member of Parliament for Bristol, the second-largest city in the country at that time and an open constituency requiring a genuine election. It was at Bristol that he famously said that a Member of Parliament should be a representative for the country, not a mere delegate pledged to obey the wishes of his constituents. He must address himself to the general good of the entire nation and act according to his own judgment and conscience. Burke held the position for Bristol for six years but later was a member for Malton, a pocket borough of Lord Rockingham's. Burke supported parliamentary reform, but his main concern was the curtailment of the powers of the crown.

The second historic issue that confronted Burke in the 1770s was the quarrel with the American colonies. When the imposition of the Stamp Act in 1765 provoked unrest and opposition, Burke's Whig group repealed it, but asserted that Britain still had the right to impose taxation. Burke's best-known statements on this issue are his two speeches, "On American Taxation" in 1774, and "On Conciliation with America" in 1775. British policy, he argued, had been both imprudent and inconsistent but, above all, legal and intransigent in the assertion of imperial rights.

Burke was sympathetic to the American colonists and thought that the British administration was short-sighted and ill-advised, so he made a historical survey of the growth of the colonies and their present economic problems. In place of narrow legalism, he called for a more pragmatic policy on Britain's part that would admit the claims of circumstance, utility, and moral principle; he thought that the British Parliament should be more conciliatory to American complaints and undertake measures that would restore the colonists' confidence in imperial authority.

The theme of his speech "On Conciliation with America" was that "All governments, indeed every human benefit and enjoyment, every virtue, and every prudent act, is founded on compromise and barter. We balance inconveniences; we give and take; we remit some rights that we may enjoy others; and, we chose rather to be happy citizens, than subtle disputants." He believed that Britain and America could be reconciled and argued that prolonged and strenuous efforts to procure peace were of greater value than the politically easy resort to war.

Whether Burke was practical in his suggestions is questionable, but his moral and political principles were, as always, lofty and impressive. He was attached to tradition and the ways of the past, but recognized the need for change and evolution rather than revolution. Perhaps his Irish background helped him to understand the colonists' relationship with their imperial power. Ireland was in a strict political dependency on Britain and internally subject to the ascendancy of an Anglo-Irish Protestant minority under which Roman Catholics were excluded from public office. Burke was always concerned to ease the burdens of his native country and consistently advocated relaxing penal regulations.

The other imperial issue to which he devoted many years was that of India. There, the British East India Company had created its own extensive empire. In the 1760s and 1770s Burke opposed interference by the British government in the company's affairs as a violation of chartered rights. However, he learned much about the company's government in 1781 while he was sitting on the Select Committee to investigate their administration of justice in India, and he concluded that the corrupt state of the Indian government could be remedied only if it was in the hands of neither the company nor the crown. He drafted the East India Bill of 1783, which proposed that India be governed by a board of independent commissioners in London. The bill was defeated, and Burke's indignation came to center on the governor-general of Bengal, Warren Hastings. It was largely due to Edmund Burke that Warren Hastings was impeached in 1787. Burke challenged Hastings's claim that it was impossible to apply Western standards to government in the East. He appealed to the concept of the law of nature, the moral principles rooted in the universal order of things, to which all races in all countries are subject. Burke's speeches about India and Hastings could be emotional and abusive, and Hastings was eventually acquitted.

The outbreak of the French Revolution in 1789 was greeted in England with enthusiasm. Burke, after a brief suspension of judgment, was hostile to it and alarmed by the favorable English reaction. In 1790, he published *Reflections on the Revolution in France*. He emphasized the dangers of democracy and the rule of numbers when unrestrained and unguided by the responsible leadership of a hereditary aristocracy. He challenged the entire rationalist and idealist temper of the movement, appealing to the virtues of the British Constitution: continuity and gradual growth; respect for a traditional wisdom; acceptance of the hierarchy of rank and property; religious consecration of secular authority; and recognition of the basic imperfection of all human societies.

Burke's long friendship with Fox came to a dramatic end in May, 1791, during the Parliamentary debate on the issue of the French Revolution; after this Burke supported William Pitt. In 1794, Burke retired from Parliament but continued to write. The war against France, he insisted, was not a war of interests but of ideologies. It was right to take up arms against ideas that were subversive of liberty. It was a war, he wrote in *Letters on a Regicide Peace*, "not with an ordinary community, which is hostile or friendly as passion or as interest may veer about: not with a State which makes war through wantonness, and abandons it through lassitude. We are at war with a system, which, by its essence, is inimical to all other Governments, and which makes peace or war, as peace and war may best contribute to their subversion. It is with an armed doctrine that we are at war." Burke's analysis was that Jacobinism was an "armed doctrine," rather as Jihad may be today.

Burke died in 1797. History vindicated his analysis of the French Revolution, which evolved into the Terror. The Napoleonic order that emerged was by no means an improvement on the ancient regime.

Thomas Paine

My country is the world, and my religion is to do good.

A share in two revolutions is living with some purpose.

—[To Washington]

THOMAS PAINE WAS BORN IN THETFORD, NORFOLK, IN 1737. His father was a Quaker and his mother an Anglican. He had very little education, just enough to master reading, writing, and arithmetic. At the age of 13, he worked with his father as a rope maker, and went on to try various other occupations, eventually becoming an officer of the Excise. His duties were to hunt for smugglers and to collect the tax on liquor and tobacco. Although the pay was barely sufficient to cover living costs, he used part of it to purchase books and various scientific tools. He had two brief marriages, and was unsuccessful and unhappy in every job he had. He was dismissed from the Excise Office in 1772 after he published an essay in support of raising the pay in order to end corruption in the service. Just when his situation seemed hopeless, he bumped into Benjamin Franklin in London. Franklin advised him to seek his fortune in America and gave him some letters of introduction.

In 1774, Thomas Paine arrived in Philadelphia and began to

edit the *Pennsylvania Magazine*. He published articles and poetry under his own name, anonymously, and under pseudonyms. His scathing denunciation of the African slave trade was signed Justice and Humanity.

Paine arrived in America when the conflict between the colonists and England was reaching its height. In his fifty-page pamphlet *Common Sense*, published on January 10th, 1776, he argued that America should not simply revolt against taxation but also demand independence. The pamphlet sold more than half a million copies within a few months. More than any other publication, *Common Sense* paved the way for the Declaration of Independence.

During the war that followed, Paine served as a volunteer aide-de-camp to General Nathanael Greene. His contribution to the patriot cause was his pamphlets and papers, 16 crisis papers issued between 1776 and 1783 – each signed Common Sense. The first, "The American Crisis #1," published in December, 1776, when George Washington's army was on the verge of disintegration, opened with the words, "These are the times that try men's souls." Washington ordered the pamphlet to be read to all the troops at Valley Forge.

In 1777, Paine was appointed Secretary to the Committee for Foreign Affairs, a post he held for two years until he became involved in a dispute with Silas Deane at the Continental Congress and was forced to resign. Still poor, he needed employment and was happy to be appointed Clerk of the General Assembly of Pennsylvania at the end of 1779. When he realized that American troops were frequently unpaid and short of food, he took $500 from his salary and started a subscription for the relief of the soldiers. In 1780 he published "Public Good," in which he appealed to the 13 states to cooperate for the well-being of the nation, and called for a national convention. In 1781 he traveled to France and brought back money, clothing, and ammunition to aid the revolution.

After the Revolution, Paine was still poverty-stricken; although his patriotic writings had sold hundreds of thousands of copies, he never made any money from them, and he sent a petition to Congress, endorsed by Washington, pleading for financial assistance. Pennsylvania gave him £500, and New York gave him a farm in New Rochelle, where he devoted his time to inventions, concentrating on an iron bridge without piers and a smokeless candle.

Forever restless, Paine left for Europe in 1787 to promote his plan to build a single-arch bridge across the Schuylkill River in Philadelphia, but he was soon diverted from this project. In 1789 he published a warning against Pitt's attempt to involve England in a war with France over Holland, reminding the English people that the one thing made certain in war was the increase of taxes, but it was really the French Revolution that concerned him. Although he had admired Edmund Burke when he supported the American Revolution, Paine was enraged by Burke's hostile reflections about the revolution in France, and expressed those views in *The Rights of Man*.

Eight editions of *The Rights of Man* were published in 1791, and the work was reprinted in the United States, where it was distributed by the Jeffersonian Society. Burke replied and Paine came back with "Rights of Man, Part Two." It began as a defense of the revolution, but evolved into an analysis of the basic reason for discontent in European society and a remedy for poverty, arbitrary government, illiteracy, unemployment, and war. Paine spoke out in favor of republicanism against monarchy and went on to outline a case for education, relief of the poor, pensions for the elderly, and public works for the unemployed, all of which would be financed by a progressive income tax. To the ruling class, Paine's proposal spelled bloody revolution, and the British government ordered the book banned and the publisher jailed. Paine was indicted for treason, and an order went out for his arrest, but he was already on his way to France, having been elected to a seat at the National Convention. He was tried *in absentia*, found guilty of seditious libel and declared an outlaw. *The Rights of Man* was ordered permanently suppressed.

In France, Paine hailed the abolition of the monarchy but deplored the terror against the Royalists, and tried quixotically to save the life of King Louis XVI, favoring banishment rather than execution.

For being the king's advocate, he was imprisoned from 1793 to 1794. It was only with the fall of Robespierre that he was released and, although seriously ill, readmitted to the National Convention.

The first part of *The Age of Reason* had been published while he was in prison. Although he made it clear that he believed in a supreme being, the work gave him a reputation as an atheist.

When Paine returned from France in 1802, he found that his services to the Revolution had been forgotten, and he was regarded as the world's worst atheist. Despite his poverty and poor health, which was worsened by occasional drunkenness, Paine continued to attack privilege and religious superstition. He died in New York in 1809 and was buried on his farm in New York.

THE COMPARISON OF EDMUND BURKE WITH THOMAS PAINE

Although both Edmund Burke and Thomas Paine were liberals in their younger years, they moved towards the right and left extremes of the political spectrum in the 1780s and 1790s. The two main reasons for their ideological shifts were the American Revolution and the French Revolution.

Paine had admired the Burke who said in 1770, "I am not one of those who think that the people are never in the wrong. They have been so, frequently, and outrageously, both in other countries and in this. But I do say, that in all disputes between them and their rulers, the presumption is at least upon a par in favor of the people." But by 1790, he became enraged by the traditionalist Burke who wrote in his *Reflections on the Revolution in France*:

> Is it now sixteen or seventeen years since I saw the Queen of France, then the Dauphiness, at Versailles; and surely never lighted on this orb, which she hardly seemed to touch, a more delightful vision. I saw her just above the horizon, decorating and cheering the elevated sphere she just began to move in, glittering like the morning star, full of life, and splendour, and

joy. Oh! What a revolution! And what a heart I must have, to contemplate without emotion that elevation of veneration to those of enthusiastic, distant, respectful love, that she should ever be obliged to carry the sharp antidote against disgrace concealed in that bosom; little did I dream that I should have lived to see disasters fallen upon her in a nation of gallant men, in a nation of men of honour, and of cavaliers. I thought ten thousand swords must have leaped from their scabbards to avenge even a look that threatened her with insult. But the age of chivalry is gone. That of sophisters, economists, and calculators, has succeeded; and the glory of Europe is extinguished forever.

In his response in 1791, Paine declared: "[Burke] is not affected by the reality of distress touching his heart, but by the showy resemblance of it striking his imagination. He pities the plumage, but forgets the dying bird." And in 1792: "The final event to [Burke] has been, that as he rose like a rocket, he fell like the stick."

Burke was a prophet of modern conservatism and the idea of democracy and the "elected representative," while Paine was ahead of his time in supporting the common man.

William Murray, 1st Earl of Mansfield   John Marshall

CHAPTER 6

William Murray, 1st Earl of Mansfield and John Marshall

—

William Murray, 1st Earl of Mansfield

The Constitution does not allow reasons of state to influence our judgments: God forbid it should! We must not regard political consequences, however formidable so ever they might be: if rebellion was the certain consequence, we are bound to say "fiat Justitia, ruat caelum" [Let justice be done though the heavens fall].

Consider what you think justice requires and decide accordingly. But never give your reasons: for your judgment will probably be right, but your reasons will certainly be wrong.

—Advice to a newly appointed colonial governor (1768)

B ORN IN 1705 TO A NOBLE, BUT IMPOVERISHED, SCOTTISH FAMILY, Murray was educated in Perth until the age of 13, when he was sent to Westminster School in London. Murray continued to Oxford University, and graduated in 1727. By 1730, he had been called to the bar in London and had gained a reputation as an excellent barrister, often representing his Scottish friends and relations in their southern lawsuits. He became involved in politics in the 1740s when he was elected a Member of Parliament and was named Solicitor General. He was regarded as one of the best speakers in the House of Commons; he became Attorney General in 1754 and unexpectedly succeeded Sir Dudley Rider as Lord Chief Justice when Rider died a few months later.

As Chief Justice, Mansfield did much to modernize the practice of law, and he made it much easier for junior barristers to present motions. He also changed the tradition that all judgments were reserved, and instead said that unless courts had doubts about the evidence presented to them, a judgment should be made immediately.

In addition, Mansfield tried to reform English mercantile law. In most European countries, the principle was that a merchant was bound by his promises in addition to signed legal documents, while English law maintained that a merchant was only legally bound by signed documents. European principle was based on the assumption of good faith on the part of merchants – or *uberrima fidas* – something lacking in English law. Mansfield's chance to reform the law came with the case of Governor Carter of Fort Marlborough in Sumatra, who took out an insurance policy for the fort should it be taken by foreign enemies. A witness testified that the governor knew that the fort was built to resist attacks from natives, but not from European enemies, and also knew that the French were likely to attack. The French did attack, and the insurer refused to fulfill the claim. Mansfield decided in favor of the insurer, saying that Carter had failed in his duty of good faith. The decision has had a lasting effect.

In 1783, Mansfield heard his first slavery case. It concerned the Zong Massacre, and was about the payment of an insurance claim for slaves that were thrown overboard by the captain of the slave ship. Mansfield summed up the jury's verdict, saying throwing the slaves overboard was the same as throwing horses overboard. But when new information was introduced, he ruled against the owners of the ship.

Mansfield's most famous case was that of Somerset. Somerset was a slave owned by Charles Stewart, an American customs officer, who had sailed to Britain for business in 1769. There, Somerset attempted to escape, but he was recaptured a few days later and imprisoned on a ship bound for Jamaica, where Stewart intended to sell him. However, three people claiming to be Somerset's godparents made an application before the court of King's Bench for a writ of *habeas corpus*, and the captain was ordered to produce Somerset before the court. Mansfield ordered a hearing in 1772, and there was a good deal of attention in the press. An abolitionist, Granville Sharp, backed Somerset, and five advocates appeared for the slave. On behalf of Somerset, they argued that while colonial laws might permit slavery, neither the common law of England or any law made by Parliament recognized the existence of slavery and, therefore, slavery was illegal; moreover, English contract law didn't allow for any person to enslave himself, and no contract can be binding without the person's consent. The argument focused on legal details rather than humanitarian principles. Mansfield, in his summing-up, ruled that a master could not carry his slave out of England by force and that "the state of slavery is of such a nature that it is incapable of being introduced on any reasons, moral or political; but only positive laws preserve its forces long after the reasons. It's so odious that nothing can be suffered to support it but positive law. Whatever inconveniences therefore may follow from a decision, I cannot say this case is allowed or approved by the Law of England; and, therefore, the slave must be discharged." This was not an end to slavery, which was not abolished in the British Empire until 1834, but it resulted in nearly 15,000 slaves being immediately freed in England. Mansfield's decision was considered to be a significant step in recognizing the illegality of slavery.

As Lord Chief Justice, Mansfield also made the process much less expensive, making it easier for people to gain access to legal aid. He was noted for his insistence that equity should be applied by all courts, not just the Court of Chancery. He established the principle that judges shouldn't blindly follow precedent, but should instead seek to find loopholes in rules that were no longer applicable. He made his judgments on the principle that the law must adapt. Although he resented the freedom of the press and refused to challenge the king, he was, in all other respects, an important reformer.

—

John Marshall

The Government of the United States has been emphatically
termed a government of laws, and not of men.

JOHN MARSHALL WAS THE FOURTH CHIEF JUSTICE OF THE US
Supreme Court, which position he held from 1801, when he was
nominated by John Adams, until his death in 1835. He was the
longest-serving Chief Justice and played a significant role in the development of the American legal system. He reinforced the principle
that federal courts are obligated to exercise judicial review by disre-
garding laws made by the states that were in violation of the Constitution. Thus he cemented the position of the American judiciary as
an independent and influential branch of government. In addition, his
court made several important decisions that affected the balance of
power between the federal and state government during the early
years of the republic. He repeatedly confirmed the supremacy of federal law over state law. Many of his decisions were unpopular, particularly among the Jeffersonian Republicans who wanted stronger
state governments.

Marshall was born in a log cabin close to Germantown, a rural
community on the Virginia frontier in 1755. The eldest of 15 children, he had eight sisters and six brothers. From a young age, he
was noted for his good humor and his black eyes, which were strong
and penetrating. He started work as a surveyor and land agent for
Lord Fairfax, a colleague of Washington's. In the 1760s, Marshall's
family moved first to Leeds Manor on the eastern slope of the Blue
Ridge Mountains and then to a small village called Salem, now
called Marshall. Although his home was modest in comparison to
the estates of Washington, Madison, and Jefferson, it was substantial
for the period.

Marshall received his early education from reading books in Lord Fairfax's library (there weren't many schools in the parish). By the age of 12, he had already transcribed Alexander Pope. The Marshall family had long decided that John was to become a lawyer, and he spent many hours reading Blackstone's commentaries on the laws of England. He served in the continental army during the Revolutionary War, first as a lieutenant, then as a captain in the 11th Virginia Regiment. He spent the winter of 1777-78 at Valley Forge with Washington, and the two became friends. After his military service, Marshall studied law under Chancellor George Wythe at the College of William & Mary in Williamsburg, Virginia. He was admitted to the bar in 1780. In 1782, he won a seat in the Virginia House of Delegates.

Marshall was selected as a delegate to the Virginia Convention responsible for ratifying the US Constitution in 1788 and led the fight in favor with James Madison and Edmund Randolph. Specifically, he was interested in defending Article 3, which established the federal judiciary. Ultimately, the Constitution was approved by the Convention. Marshall identified with the new Federalist Party, which supported a strong national government and commercial interests, and opposed Jefferson and the Republican Party, which advocated for states' rights and the everyman.

During this time, Marshall continued to practice as a lawyer. He represented the heirs of Lord Fairfax in a Supreme Court case in Virginia involving a large tract of land. He appeared before the US Supreme Court in 1796 in a case involving the validity of a Virginia law that called for the confiscation of debts owed to British subjects. Marshall argued that the law was a legitimate exercise of the state's power. The Supreme Court ruled against him, but he was admired for his arguments and delivery.

In 1795 Marshall declined the position of Attorney General of the United States, and, in 1796, the Minister of France. He eventually did accept, in 1797, a position on a three-member commission to France, which was assembled by John Adams. It was a failed mission, although Marshall's conduct, as well as the resentment towards the French made him popular with the American public. In 1798 he declined a Supreme Court appointment and instead ran for a seat in the House of Representatives. He won, but made only one speech before being appointed Secretary of War in 1799. In May of that year, at the end of Adams's four-year presidency, he was appointed Secretary of State. He took office in June and, shortly before Adams left office on January 31st, 1801, was appointed the fourth Chief Justice.

Marshall continued to serve as Chief Justice for 34 years and through the administrations of six presidents – John Adams, Thomas Jefferson, James Madison, James Monroe, John Quincy Adams, and Andrew Jackson. He remained a stalwart advocate of Federalism and opposed the Jeffersonian school of government. He participated in over 1,000 decisions and wrote 519 opinions himself. He helped to establish the Supreme Court as the final authority on the meaning of the Constitution, and his impact on constitutional law is unmatched.

Soon after becoming Chief Justice, Marshall changed the manner in which the Supreme Court announced its decisions. Previously, each justice would offer a separate opinion, as is the practice in the UK and Australia today. Under Marshall, however, the US Supreme Court adopted the practice of handing down a single opinion, allowing it to present a clear verdict, although individual justices were allowed to dissent. Marshall's forceful personality also helped him to steer his fellow justices, and only once in 35 years did he find himself on the losing side in a constitutional case.

As his contemporary Oliver Wolcott observed, Marshall had the knack of putting his own ideas into the minds of others. He had charm, humor, intellectual agility, and an ability to bring men together. His sincerity and his presence commanded attention. His opinions were workmanlike rather than eloquent or subtle. Marshall was attentive while listening to oral arguments, but he wasn't widely read in the law and seldom cited precedents. Often he asked Justice

Joseph Story to deal with the chore of locating the precedent by saying, "There, Story, that is the law of this case. Now go and find the authorities."

The Marshall Court struck down an Act of Congress in only one case, which established the court as a powerful check on congress and the presidency. The case was *Marbury vs Madison*, ruled unconstitutional in 1803. President Jefferson believed that the court could not give him an order even if it had jurisdiction. Jefferson lamented that allowing the Constitution to mean whatever the courts say it means would make the Constitution "a mere thing of wax in the hands of the judiciary which they may twist and shape into any form they please." Chief Justice Marshall put it this way, "It is emphatically the province and the duty of the judicial department to say what the law is. Those who apply the rule to particular cases must often of necessity expound and interpret that rule. If two laws conflict with each, the courts must decide on the operation of each." The Constitution did not explicitly give judicial review to the court, and Jefferson was furious with Marshall because (for all his revolutionary ideas) he believed the president should decide whether his acts were constitutional or not. Most historians agree that the framers of the Constitution planned for the Supreme Court to have some sort of judicial review, and Marshall solidified the founder's intentions. His opinion expressed a basic theory: government under law.

Marshall also presided over the conspiracy trial of Aaron Burr in 1807. The former vice president was charged with treason and high misdemeanor. Prior to the trial, President Jefferson had condemned Burr and strongly supported his conviction. Marshall, however, narrowly construed the definition of treason provided in Article 3 of the Constitution. He noted that the prosecution had failed to prove that Burr had committed an overt act, as the Constitution required. As a result, to Jefferson's disgust, Burr was acquitted.

Marshall presided over a number of other significant cases, among them *McCulloch vs Maryland*, which established the balance of power between the federal government and the states, affirming federal supremacy; Gibbons vs Ogden, which overturned a monopoly of New York steamships, establishing the rule of federal commerce; Johnson vs M'Intosh, which held that private American citizens couldn't purchase tribal lands directly from Native Americans – only the government could do so.

In addition to his judicial activities, Marshall wrote an influential five-volume biography of George Washington that was published in 1832. He spent most of his retirement, brief as it was, in Richmond, and became first president of the Richmond branch of the American Colonization Society, which was dedicated to resettling freed American slaves in Liberia. In 1829 he was again delegate to the state constitutional convention at the age of 74, along with his contemporaries, Madison and Monroe. His wife died in 1831, and his health quickly declined afterwards, though he continued to sit on the Supreme Court until he died on July 6th, 1835. The title of Chief Justice does not appear on his tombstone, which lists only his parents and his wife. He was one of the last surviving Founding Fathers, and the last surviving Cabinet member from John Adams's administration.

Marshall laid the foundations of the American legal system, which is unlike that of any other country. Perhaps the United States is a more litigious country (with a higher proportion of lawyers in its population) than any other nation, even the United Kingdom – but that is based on the veneration and respect for the law, which began with John Marshall and the Founding Fathers.

THE COMPARISON OF WILLIAM MURRAY, 1st EARL OF MANSFIELD WITH JOHN MARSHALL

In *Parallel Lives* Plutarch included not only statesmen, orators, generals, and founders but also lawgivers, and when we consider who has contributed most to the centrality of law in Britain and America, we must recall the great eighteenth-century jurists and judges.

John Marshall, the fourth Chief Justice of the Supreme Court of the United States, laid the basis for US constitutional law and made the US Supreme Court a branch of government equal to the legislative and executive branches. The equivalent and contemporary British figure – indeed, the only British jurist who matches that high standard – is William Murray, 1st Earl of Mansfield.

Both men had a seminal impact on the justice system in their countries and were original, fearless thinkers who were prepared to uphold justice.

Lord Melbourne

James Madison

CHAPTER 7

Lord Melbourne and James Madison

Lord Melbourne

When in doubt what should be done, do nothing.

"Lord Melbourne looked as if he enjoyed himself," said a surprised observer who had watched him beaming at some tedious city banquet. "There is nothing Lord Melbourne does not enjoy," was the reply. Along with his pleasure in life went a pleasure in his fellow creatures. Most cynics have a fundamental antipathy to their kind; not so William. "The worst of the present day," he once said to a friend, "is that men hate one another so damnably. For my part I love them all!"

LORD MELBOURNE WAS BORN IN 1779 AS WILLIAM LAMB, THE younger son of the first Lord Melbourne, who was a member of the tightly knit group of Whig aristocrats with vast landed estates and an inherited right to sit in Parliament. Lamb was the second son and didn't expect to succeed, so he was called to the bar in 1804 when he was 25. A year later, his older brother died, and he entered politics, becoming a Whig Member of Parliament for Leominster in 1806.

Around this time Lamb married Lady Caroline Ponsonby, who was a wayward, passionate, and unpredictable wife, and a thorn in his side for the next 20 years. She eventually went mad and died at the age of 40. Among her various lovers was Lord Byron. Melbourne's appealing character is nowhere so much admired as by his long suffering tolerance of his unbalanced spouse.

Lamb did not achieve political office until he was 46, when he became secretary for Ireland in George Canning's short-lived administration. He performed well, and his unflappable, tolerant, and easygoing manner endeared him to the Irish.

In 1830, Lord Melbourne, as he was called after succeeding to the title in 1828, was appointed Home Secretary. He was in no sense a reformer, and as a true conservative, believed in generally leaving things alone, but in 1830, during the Industrial Revolution, the demands of the middle class for a greater voice in political affairs was undeniable.

Melbourne realized that, although he disliked reform, it had become politically necessary. "If you can't beat 'em, join 'em," was the motto of the aristocratic Whig. As Home Secretary, he expressed a firmness and clearness of policy that nobody who knew him and his languid, cynical approach to life had expected. He put down popular unrest in rural areas in 1830, and again in 1834 with the Tolpuddle Martyrs.

So, in 1834 when Lord Grey's administration was in difficulties, the only person who seemed to fulfill the needs of the hour (and the best of King William IV's choices) was Melbourne. Melbourne himself was reported to have described the prospect of being prime minister as a "damned bore," and hesitated to accept the position. It was quite an achievement that he was able to hold the government together at all. In circumstances where he had to balance the autocratic instincts of some of his peers with an uneasy cooperation with the radicals and the Irish under Daniel O'Connell, Melbourne's policy was to wait to act until absolutely driven to it. His good looks, persuasive charm, and flair for personal relations helped him to navigate these difficult political times.

King William IV soon decided to dismiss Melbourne and persuaded the Duke of Wellington to form a government until Sir Robert Peel returned from his holiday in Italy. Melbourne had a few months out of office but was soon back after Peel was defeated in 1835. Like Abbot Sieyès, who, when asked what he had done during the French

Revolution, replied that "he had survived," Melbourne could make the same claim for his government. In the eyes of his contemporaries, the responsibilities of government were confined to keeping order, raising taxes, dealing with foreign policy, and directing war. There was no pressing need for social change or for legislation in the 1830s.

After 1837, Melbourne became a mentor to Queen Victoria, a responsibility for which he was very well suited. It is argued by some historians that the role Melbourne played in the first four years of Queen Victoria's reign, as her guide to being a constitutional monarch, was critical to the success of her reign. Every morning they discussed political business, and Melbourne spent much time riding and dining with her at Windsor. Although the Queen had a much more "black and white" moral barometer than Melbourne, he tried to pass on some of his own tolerance towards human frailties. Even after he had to step down as prime minister in 1841, they continued their correspondence, and by the time he died at the age of 69 in 1848, she was under the sway of Prince Albert, who awakened in her an understanding of the social problems that confronted the new industrial and urban Britain. As prime minister, Melbourne oversaw her succession and the beginning of perhaps the longest and most successful reign in British history.

———

James Madison

If men were angels, no government would be necessary.

"MRS. MADISON IS A FINE, PORTLY, BUXOM DAME WHO HAS a smile and pleasant word for everybody . . . but as to Jemmy Madison, ah Poor Jemmy – he is but a withered little applejohn." Thus did Washington Irving describe the president and his wife in a letter written in 1811. An applejohn is an apple considered to be perfect only when it is withered and shriveled, and the president fitted the description. He was the smallest president, standing only five feet, four inches, and weighing about one hundred pounds. An unprepossessing figure – more of a mind than a man – he had a tiny, almost inaudible voice, but bright blue eyes and a lively, humorous character. He was gentle, kind, and scholarly, shy but with a quiet strength. He suffered from epilepsy and was a hypochondriac who was always worried about his health. Nevertheless, he lived to the age of 85.

Madison was born in 1751 into an old Virginia family. They had 5,000 acres in Orange County, Piedmont, where they planted tobacco and grains, and they owned 100 slaves. Their lives were leisurely, rich, and hospitable.

In 1772, Madison graduated from Princeton with a Bachelor of Arts. He was in the Virginia Convention in 1774 and then the Virginia Council of State in the late 1770s. He attended the Continental Congress in 1780. Though a believer in a strong central government, Madison was, nevertheless, a disciple of Jefferson's and believed in states' rights and democratic principles.

At the Virginia legislature in 1783, he worked to enact Jefferson's statutes of religious freedom. It was this experience that made him realize that the executive branch needed the power to enact such important laws. In the constant debate about the balance of power between states and central government, Madison came down against democratic demagoguery. Perhaps having also observed the excesses of the French Revolution, he wanted a stronger and more balanced central government. He proposed an electoral college, and – in addition to the legislature – a strong executive and a strong judiciary.

George Washington provided the crucial example of an executive with restraint and moderation in exercising his power and set the pattern for presidents to come, but Madison opposed Hamilton's strong financial policies and the executive privilege of the Treasury. Hamilton believed that there should be a prime minister figure under the president, such as a Pitt, a Richelieu, or a Colbert. Madison believed in a pure republican democracy in which no single man had too much power. During the war between France and Great Britain that continued from 1793 to 1815, the executive power of the president increased, as it does in times of war. Under Jefferson's administration (1801–9), Madison took the key role of Secretary of State.

While Secretary of State, Madison was involved in the Louisiana Purchase in 1803 and in the embargo of exports of 1807–9. The Louisiana Purchase marks the difference in American policy to that of the European states that had preceded it. The Americans did not go to war to conquer territory; they purchased it. This had never been done before, and it was an unusually peaceful way of acquiring vast areas of land, which continued with the purchase of Florida, Alaska, and other territories that they acquired when America became a great power: Hawaii for instance was annexed in 1898.

In 1809, James Madison was elected the fourth president of the United States (following Washington, Adams, and Jefferson). Like Washington and Jefferson, he was a landed, slave-owning Virginian aristocrat. To some extent he followed in the somewhat radical policies of his mentor Thomas Jefferson.

Madison had a weak cabinet until Monroe took over as Secretary of State in 1811. They faced the greatest crisis of the twenty-year-old Republic when, in 1812, Madison asked Congress to declare war on Britain. But Madison was unable to prepare the American army for war. The result was a swift defeat of the American invasion of Canada, a surrender at Detroit, and finally, in August, 1814, the capital, Washington, DC, was abandoned by the government and burned by British forces. Madison was then 63 and in poor health. He took refuge in the countryside in Virginia, and after a few weeks, he was able to return to the capital, which, however, needed to be rebuilt.

As one of his contemporaries wrote, the president was "virtuous, able, and patriotic" but found it difficult to enact his republican axioms of virtue during the emergency of war. His popularity, nevertheless, recovered in 1815 when Andrew Jackson won the decisive victory of New Orleans on January 8th, 1815, not knowing, because of the slow progress of communications, that a truce had already been signed on Christmas Eve between Britain and America. Finally, the peace treaty was signed in February, 1815. It was a decisive victory for the Americans to acquire the western lands. The War of 1812 – 33 years after the surrender at Yorktown – is often called the second war of independence and marks the low point in the relationship between Britain and America, which, from that point on, began to grow closer, until they eventually became allies in 1917.

Madison's appointments and legislative program sustained his republican idea of government. He championed the Bill of Rights (the first ten amendments). He enacted commercial treaties and tariffs. He established a national university. He showed non-partisan leadership that was neither federalist nor democrat.

In 1817, Madison retired to Monticello. He became known, in old age, as the Father of the Constitution because of his contribution to the Federalist papers and his establishment of checks and balances between the executive, congressional, and judiciary branches.

Although he lacked executive ability, Madison was a "great little man," to quote Aaron Burr, who, incidentally, introduced Madison to his wife, Dolly Payne Todd, the widowed daughter of a Philadelphia boardinghouse keeper. Had it not been for Dolly, her husband's regime would have been a dull one, but she was as flamboyant and colorful as he was drab. She was endowed with the social touch, gave brilliant parties, and dressed the part. Her trademark was the bejeweled and feathered turbans that matched her Parisian dresses and cost her $1000 a year. Much to the disgust of the ladies who remembered her humble Quaker origin, she dipped snuff and used rouge and lipstick. Warm-hearted and lively, she ruled her court with charm and had a rare memory for names and faces. She had great tact too, for she lived in harmony under the same roof with her mother-in-law for many years.

Madison was twenty-one years older than Dolly and shorter by a head. While he was reserved, dignified and precise, she was cordial, gay and amiable. Despite their different natures, they were devoted to each other all their lives. Dolly referred to the president with affection as "my darling little husband." James Madison died in 1836.

THE COMPARISON OF LORD MELBOURNE
WITH JAMES MADISON

Lord Melbourne was a member of the British aristocracy, as was James Madison a member of the Virginian elite. As contemporary leaders who had similarly scholarly and literary interests, they were detached from the exercise of power in the political field.

As to the issue of slavery, Madison did not allow his abhorrence of it to change his way of life. Melbourne once remarked to Archbishop Whatley, "I say, Archbishop, what do you think I would have done about this slavery business if I had my own say? I would have done nothing at all. I would have left it all alone. It is all a pack of nonsense. There always have been slaves in most civilized countries, the Greeks, the Romans. However, they would have their own way and we have abolished slavery. But it is all great folly."

Cynical as this sounds, Melbourne moved with the times. And in 1833, he voted for the abolition of slavery in the British Empire. James Madison, though a radical democrat in the Jeffersonian tradition, took no action during his presidency (nor did Jefferson) to tackle the overwhelming issue of slavery in the United States. It was perhaps too early for the colonial society to undertake such radical reforms, which took the Civil War and the greatness of Abraham Lincoln to achieve.

George Canning   James Monroe

CHAPTER 8

George Canning and James Monroe

—

George Canning

Such is England herself: while apparently passive and motion-less, she silently concentrates the power to be put forth on an adequate occasion.   [on Naval Men-of-War]

G EORGE CANNING WAS BORN IN 1770, AND RAISED IN IMPOVER-ished circumstances as his father died when he was a year old. His mother remarried a disreputable actor, but Canning was rescued by a rich uncle, Stratford Canning, a city banker, and educated at Eton and Oxford, where he met a number of prominent Whigs.

Canning was called to the bar in 1791, and entered Parliament in 1794 for the safe seat of Newtown on the Isle of Wight. Already friends with many young Tories, he was converted by Prime Minister William Pitt the Younger. Even so and despite his air of perfect breeding, he was still reviled by some of the aristocratic Tories for his "common" background.

Canning had an elegant figure and an expressive face. He reveled in vituperation, invective, and satire, and was the author of jokey verses such as:

> But of all plagues, good Heaven, thy wrath can send,
> Save, save, oh! Save me from the *Candid Friend*!

On the question of Catholic emancipation, he had another joking line:

> Though they sleep with the devil, yet there is the hope,
> On the downfall of Britain to rise with the Pope.

Canning was able to change his party with wicked laughter. But young George was sometimes criticized as something of a bounder and not always taken seriously.

Shortly before Canning took office as Foreign Secretary, in 1807, he was described by a European diplomat as "very clever and very essential to government but hardly yet a statesman because of his dangerous habit of quizzing." Canning's reputation for quizzing, or destructive criticism, dragged the ministry into fierce trouble in 1809, when he fought a duel with Lord Castlereagh, who was at the war office. Eventually, in 1814, he was appointed Ambassador to Lisbon.

Canning was disliked by King George the IV because he had proclaimed his loyalty to Queen Caroline, whom the king had divorced in 1819. When Canning finally "kissed hands" with the King as Foreign Secretary in 1822, Canning likened his appointment by the reluctant sovereign to receiving an entry card to society's most gentlemanly club, and finding written on the back, "Admit the rogue."

Canning was a Tory but he also stood for a commercial seat in Liverpool and was fully conversant with new trends in free trade. He was against agricultural grandees and the European system of repressive monarchies. Canning's policy in Europe was nonintervention, and he sent the Duke of Wellington to the Congress of Vienna in 1822 with those instructions. "So things are getting back to a wholesome state again," he wrote. "Every nation for itself, and God for us all." He was in all things a patriot; and to this day, there is a Canning Club, which Tories are proud to belong to.

Canning soon won the King's goodwill and, in contrast to his desire to extricate England from continental entanglements, he was determined to have British commercial attachés sent to the newly independent Spanish colonies in South America, in the hope that England would win the lion's share of trade in the new and rich region. Canning said that he had "called the New World into existence to balance the Old." By December, 1824, he had a cabinet majority for his policy. "I am really quite knocked up by it," he wrote. "The fight has been hard but it is won . . . The deed is done; the nail is driven; Spanish

America is free; and if we do not mismanage our affairs, she is English."

In 1826 Canning dispatched troops to defend Portugal against a potential Spanish invasion. He also sponsored lower trade duties in opposition to the Dutch minister, and turned to verse again:

In matters of commerce the fault of the Dutch
Is giving too little and asking too much;
With equal advantage the French are content,
So we'll clap on Dutch bottoms a twenty per cent.

Canning was not well liked and had difficulty gaining a following in the collegial House of Commons. His best days occurred during his time as Foreign Secretary from 1822 to 1827. However, on April 12th, 1827, he became prime minister. He served for only 119 days, the shortest term of any British prime minister.

Canning eventually succumbed to "the odious lumbago," as the King called it, and was sent down to the villa in Chiswick where Fox had died 20 years earlier. Canning died on August 8th, 1827. His reputation stood high, and he undoubtedly had a strong influence on the succeeding generation – Peel, Palmerston, Gladstone, and Disraeli.

—

James Monroe

The history of all ages proves that . . . at least one half of every century, in ancient as well as modern times, has been consumed in wars, and often of the most general and desolating character.

The revolution of France undoubtedly took its origin from that of the United States. Her citizens fought and bled within our service. They caught the spirit of liberty here, and carried it home with them.

The Navy is the arm from which our government will always derive most aid in support of our neutral rights. Every power engaged in war will know the strength of our naval force and pay due consideration to that argument.

S EVEN OF THE FIRST TEN US PRESIDENTS HAILED FROM VIRGINIA. James Monroe was the last of the Virginia "aristocrats" – following Washington, Jefferson and Madison – to hold the office.

Born in 1758, Monroe's family had Scottish origins. He went to William & Mary College in 1774. In 1775, at the age of 17, he enlisted – under Washington – and fought in the Revolutionary War.

He was six feet tall, and a dignified, plain man. When he was young, he met Thomas Jefferson, who was almost 15 years older than him, and became a close associate of Jefferson's.

Monroe studied law and, in 1782, when he was 24, entered the Virginia legislature. At 28 years old, he married Elizabeth Kortright, the daughter of a New York merchant, and they had two daughters. Not particularly rich, he aspired to live like Jefferson and Madison, who had vast estates. In 1789, he was able to buy a small plantation in Albemarle County with the savings he had made from his legal career.

In 1790, Monroe entered the US Senate, and he was appointed as Minister to France by George Washington in 1794. Although this was at the end of the Terror in Paris, Monroe was enthusiastic about the revolutionary movement, and Washington recalled him quite quickly because of these sympathies.

In 1799 Monroe became governor of Virginia. During that time, he bought a 2,500-acre plantation called Highlands, adjacent to Jefferson's Monticello, where he was able to live out his dream of being a landed Virginian aristocrat.

In 1803, Jefferson appointed Monroe as Envoy to France, and he arrived just in time to sign the Louisiana Purchase, perhaps the most important single foreign-policy initiative taken by the young American republic. It bought all the land west of the Mississippi River from Napoleon for $15 million, money needed to finance his military ambitions. Monroe's forte was in diplomacy. He became Minister to Great Britain in 1805, returning to America when Madison became president to take on the role of Madison's Secretary of State from 1811 to 1817. It was during this time that he enunciated the Monroe

Doctrine – "The American continents . . . are henceforth not to be considered as subjects for future colonization by any European powers." The Doctrine envisioned that the South American continent would be free of European influences and, therefore, in effect, under "Yankee" dominance for the next 150 years. (But as we have seen from Canning's proclamation about South America, this "doctrine" was by no means accepted by all European powers.)

Monroe became president in 1817 and served for eight years with John Quincy Adams as his Secretary of State. He was the first president to tour the nation and, following the War of 1812 with Britain, was particularly interested in establishing forts along the coast and a proper standing army to defend the country. He restored formality to the White House, as Washington had had it, following the rather informal era of Jefferson. The president's salary was only $25,000 a year, which was inadequate to entertain, but Monroe did so anyway and left the office in debt. He also authorized the construction of roads and canals, a new initiative on the part of the federal government, which was still a very small part of the total economy.

In conclusion, James Monroe was a successful president at the end of almost four decades of Virginian and Federalist Party dominance.

THE COMPARISON OF GEORGE CANNING WITH JAMES MONROE

George Canning held office as Foreign Secretary for five years (1822–27) and was prime minister for barely three months before he died. James Monroe was Secretary of State for seven years (1811–17) and president for a further eight years (1817–25).

While Monroe was annunciating his Doctrine, Canning was trying to ensure that British interests were protected in the new South American republics – independence came suddenly to the Latin republics, and Canning quickly established trade ties. Monroe's Doctrine spun Canning's policies (and British sea power) to US advantage. The two statesmen wanted to keep Continental powers out of the Caribbean and Latin America; they had the same objective, but different purposes.

Britain didn't have any colonies in South or Central America (apart from British Honduras and British Guiana) but, from 1810 to at least 1914 Britain's traders, merchants, and shipping lines dominated South American commerce. It was the British who built the railways (especially in the Pampas of Argentina) and the British Vestey family who organized the frozen-meat business.

Canning's greatest influence was in his role as Foreign Secretary after the end of the Napoleonic Wars and the collapse of Spanish and Portuguese power. Similarly, Monroe was a dominant figure in US foreign policy, especially with regard to Britain and South America.

CHAPTER 9

William Wilberforce and John Quincy Adams

—◆—

William Wilberforce

Our social hours were enlivened by his wit, and by the innocent playfulness of his brilliant fancy. His whole manner and expression of countenance were the index of the sunshine of a mind at peace with God, and cherishing no thoughts but of kindness and love to his fellow-creatures.

—John Harford, *Recollections of William Wilberforce*, 1865

A VISITOR TO KINGSTON-UPON-HULL, IN SOUTH YORKSHIRE, MAY struggle to find the old red brick house where William Wilberforce was born in 1759. Hidden away in old town is the fine Jacobin house that had been in Wilberforce's family for many years, a typical home of a prosperous eighteenth-century merchant – comfortable and spacious. Later it became the office of the family trading business, which dealt with the Baltic.

The room in which Wilberforce was born now carries the inscription, "Statesman, orator, philanthropist, saint, one of the greatest Parliamentarians in a great age, a friend of Pitt and Burke, of Fox and Canning."

The next room contains the gruesome paraphernalia of slavery: branding irons, whips, shackles, runaway-slave collars, and the inventory of a plantation, including the poignant entry "Quamina," a good watchman with bad legs valued at sixpence. There is also a model of a slave ship, used by Wilberforce in his speech to the House of Commons to demonstrate the cruelty of the trade.

William Wilberforce   John Quincy Adams

In the last room there is an effigy of Wilberforce sitting behind his desk. Above is the painting of a slave in chains that he used to illustrate lectures. Also in the room are portraits of Wilberforce and John Newton, the former captain of a slave ship who converted to the gospel, devoted himself to the abolitionist movement, testified against the slave trade before the House of Lords, and wrote "Amazing Grace."

A few doors down the narrow cobbled street is a pub called The Old Black Boy with a sign depicting a slave. Such is the incongruity of Wilberforce's home city, a tough commercial place, from which this sweet, gentle, Christian soul emerged to change the world.

Wilberforce's father died when he was eight, and he was sent to live with his childless uncle and aunt in London. During his years with them, he was influenced by evangelicalism and Methodism. "If Billy turns Methodist, he shall not have a sixpence of mine," said his grandfather. But, at 12 years old, William stuck to his religious beliefs. Growing up, he enjoyed the pleasures of society and returned to the Church of England, but always retained the evangelical influence that later motivated him in his crusade against the slave trade.

At Cambridge, Wilberforce became friends with the younger William Pitt. Both decided on graduation to enter politics. Pitt would become prime minister at 24. Wilberforce on the other hand never rose higher than MP for Hull and, with frequent bouts of ill health, was not really suited to parliamentary life.

Wilberforce's Cambridge tutor, Isaac Milner, introduced him to Philip Doddridge's *Rise and Progress of Religion*, which deeply influenced him, and at 25, he became "born again." John Newton came into his life at this time.

Although Wilberforce was a wealthy gentleman who more or less inherited a seat in Parliament in 1780, he was also a man tortured by religious doubts. At the age of 26, he gave up his clubby social life with friends such as William Pitt the Younger to join the Evangelical wing of the Church of England. It was this conversion that inspired his efforts to reform British society (for example, in observing the Sabbath). By 1787, however, his attention had become focused on what would ultimately be his life's calling: the slave trade.

Wilberforce's conversion to the abolitionists' cause occurred (by his recollection) while talking to Pitt under an old oak at Holwood above the vale of Keston. After this, Wilberforce devoted the rest of his life and parliamentary career to bringing forward motions to abolish first, the slave trade (achieved in 1807) and, finally, slavery itself (1833).

After the horrifying events on the slave ship Zong, in 1783, the abolitionists formed a committee in the House of Commons to move for abolition. Thomas Clarkson was one of the most energetic members of the committee in collecting information to condemn the slavers and had a great influence on Wilberforce. Pitt, though sympathetic to abolition, was constrained by the domestic political situation of the time and, after 1793, by the war with France.

Wilberforce gave his first great speech on the subject in the House of Commons in 1789. He revealed that more than 38,000 slaves were carried in British vessels from Africa to the Caribbean each year under horrible conditions which caused many of them to die. He also told them that there were over 250,000 slaves in Jamaica and more on the other British islands. The final bill for the compensation of slave owners in 1833 exceeded £20 million (a modern equivalent of $20 billion), so it was an enormous undertaking to challenge slavery when so many people had vested interests. One of the concerns the British ruling class had was that, if they abolished slavery, the French would profit instead.

In 1791, Wilberforce delivered a four-hour speech in the Commons, in which he demonstrated complete mastery of the extensive evidence against the slave trade gathered at that point. After another speech and a debate in April, 1792, the House of Commons decided by a large majority that some form of abolition was necessary, but it was repeatedly postponed over the next 40 years by MPs who didn't want to disturb business interests. During this time, Wilberforce's life was threatened by two West Indian captains, and his health suffered from the strain of leading the movement.

Like some of his contemporaries among the romantic poets, Wilberforce was dependent on laudanum, or opium, to maintain his rather weak constitution. This continued until he was 37, when he married and had four sons and three daughters. The Wilberforces had a very happy family life, with a villa in Wimbledon and regular visits to Yorkshire to see the extended Wilberforce family. Wilberforce's life, however, centered around the House of Commons.

Wilberforce continued to bring up the abolition of the slave trade almost every year in Parliament with little success. However, as the Napoleonic War began to move in Britain's favor, the strategic and military advantage became more compelling. Finally, in 1806 the abolitionists gained the active support of the government and were able to pass the bill abolishing the slave trade. This was a triumph for Wilberforce, although it took another 27 years before slavery itself would be abolished in the British Empire. It was passed entirely as a result of the moral force of the abolitionists' campaign and the idealism of Wilberforce, Clarkson, and their peers.

Wilberforce's first political action as a young man in 1780 had been to oppose the war against the American colonists. He recognized and appreciated the American contribution, particularly from the Quakers, towards the abolitionists' movement and wanted the two countries to join in enforcing abolition. In 1812 he was horrified by the outbreak of war between Britain and America, saying, "I'm sick at heart from the sad prospect of a war with America."

In his old age, Wilberforce, an indulgent parent (like William Penn), spent most of his fortune to pay the debts of his son William. He accepted this, at the age of 70, with Christian resignation and, just before he died, made his last speech in public against slavery. The bill for the abolition of slavery passed on July 26th, 1833; Wilberforce died on July 29th.

William Wilberforce never held high office and was an infrequent attender of parliament, due to his ill health, but his moral influence and example for nearly 50 years (from 1785 to 1833) were significant. He achieved one great thing, and he changed the history of the western world. By his eloquence and courage, his industry and pertinacity, William Wilberforce did more than anyone else to bring about the abolition of slavery throughout the British Empire. No Englishman has done more to evoke the conscience of the British people and to elevate and ennoble British public life.

—

John Quincy Adams

The soul of one man cannot by human law be made the property of another. The owner of a slave is the owner of a living corpse; but he is not the owner of the man.

Slavery is the great and foul stain upon the North American union, and it is a contemplation worthy of the most exalted whether its total abolition is or is not practicable.

JOHN QUINCY ADAMS WAS BORN IN 1767. PERHAPS NO MAN EVER had such a precocious and rapid introduction to the world of diplomacy and politics. At the age of seven, he was taken by his mother, Abigail, to watch the Battle of Bunker Hill to "better understand the price of freedom;" when he was ten, he accompanied his father, John Adams, to France, where they stayed with Benjamin Franklin. At the age of 14, he was already fluent in French, so he went with Francis Dana, who was appointed ambassador to Russia in 1781, to St Petersburg. His letter and diaries of the time he spent in Europe are a veritable mine of information on the eighteenth century. "There is nobody here but princes and slaves . . ." he wrote to his father from St Petersburg. He was unable to find a decent school, so he educated himself by reading Cicero, Voltaire, Pope, Addison, Dryden,

Hume, and Macaulay, and taught himself German, French, Latin, and Greek.

At the age of 16, Adams was again in Paris; he dined frequently with Thomas Jefferson, and assisted in drawing up the papers for the 1783 Treaty of Paris, which ended the War of Independence with recognition of the United States.

In 1784, Abigail Adams sailed for Europe, where she saw her husband, John, and son, John Quincy, now 17, for the first time in four years. She was shocked to encounter, instead of a little boy, a tall strapping young man who had attended parties and experienced diplomatic life in Russia and Sweden.

When his father was appointed US Ambassador to Britain in 1785, John Quincy sailed home to enroll in Harvard. By 1790, he had opened a law office in Boston, and almost became engaged to a beautiful girl named Mary Frazier, but, at his mother's insistence, he broke it off.

Like his father, John Adams, the younger Adams espoused a Federalist viewpoint, as opposed to Republican. In the 1790s, this was seen by some American Republicans as being in favor of monarchy, aristocracy, and elitism.

By 1794, at the age of 27, John Quincy Adams had already been named by President Washington as US Minister Resident in the Netherlands, and he invited his brother Tom, five years his junior, to join him there. In 1797, he married Louise Johnson, daughter of the American Consul in London. She was from an English family, and Abigail didn't approve of her. But by that point, John Quincy had decided that his mother's approval mattered less than his personal decisions and need for happiness.

The same year, his father, John Adams, became the second president. While I have not included John Adams as one of the American biographies in this modern version of Plutarch's parallel lives, he is a significant figure; and the Adams family is one of the great founding families of the United States. One aspect of their story is their strict Christian morality; another was their high expectations – only John

Quincy (who rebelled when young) and, of his children, only Charles, were able to meet these expectations. Although John Adams was a one-term president (both father and son shared this unhappy distinction), he played a central role in the constitutional and practical founding of the country. He was nicknamed "His Rotundity" by congressmen because of his love of titles and ceremony (as well as his short, tubby figure). Coming as he did between the tall Washington and the tall Jefferson, he struggled to maintain his dignity and presence and popularity, but was nevertheless an effective president during a difficult period (1797–1801).

Meanwhile, John Quincy became minister plenipotentiary to the Kingdom of Prussia in Berlin. While John Adams was defeated for re-election by Thomas Jefferson, the happy news arrived from Berlin of the birth of his first grandson (George Washington Adams).

In September, 1801, John Quincy returned to the United States and again set up a law practice in Boston. Without campaigning, he was elected to the US Senate in 1803. In 1806 he also became Boylston Professor of Rhetoric and Oratory at Harvard. Meanwhile, he continued to demonstrate an independent streak: he voted against the Louisiana Purchase, and for President Jefferson drafted an embargo against the British that deeply alienated his Federalist Party colleagues. By 1808, he was forced to resign his Senate seat. The new president, James Madison, asked him to be Minister to Russia, which he accepted, but left his two eldest boys, George and John (aged eight and five), behind in Boston. They both suffered from this deprivation of family life, and his wife Louisa felt deeply guilty about it. Both boys were to have unhappy and short lives.

Adams was an effective diplomat and got on very well with the Tsar, Alexander I. In 1812, Napoleon invaded Russia, and Britain and the US went to war against each other. John Quincy's beloved one-year-old daughter, Louisa, died in St. Petersburg. The Adamses moved to the Netherlands where, in 1814, Adams was involved with the American delegation to make peace with Britain. In 1815, Adams was ready to return home but was made Minister to Great Britain, where he met Lord Liverpool, the Prime Minister; Castlereagh, the Foreign Secretary; and George Canning, as well as William Wilberforce.

By 1817, Adams took on perhaps his greatest role, that of Secretary of State under President James Monroe. His deep belief was in Manifest Destiny, in independence and union, with one nation, one language, united under a democratic system of government. One of his achievements was to establish the boundary in the northwest along the 49th parallel over the Rocky Mountains, which would eventually become the "Oregon Country."

In 1819, Adams defended General Andrew Jackson's aggressive actions in Florida and successfully negotiated with Spain to purchase Florida – for $5 million – while abandoning its claim to Texas (at least for the next 15 years). In 1821, with revolutionary movements sweeping across South America, and President Monroe's doctrine in place, Secretary Adams pressed for an end to colonization in the Americas and also – an allied question – an end to the slave trade. Adams was, therefore, influential in establishing America's boundaries, preserving peace with Britain, and delineating the principles of non-interference in the New World by European powers. By 1824, though his reputation was at its height, his presidential election was hotly contested. Although Andrew Jackson won the popular and electoral college, no candidate had the majority of the electoral college. Henry Clay, however, swung his support behind Adams and (probably by secret agreement) was appointed Secretary of State in the new administration.

This "corrupt bargain" (as Jackson called it) soured the atmosphere of Adams's presidency from the beginning. Andrew Jackson resigned from the Senate and returned home to Tennessee, vowing to have his revenge in the 1828 election (which he did).

Adams was, nevertheless, a conscientious chief executive who worked from 5 a.m. to 11 p.m. each day, read the Bible, walked three or four miles, and met Congressmen and visitors. He also used to swim regularly in the Potomac River, nearly drowning on one occasion. But he was fundamentally a cold and rather proud man, not a warm father or husband. He never campaigned to voters or made himself personally popular or sociable.

In his inaugural address, Adams proposed many new federal institutions, such as a national university, an observatory, the West Point Military Academy, and new surveys of the coastline, many of which were rejected by Congress. Many Southern leaders feared that Adams supported the suppression of the slave trade.

In 1826 his father, John Adams, died on the Fourth of July, the same day as Thomas Jefferson, but John Quincy wasn't able to reach Quincy, Massachusetts in time to see him. His mother, Abigail, passed away two years later, and he didn't attend the funeral.

When Andrew Jackson was elected president in the election of 1828 – an especially bitterly fought contest with scurrilous rumors circulating about both candidates – he refused to have the courtesy to call on the outgoing President Adams, who (like his father in 1800) became one of only two departing presidents to boycott the inauguration of his successor.

Adams's unhappiness was further deepened by the suicide of his eldest son, George Washington Adams, and the alcoholism of his younger son, Johnny. "I have been deserted by all mankind," he wrote. "I have nothing to rely on but the mercy of God."

His youngest son, Charles Francis, was some consolation to him, and had a successful marriage and career. His friends in Quincy suggested to the disconsolate ex-president that he should run for Congress, an idea he initially rejected; but he was persuaded and elected with a large majority – "a call to public service," he called it. It was the only instance in US history of a former president becoming a congressman.

Foreshadowing the Civil War 30 years later, South Carolina threatened in 1832 to secede from the Union over the tariff question. Adams played a central role in Congress in preventing this outcome.

In 1834, following the death of his younger son, Johnny, from alcoholism (his brothers, Charles and Tom, had succumbed, too),

Adams buried himself in work and made a memorable three-hour speech attacking Daniel Webster. He became known as "old man eloquent" by his fellow Congressmen.

The final great crusade of his long political career was slavery. In 1833, the British parliament finally passed the bill abolishing slavery in the British Empire. The abolitionists, driven by religious fervor, became more vocal and demanded the end of slavery in America, starting with the District of Columbia.

Like Lincoln, Adams later realized that the existence of slavery threatened the existence of the Union. He saw the Democratic Party, as created by Van Buren and Andrew Jackson, as an unholy alliance of Southern plantation owners and Northern republicans. Respected because of his age and for being an ex-president, he became a lone voice resisting the Southerners' push to "gag" any petition in the House to abolish or restrict slavery. He became a hero for many ordinary Americans, with a degree of popularity he had never enjoyed before. A large banner appeared in Cincinnati: "John Quincy Adams, Defender of the Rights of Man."

In 1836, Texas applied to join the Union as a slave state. Adams spoke out strongly against it: "Are you not large and unwieldy enough already? Do not 2 million square miles cover surface enough for the insatiate appetite of our land jobbers? Have you not Indians enough to expel from the land of their father's sepulchers and to exterminate?"

Adams' efforts to win the freedom of 39 African captives aboard the slave ship *Amistad* led him to appear before the Supreme Court, where he reiterated the Declaration of Independence and the right of every man to life and liberty. He won the case and in doing so established the clear principle that Africans were citizens and human beings with rights, not simply property.

Adams opposed the Mexican War of 1846. Following his speech opposing a resolution of the war, he collapsed while registering a protest and died at age 81 on the steps of the Capitol.

Modern readers might regard the Adams clan as a cold, dysfunctional family. But it is probably unfair to pass judgment on a strongly religious eighteenth-century background that nevertheless bred two outstanding presidents, patriots, and public servants of the caliber of John Adams and his son John Quincy Adams.

In Plutarchian fashion, we can, however, opine that John Quincy Adams failed, during his presidency, to achieve his aims; his real political achievement came earlier in his career, as Secretary of State under James Monroe, in determining and mapping the Union and its borders – both South and North – and in enunciating the clear principles of non-interference by European powers in the New World. He was a great statesman and diplomat but not perhaps a great president. Like his father, John Adams (and, later, Woodrow Wilson), he lacked the popular touch and the ability to corral Congressmen and Senators to pass legislation (the "schmoozing" perfected by Lyndon Johnson). If we judge greatness by the enactment of laws, rather than conception, vision and leadership of ideas, John Quincy Adams falls short. But I would suggest that he is at the top of the second division of presidents and statesmen in the American pantheon.

THE COMPARISON OF WILLIAM WILBERFORCE WITH JOHN QUINCY ADAMS

William Wilberforce and John Quincy Adams played seminal roles in their respective movements to combat the slave trade and emancipate the slaves. In 1807, Parliament struck down the slave trade. In 1833, Wilberforce's great triumph before he died was the final abolition of slavery itself throughout the British Empire. One might have expected a more immediate impact on American public opinion, but the abolitionist movement in the United States lagged behind the British evangelical impetus and parliamentary opinion by more than a generation. It would be another 30 years and a civil war costing 600,000 lives before Lincoln's great Emancipation Proclamation of 1863. During these three decades, the abolitionists slowly gained ground, and John Quincy Adams's brave and lonely stand in

Congress in the 1830s and 1840s surely paved the way.

John Quincy Adams was influenced by Wilberforce's work, but he was a career politician for whom slavery was only one issue. Wilberforce made abolition his life's work. Their dedication to public servicdemay have also been partially responsible for the problems they both had with their children.

Spencer Perceval   James Garfield

CHAPTER 10

Spencer Perceval and James Garfield

﹏

Spencer Perceval

I have nothing to add to the nothing that has been said.

ORN IN 1762, SPENCER PERCEVAL, AS THE YOUNGEST SON, expected no inheritance and to have to make his own way. After attending Harrow and Cambridge, he read for the bar, becoming a King's Counsel, or senior barrister, in 1796. He was a very successful lawyer, earning up to 5,000 guineas a year (approximately $10 million today).

Once he became an MP, he rose rapidly up the ladder of preferment, to become Solicitor General in 1801, Attorney General from 1802 to 1806, and eventually Chancellor of the Exchequer, in 1807. He succeeded to the premiership in October 1809, but he has largely been forgotten by history.

Perceval had a robust attitude towards the war with Napoleonic France. On the home front, he stood firm against the Luddite Riots, an effect of the rapid industrialization of England when many workers were unemployed and started to destroy the new machinery. Despite his liberal and Evangelical sympathies, Perceval believed it was essential to maintain order. He was against the slave trade and in favor of trade with South America. He tried to improve the conditions of convicts going to New South Wales, and, as a protégé of Pitt the Younger's, he espoused sound finance as well as strong military and naval power.

Having been mentored by Pitt, he himself was a mentor to William Peel and Viscount Palmerston. He was loved by nearly all his colleagues and friends, and, to everyone's surprise, managed to maintain his position as Prime Minister for two and a half years.

One day in May, 1812, a man named John Bellingham, who had lost all his money trading in Russia and nursed a grievance against the British government, entered the Members' Lobby outside the chamber of the House of Commons, and fired a revolver at point-blank range at the prime minister, who died almost instantly. Perceval was 49 years old.

Bellingham was hanged within the week. Perceval was eulogized as "the model of a high-minded, high-principled, truthful, generous gentleman, sans peur et sans reproche," and Parliament voted that a large sum of money be given to support his widow and family.

Perceval was a devoted family man with six sons and six daughters. He should be remembered as a man of great integrity, hard work, and professionalism; for laying the foundation for the long premiership of his successor the Earl of Liverpool; and for his disciples, Peel and Palmerston, who would maintain British power and financial integrity.

⏤

James Garfield

I am receiving what I suppose to be the usual number of threatening letters on the subject. Assassination can be no more guarded against than death by lightning; it is best not to worry about either.

JAMES GARFIELD WAS BORN IN 1831 IN A LOG CABIN ON THE FRONTIER in Ohio. He had little or no education, and as a sixteen-year-old was briefly a canal driver, which required him to drive a horse pulling a boat along the new canal from Cleveland to Pittsburgh. After teaching himself, he enrolled in and eventually graduated from Williams College and became Professor of Classics and then President of Hiram College in Ohio.

In 1859, at the age of 28, Garfield entered politics as an abolitionist Republican. He entered Congress in 1863 and became Senator for Ohio in 1880. During the Civil War, he served as a competent general on the Union side, but he found seeing young men killed traumatic. He was a thoughtful, enquiring gentleman who was married and had five children.

Garfield never campaigned for the presidential nomination. He had "a sense of dread" about it. Modest, unassuming, and unambitious, he was perhaps the best and the most well-read man ever to run for president, having steeped himself in Greek, Latin and English classics. He was nominated as a dark-horse compromise candidate – on the 36th ballot of the 1880 Chicago Republican Convention – after making a nominating speech for John Sherman: "You ask for his monuments, I point you to twenty-five years of national statutes. Not one great beneficent statute has been placed in our statute books without his intelligent and powerful aid." Garfield made the rather questionable figure of Chester Arthur his running mate because he was one of the lieutenants of the Senator from New York, Roscoe Conkling, and a stalwart Republican in the days of "smoke filled rooms" and behing the scenes of political deals.

However, on July 2nd, 1881, only four months after his inauguration, a disappointed office-seeker named Charles Guiteau shot President Garfield, who died two months later in great pain. Joseph Lister had already invented and tested antiseptic in London, but Garfield's doctor refused to use it, so he died of blood poisoning.

Garfield had flagged up his enduring political legacy: "The civil service can never be placed on a satisfactory basis until it is regulated by law. For the good of the service itself, for the protection of those who are entrusted with the appointing power against the waste of time and obstruction to the public business caused by the inordinate pressure for place, and for the protection of incumbents against intrigue and wrong."

Like Lincoln, Garfield had been a storybook president, rising from a humble log cabin to the White House. He was also one of the few scholarly men to obtain the highest office.

THE COMPARISON OF SPENCER PERCEVAL WITH JAMES GARFIELD

Spencer Perceval and James Garfield are both little-known political figures. They were both also dignified men who were well-read and well-educated, and generally well-meaning. Both were promising, idealistic, and capable. Perceval and Garfield are the outstanding "might-have-beens" of British and American political history.

Charles James Fox   Aaron Burr

CHAPTER 11

Charles James Fox and Aaron Burr

⁓

Charles James Fox

How much the greatest event it is that ever happened in the world! And how much the best! —[on the French Revolution]

Humanity ... does not consist in a squeamish ear. It belongs to the mind as well as the nerves, and leads a man to take measures for the prevention of cruelty which the hypocritical cant of humanity contents itself in deploring.
> —[House of Commons debate on the slave trade]

CHARLES JAMES FOX WAS AN INVETERATE GAMBLER AND WOMAN-izer, and consumed large quantities of alcohol, sometimes in all-night drinking sessions before appearing in the House of Commons the next day to make an eloquent speech. He borrowed large amounts of money from his friends and rarely, if ever, repaid them. Yet, he was loved and revered by some of the leading men of his time.

Fox was born on January 24th, 1749, in London, the second surviving son of Henry Fox (first Baron Holland) and Lady Caroline Lennox, the daughter of the second duke of Richmond. Lord Holland had made a fortune in politics and was an indulgent father, saying of Charles: "Let nothing be done to break his spirit. The world will do that business fast enough." When the child threatened to smash a watch with a hammer, Lord Holland said: "Well, if you must I suppose you must." At 12 years old, Charles negotiated his first loan, signing a document still in the Holland House papers: "December 15, 1761. Receiv'd, advanced to me by my Father as part of my Fortune two hundred pounds, CJ Fox."

Fox went to Eton in 1758, but was asked to leave five years later due to his misbehavior, and then left Oxford without a degree (though that was hardly uncommon at that time for well-connected and well-heeled young men). While at Eton, when he was 15, he was taken by his father on a Continental tour, and at Spa, Lord Holland provided him with five guineas a night to spend on dice and cards. His mother, Lady Caroline, feared the consequences of such an upbringing: "I have been this morning with Lady Hester Pitt, and there is little William Pitt, not 8 years old [10 years younger than Fox], and really the cleverest child I ever saw and brought up so strictly and so proper in his behavior that, mark my words, that little boy will be a thorn in Charles's side as long as he lives."

From 1766 to 1768, Fox undertook a grand tour of the Continent. His attitude towards many things, from women to wit, aligned with that of the libertine French society he so enjoyed.

Fox was elected to Parliament in 1768 in a constituency (Midhurst, Sussex) purchased for him by his father. Since his father had been at odds with the Rockingham government, Fox sided with Lord North and the Tories. He seemed set on a bright political career, but he paid a high political price for his extraordinary character. George III came to hate him both for political and personal reasons, as a Whig and also as a corruptor of the Prince of Wales. Fox was one of the most talked about and caricatured men in eighteenth-century Britain.

Several things made Fox a Whig. First, religion: Fox was too much a libertarian ever to tolerate religious bigotry. From the 1780s onwards, he was a staunch supporter of the dissenters (those who distanced themselves from state religion), and he also supported Catholic emancipation. Nurtured by the ideals of the French philosophes and America's Founders, this developed into a commitment to natural liberty, and Fox became one of the earliest supporters of Wilberforce's campaign against the slave trade. At the same time, fellow Whig Edmund Burke sought Fox out in 1774 and, for some twenty years, was Fox's closest intellectual companion.

But the most important issue to him was the developing crisis in the American colonies. Fox came to believe that George III intended to establish an autocracy in Britain, that the power of the executive had grown too great, and that the American colonists were right in their opposition to it.

Once the War of Independence began in 1776, Fox believed that it would be long and difficult. He also believed that the Americans had a strong chance of winning and that instead of going to war, it would be better to grant the Americans their independence. In 1778, he moved that no more of the "old corps" (Britain's peacetime forces) be sent to America, and condemned the British handling of the dispute.

Fox's criticisms helped topple the government in 1782. This paved the way for a Rockingham–Shelburne government in which Fox was foreign secretary. But matters did not improve and even before Rockingham's death in July ended the administration, Fox was determined to resign. Fox, who after Rockingham's death was leader of the Whigs, opposed Shelburne's new administration.

Fox returned to power in a coalition with Lord North but the government did not last long – from March to December, 1783. Fox's belief that the king took every opportunity to bring his government down was hardly far-fetched: the crisis over the East India Company administration was defeated in the Lords (after the king personally appealed to the peers) by 19 votes. Fox spoke against this abuse of royal prerogative, and when the king nominated Pitt as the new prime minister in December, Fox used his majority in Parliament to obstruct all of Pitt's measures. In 1784, the king dissolved Parliament, and in the next election of Pitt returned with a substantial majority (Fox claimed that there had been electoral manipulation).

It was about this time that Fox met Elizabeth Bridget Armistead, a former mistress of the Prince of Wales. They lived together for about ten years, and were secretly married in 1795. Fox acknowledged the marriage publicly in 1802. Armistead domesticated Fox somewhat, and from the late 1790s they lived together in a villa in Surrey.

Fox's supporters who survived the 1784 election called themselves 'Foxites' rather than Whigs, a reflection of the degree to which personal attachments flavored Fox's politics. By the 1790s, the Foxites also came to be known as 'Fox's Martyrs.' Fox now argued for the supremacy of the legislature, particularly in the nomination of ministers; nor were his arguments only a case of 'people' versus 'King'; actually, he was pressing the case for oligarchy against despotism.

Between November, 1788, and March, 1789, George III suffered a bout of madness. Fox was in Italy and did not reach England until late November, and then was ill (and in Bath) until late February. Fox demanded that the Prince of Wales (who was a convinced Whig and a friend of Fox) be given full right of regency without conditions attached by the Commons. But the king recovered and Pitt remained prime minister.

Undoubtedly, Fox was a skilled orator. Horace Walpole wrote: "No man ever excelled him in the clearness of argument, which flowed from him in a torrent of vehemence, as declamation sometimes does from those who want argument." Burke once called him "the greatest debater the world ever saw." Sir James Mackintosh described him as "the most Demosthenean speaker since Demosthenes." But while Fox was capable of putting on a first-rate show wherever he was – whether at Brooks's club or the Commons – he wasn't a strong leader. His stays in office were short, and his interest in many issues was fleeting. The only holding power he had was that of friendship. Fox was close with European liberals such as Lafayette and Talleyrand. He was also close to Jefferson and Franklin, and Lafayette had fought in America with Washington, so Fox was a member of an international band of Franco-Anglo-American liberals; he regarded himself as a citizen of the world.

Many of these men celebrated the French Revolution. Between 1789 and 1791, it looked as if France would establish a government on "Whig" principles. When the Bastille fell, Fox assumed that the revolution would establish the supremacy of the legislature over the executive. Burke was one of the few people who understood how horrific the French Revolution really was; Fox disagreed. Fox's misinterpretation – and the stands in Parliament that went with it – split the Whigs for many years and ended his involvement in Parliament.

On May 6th, 1791, Burke moved to consider the deplorable

state to which France had sunk and the sad situation of her king. Fox defended the principles of the French Revolution. Burke's reply was to vindicate his own ideas and opinions, claiming that Fox had torn him apart in debate and had commanded his lieutenants to do the same. When Fox whispered there was no loss of friendship, Burke replied there was, and that by doing his duty, their friendship was at an end. Fox rose to reply, stood silent for several minutes, and wept. Most of his reply was a protestation of his intellectual debt to Burke and his friendship. Burke never spoke to Fox again, even refusing a last interview on his own deathbed in 1797.

When the French monarchy was overthrown in 1792, Fox moderated his views – especially since the Jacobin Republic inaugurated a Terror that claimed the lives of many of his friends. He recognized that there was no longer any genuine commitment to parliamentary values in France.

Even as the Whigs disintegrated politically, many of Fox's friends banded together to pay off his debts and purchase him a large annuity. It was a miracle that Fox held the Whigs together until June, 1794. Until 1792, they had agreed that the French were treading a well-worn English path. When that view was overthrown by the French themselves, they still sided with Fox because they had so little love for Pitt. By 1794, however, their fear of France became greater than their fear of Pitt and George III, and they began to defect.

Between the electoral battering of 1784 and the mass defection of 1794, there was little left of the Foxite Whigs – perhaps a few dozen MPs, which amounted to a lobby rather than an opposition. Fox took refuge in a few key issues. The first of these was that of civil and political liberty. Pitt had put civil liberty into abeyance in a series of acts between 1792 and 1794, which Fox viewed as George III's path to absolute tyranny. The Foxites therefore gave unstinting aid to those who ran afoul of these measures. Fox also established contacts with those like Wilberforce who were interested in reform and peace.

Fox kept pressure on the government to conclude a peace with France, in the belief that France, once the pressure was off, would be-

come a more reasonable and peaceful country. But Fox effectively retired from parliamentary affairs from 1797 until 1801. His political
position was represented by his nephew. In Fox's mind, the game was
over: George III had won, many of his friends were in prison, and the
European monarchs had assembled to destroy whatever cause liberty
still had left in France. Pitt's resignation in 1801, however, opened the
way for Fox's return to politics, as it split the king's supporters.

With the resumption of peace, many Foxites took the opportunity to visit France, as Fox did in 1802, where he was so well received
that the British Embassy kept surveillance on him. Talleyrand and
Lafayette were his hosts and introduced him to important new revolutionary figures, and even arranged for interviews with Napoleon.
They met on three occasions, and during each, Napoleon aimed to
please and Fox left dissatisfied. Conversation invariably turned to issues that frustrated Fox: how free the press ought to be, how useful a
standing army was, and so on. Napoleon's answers could hardly have
satisfied the old Whig. Fox eventually concluded that there could be
no cooperation with such a tyrant.

In 1804, Fox entered into negotiation with the Grenville Party.
Grenville supported Catholic emancipation, opposed kingly preroga-
tives and wanted the slave trade abolished – all issues dear to Fox.
This laid the foundation for the "Ministry of All the Talents" of 1806,
in which Fox returned to office (once more as foreign secretary). Even
then, Fox still thought that peace with France was possible, though
he was eventually disabused of this belief.

Fox was more successful in tying the abolition of the slave trade
to the broader issue of waging war against France, which helped ensure the success of the act in 1807. Indeed, this was the only bill –
aside from the Libel Act of 1792 – that may be directly ascribed to
Fox. It was the final act of Fox's life. When he accepted office in January, 1806, he was increasingly ill, probably from psoriasis of the
liver. He became swollen with fluid, which was "tapped" on occasion
to provide temporary relief. He died on September 13th, 1806, and
in his will left his money to, among others, a Robert Stephen and a

Harriet Willoughby, whom historians conclude are his illegitimate children. He had a private funeral, though his supporters were cheered that the attendant crowds appeared to equal those of Fox's old rival, Pitt (who had died just months before).

Although loved in his lifetime and a cult-figure afterwards, Fox left little lasting legacy in terms of political reform or legislation. Part of the reason was perhaps his dissolute life and character; he simply didn't devote the time or attention to politics that, for example, his great rival, Pitt, did. The bust of Charles James Fox that still presides over Brooks's Club in St James is rather the symbol of his hours spent there gambling, drinking, and enjoying time with his aristocratic and Whig friends than any testament to his political genius or influence. Fox was the great foil to Pitt. Pitt had few friends, while Fox had many. Long after his death, the poet Samuel Rogers recorded an elderly Fox-ite bursting "into tears with a vehemence of grief such as I hardly ever saw exhibited by a man," and added that he "was their world."

—

Aaron Burr

I am dead.
Thou livest. Report me and my cause aright
To the unsatisfied ...
  what a wounded name,
  Things standing thus unknown, shall live behind me!
  If thou didst ever hold me in thy heart
  Absent thee from felicity awhile,
  And in this harsh world draw thy breath in pain,
  To tell my story.
                                        —Hamlet V.2.333–4, 344–9

Political opposition can never absolve Gentlemen from the necessity of a rigid adherence to the laws of honor and rules of decorum.   —To Alexander Hamilton, June 21st, 1804

ONE OF BURR'S FAVORITE STORIES FROM HIS CHILDHOOD WAS about the time when, at ten years old, he tried to run off to sea to escape his uncle's strict upbringing. Burr successfully made it onto a ship. When his uncle climbed aboard to fetch him, Burr hoisted himself to the top of the ship's mast and negotiated a truce. His uncle agreed to let him return home without a beating. An older Burr would look back at the event as signifying early on his ability to persuade others and to go to great lengths and heights to achieve his goals.

Born in New Jersey in 1756, Aaron Burr was the son of the Reverend Aaron Burr, Sr, President of the College of New Jersey (now Princeton), and Esther Edwards, daughter of the famous Calvinist theologian Jonathan Edwards. He was a sickly child, who nearly died when he was only eight months old, causing his mother to write in her journal, "I look on the Child as one given to me from the dead." He was to lose both his parents by the time he was two years old.

He graduated from Princeton in 1772 with a degree in theology but decided to switch to law, at which he proved a brilliant student. However, the war intervened, and in 1775, Burr was part of General Arnold's difficult winter expedition into Canada that failed to capture Quebec. Burr distinguished himself by his courage in action and would continue to do so.

His bravery came to the notice of George Washington, who wanted to appoint Burr to his staff. But Washington and Burr clashed – some historians say they took an instant dislike to each other – and after further heroic service at the Battle of Monmouth in 1778, Burr retired from the army.

During the war, Burr met his future wife, Theodosia Prevost, ten years his elder. He admired the cultured, well-educated Theodosia and their relationship grew from friendship into love after the death of Theodosia's first husband in 1781. The two shared an admiration for the work of Rousseau and Mary Wollstonecraft, and valued rigorous education for men and women. Based on their letters, their relationship was close and intellectually engaging.

In preparation for marriage and family, Burr studied law in earnest. In April, 1782, he opened a law office in Albany, New York, and in July, married Theodosia. The newlyweds settled in Albany and, in 1783, Theodosia gave birth to a girl, whom they named Theodosia. Young Theodosia's academic and cultural development became one of Burr's passions.

Burr spent the 1780s building up his law practice. In 1783, he moved it to Manhattan. He felt law was tedious and a waste of his intellectual talents, yet continued to pursue cases to support his family. Nineteenth-century biographer James Parton described him as "a soldier by nature, a lawyer from necessity," and argued that his conduct in court had a militant tenor.

In 1784, Burr was elected to the New York Assembly, and he became New York's attorney general in 1789. The position gave him visibility and paved the way for him to become Senator for New York, defeating the incumbent, Alexander Hamilton's father-in-law Philip Schuyler. By displacing Hamilton's father-in-law, Burr became the target of Hamilton's malice and, during the following year's New York gubernatorial race, Hamilton retaliated. In a particularly bitter contest, Hamilton convinced political operatives to withdraw support from Burr, ultimately compelling Burr to quit the race. In spite of this setback, Burr served actively in the senate.

Even though Hamilton's prestige was far greater, he seems to have been threatened by Burr in some deeply personal way and went out of his way to attack him. Hamilton already disliked him but, seeing him rise as a member of the Republican Party to a position that might push him into national prominence, he went on the attack. He started a letter-writing campaign calling Burr an "embryo Caesar" and claiming that he had heard "rumors" that Burr was "unprincipled as a private and public man."

In 1793, Burr moved his family into the Richmond Hill estate. Spreading over 26 acres, the grounds included English-style gardens, meadows that stretched to the Hudson, and a man-made pond. The two-story mansion had neoclassical features and an Ionic portico.

Burr supervised the transformation of the home into a political statement, an extension of his private tastes and public persona. Then, in 1794, at the age of 48 and after 12 years of marriage, Theodosia died.

Burr soon attracted negative publicity for his campaigning style. Unlike other leading politicians of his era, Burr actively campaigned. He had an eye for detail and a love of the political game. In the 1796 presidential contest, more than any other candidate, Burr waged political warfare. He conducted interviews in New England for several weeks, ostensibly for Thomas Jefferson and the Republicans, and also met with powerful state politicians (of both parties) who might influence the selection of electors. Burr's term in the Senate expired in 1797, and he returned to New York. Many assumed his political career was over.

Leading up to the 1800 presidential election, Burr continued to pursue his legal career and involved himself in local and state politics. In his campaign efforts, he embarked on a street campaign. Most politicians kept a considerable distance from campaigning and allowed others to fight their battles. This remote approach was viewed as the more honorable, less pandering route. Burr, however, canvassed voters, personally collecting useful information and talking to constituents to win votes. Drawn to the political battlefield, he enjoyed campaign tactics and strategy. He converted his home into a campaign headquarters, supplying volunteers with coffee, food, mattresses on the floor, and guidance on political endeavors. He also compiled a roster with the name of every New York City voter and distributed it to his young followers, who went door-to-door. On the one hand, this made Burr an invaluable ally in the political arena, but on the other, he became distrusted by many and caused his contemporaries to question his principles. His hands-on approach led to the lasting characterization of him as a wheeling-and-dealing intriguer. The reality was that politics also afforded Burr "a great deal of fun and honor & profit," and he mingled among a limited circle of social equals whom he charmed into supporting him.

The results of the election ended in a tie between Jefferson and Burr with 73 electoral votes each, and the final decision was sent to the House of Representatives. Rumors spread that Burr had double agents who were making secret deals with Republicans and Federalists to steal the presidency from Jefferson. After 36 ballots, the contest finally ended with Thomas Jefferson voted into the office of president and Burr as Vice President. Claims that Burr tried to steal the presidency plagued him for years thereafter. He had certainly made one political mistake: he had done nothing to hide his interest in the office. The proper stance for a candidate of high office was silence and passivity. Burr never put on such a show.

In the February, 1804, Republican caucus, not a single Republican voted for Burr to return as Jefferson's vice president, and they instead chose George Clinton. Burr then ran against George's son, DeWitt Clinton, in the 1804 New York governor election, and was again defeated. During this contest, Burr and Hamilton reignited a personal battle that would end in a duel. Burr issued a challenge and both men put their affairs in order in preparation for their deadly appointment. On July 11th, 1804, the political rivals met in Weehawken, New Jersey, the usual location for duels – the practice was illegal in New York. There's some dispute about who fired first, but the outcome is that Burr's bullet hit Hamilton above the right hip, lodged in his spine, and soon after led to his death.

Public interest in the Hamilton–Burr altercation compelled their second-in-commands to draft accounts of the duel immediately after Hamilton died, which of course contained discrepancies. Clintonians and Hamiltonians took advantage of the ambiguity and condemned Burr as a murderer. Burr headed south to escape the public outcry, defamations, and indictments for murder and violation of dueling laws.

In the winter of 1804–5, Burr returned to Washington, DC. Though Federalists shunned him, many Republicans welcomed him back, because they welcomed the elimination of Hamilton. Jefferson invited him to dinner parties, and Burr took part in his final duties as vice president. On March 2nd, Burr made his last official appearance as vice president, delivering a speech to the Senate that voiced his profound respect for his fellow politicians and apologized for any negative feelings left in his wake. This was only two years after the Louisiana Purchase of 1803, and much of the newly acquired territory was unknown to its legislators.

Now that participation in national politics was impossible, Burr turned his focus south and west. He began working on accumulating contacts and resources to lead a filibuster campaign in Mexico and Florida in case the US went to war with Spain. Burr's ambitions aligned with the expansionist ambitions of the young republic: he claimed he did not want to conquer land or divide the US, but rather wanted to spur independence movements in the Spanish colonies and make Florida a part of the Union.

On an information-gathering mission that began in 1805, Burr traveled for seven months, over 3,000 miles, down the Ohio and Mississippi Rivers and through west Florida. Though tensions with Spain began abating and dispelled potential war, Burr continued recruiting and planning his filibuster in case that changed. However, his actions attracted attention, which led to charges of conspiracy.

In October, 1806, the postmaster-general Gideon Granger said that Burr's plans went beyond Mexico and Florida, and actually sought to topple the administration and declare the western states separate from the US. Though Burr had sometimes commented on the weakness of Jefferson's government and argued it might lead to the destruction of the union, no reliable evidence exists that Burr's plan went to this extreme. In 1807, Jefferson accused Burr of leading an illegal expedition and engineering a conspiracy. Reports circulated that Burr had an army of 20,000, but when the Ohio militia seized several of Burr's vessels, they found only about a hundred men and a cache of books, not weapons.

Chief Justice Marshall presided over Burr's trial. Though Jefferson wanted a conviction, Marshall ruled that, although evidence substantiated the accusation, the prosecution failed to provide convincing evidence of an "overt act" of treason.

Soon after the trial, former friends and supporters pressed Burr for repayment of loans or bills in a civil suit totaling $36,000. Unde-terred, and determined to reinstate his plans for a filibuster, Burr made plans to travel to England to seek foreign aid. So began his years of exile.

In 1808, he sailed for Britain and worked to establish social net-works with powerful members of British society and politics. How-ever, he failed to gain political backing and was ordered to leave Britain in 1809. Burr then sailed to Stockholm and spent five months there. He went on to Copenhagen. In both Sweden and Denmark, he received warm welcomes and had many admirers. However, the rest-less Burr refused to settle down. He spent the Christmas of 1809 in Germany, and was granted a passport to Paris in 1810.

War between Britain and the US loomed, and Burr wanted Napoleon to give him two or three frigates. He met the emperor's brother, Jerome, but it led to nothing. Burr decided to apply for a passport to return to the US, but access was denied. Trapped in Paris, he lived with an old American friend, artist John Vanderlyn.

Burr eventually returned to Manhattan in 1811 under a false name, hoping to evade long-standing creditors. Having failed to gain support for a filibuster, he turned his attention to re-establishing his law practice. In July, Burr discreetly announced the reopening of his law offices but in the same month, family tragedy again struck. Aaron Burr Alston, Burr's only grandson and namesake, died at the age of eleven. A devastated Theodosia made plans to travel north to be with her father and set sail on the ship *Patrio*. Caught in a violent storm, the ship was lost at sea.

To overcome his loss, Burr threw himself into his law practice. He also adopted several people to mentor, including Theodosia's cousins Phoebe and Kate Bartow. Burr adored children and looked for ways to recreate a sense of the family that had been lost. Additionally, he adopted rising lawyer and politician Martin Van Buren as his protégé. They shared many political and moral beliefs and the similarities ex-tended to physical appearance: both were small of build and dressed meticulously; false rumors circulated that Van Buren was Burr's bastard. Burr also mentored two adopted sons, both of whom were also reputed to be his biological children: Aaron Burr Columbe (who later changed his name to Aaron Columbus Burr), the son of a French woman who arrived in the US around 1815; and Charles Burdett, born in 1814.

In 1833, at the age of 77, Burr married Eliza Jumel, a wealthy New York widow. At 58 years old, her life was summed up as: "Born a bastard, in youth a prostitute, in middle age a social climber, died an eccentric." They honeymooned in Connecticut, but six months after marriage, separated and ultimately divorced. Jumel charged her husband with adultery; Burr countered that Jumel caroused with different men. The divorce was eventually approved and came through on September 14th, 1836, the day Burr died.

THE COMPARISON OF CHARLES FOX WITH AARON BURR

Aaron Burr's imperial ambitions in the western United States were initially supported by Britain. However, in 1806, when Charles James Fox became the new British foreign secretary, he ended the government's support of Burr.

Both Fox and Burr were scions of gentility. But while Burr was a man who could never be idle, who rose early, and worked conscientiously through the day and often into the evening, Fox was a gambler and womanizer who sometimes drank all night.

Friendship was at the heart of their politics. Both were revered for it. At his death many of Fox's friends, like his nephew Henry Holland, were a decade or more younger than him. Burr's charisma had also enabled him to attract a band of young supporters and followers.

Most of Burr's contemporaries believed in principles, such as Federalism or Republicanism, before personal commitments. Burr committed neither to Federalists, nor Republicans; he sought office at any cost and was happy to accommodate anyone willing to support him. Burr saw the bond of friendship as stronger than political ties. He adhered to it over political affiliations. Fox was similar in this respect. He could treat politics as an arena in which to settle personal scores.

Ultimately, both men – perhaps like Alcibiades and Coriolanus in Plutarch's original *Lives* – lacked the moral fiber and integrity to succeed to the highest office. They were clever libertines who had many friends and supporters but lacked good judgment, one on the French Revolution, the other on the secession of the South.

Sir Robert Peel   Andrew Jackson

CHAPTER 12

Sir Robert Peel and Andrew Jackson

— ◆ —

Sir Robert Peel

There is not a man in the House more sensitive on the subject of honour than Sir Robert [Peel]. You may apply to him epithets which are synonymous with fool, blockhead, etc., if you please, and he utters not a word of complaint; you may brand him with the name of bigot, either in politics or religion if you are so inclined, and he murmurs not a word of resentment; but charge him with anything, either in his private or public capacity, inconsistent with the character of a man of honour, and that moment he demands an explanation.   —JAMES GRANT

ROBERT PEEL WAS THE FIRST MODERN BRITISH PRIME MINISTER. He introduced modern administrative practices and founded the British police force (known as "Peelers" or, as they still are called today, "Bobbies").

"There seem to me very few facts, at least ascertainable facts, in politics," Peel said, perhaps foreshadowing Macmillan's "Events, dear boy, events." Lincoln would admit, "I plainly confess I have not controlled events, events have controlled me." Peel's opinion was that "The great aim of government is to work by such instruments as the world supplies."

Peel's pragmatism probably came from his childhood as the son of a wealthy Lancashire cotton-spinner and manufacturer. He was polished at Harrow School and Oxford, but always spoke with a Lancashire accent. His exact contemporary at Harrow was Byron. No two men could have been more different. Byron's romantic temperament was volcanic; from it, lava flowed. The mind of Peel was the opposite: his opinions accumulated daily like the deposits of a rich alluvial soil, as Bagehot said: "You scarcely think of [Peel's] mind as acting; it always seemed acted upon." Unlike Byron, Peel's love life was simple, and in 1820, he married the beautiful Julia Floyd (whose portrait by Gainsborough hangs in the National Gallery). They had five sons and two daughters.

In 1832, opposing popular demand for a wider franchise, Peel said, "No government can exist which does not control and restrain the popular sentiments." However, he was deeply interested and concerned about the workers in Britain's factories. He never tried to hide his own background as the son of a cotton-spinner and was taunted by some Tories with the nickname "The Spinning Jenny." His response:

> What was the grand charge against myself – that the King had sent for the son of a cotton-spinner . . . in order to make him Prime Minister of England. Did I feel that by any means a reflection on me? . . . No; but does it not make me, and ought it not make you, gentlemen, do all you can to reserve to other sons of other cotton-spinners the same opportunities, by the same system of laws under which this country has so long flourished, of arriving by the same honourable means at the like destination?

Peel became the first prime minister to come from a non-aristocratic background. He changed his mind on great questions like parliamentary reform and the Corn Laws. He effected a minor revolution, repealing the Corn Laws in 1846, sacrificing his career to make food cheaper for the people. This, his greatest and most controversial act, led to him being called "a great doer of the impossible" by the social reformer Harriet Martineau. His reforms laid the foundations for Victorian prosperity for the rest of the 19th century.

In his speech against the law Peel said:

I shall leave a name execrated by every monopolist who . . . clamours for protection because it accrues to his individual benefit; but it may be that I shall leave a name sometimes remembered with expressions of goodwill in the abodes of those whose lot it is to labour, and to earn their daily bread by the sweat of their brow, when they shall recruit their exhausted strength with abundant and untaxed food, the sweeter because it is no longer leavened by a sense of injustice.

It was said of Peel's oratory: "No man in the House can appeal with a tittle of the effect with which he can, to the fears of his audience . . . The deepest stillness pervades the House while he is speaking. Even in the gallery, where there is generally a great deal of noise from the exits and entrances of strangers, the falling of a pin might be heard. All eyes are fixed on Sir Robert."

Peel's closest political colleague, though 20 years his senior, was the Duke of Wellington, who testified to his veracity: "I never had, in the whole course of my life, the slightest reason for suspecting that he stated anything which he did not firmly believe to be the fact" – a degree of honesty rare among politicians.

The repeal of the Corn Laws in 1846 ended Peel's political career. In 1850, he was riding his horse in Hyde Park, and expired soon after falling on his head.

Andrew Jackson

In the person of Andrew Jackson, the West had reached controlling power. Here at last was an American President who had
no spiritual contacts whatever with the Old World or its pro-
jection on the Atlantic shore, who represented at the White
House the spirit of the American frontier. To many it seemed
that democracy had triumphed indeed.

There were wild scenes at Washington at the inauguration of
the new President, dubbed by his opponent Adams as "the
brawler from Tennessee". But to men of the West, Jackson was
their General, marching against the political monopoly of the
moneyed classes.

—CHURCHILL, *A History of the English-Speaking Peoples*

ANDREW JACKSON REPRESENTS THE RISE OF THE BACKWOODSMAN
and the frontier into American political life. Following the
first six presidents (Washington, Adams, Jefferson, Madison,
Monroe, and John Quincy Adams) and 50 years after the Declaration
of Independence, the aristocratic Virginian plantation owners and the
Massachusetts lawyers were suddenly supplanted by "Old Hickory,"
a rough frontier fighter, child of the Carolina backcountry, and Tennessee landowner.

As an experience, myth, and symbol, the Frontier continues to
dominate American thought. The movement, progress, energy, expec-
tation, confidence, prosperity, and hope that it represents still remains
central to American culture.

As the results of the 1828 US presidential election came in, it
could be seen that John Quincy Adams had won practically nothing
outside New England. The West had finally had its say. Though a self-
taught lawyer, Jackson represented a significant democratic break
with the political tradition of the Virginians (and the Adams family)
who had dominated the early years of the republic.

Jackson's portrait of 1835, with its shock of stiff white hair, deeply lined leathery face, black eyes, and clinched lips over toothless gums, emanates melancholy and determination. Under the white hair was a deep and nasty scar he had received when he was a boy soldier of only 13. Captured by the British, he refused to clean an officer's boots, claiming the status of a prisoner of war, and received a sword slash across his skull and fingers. To Jackson, it was a source of pride in his patriotic suffering and dedication.

Jackson treated Native Americans in a very different manner than the first six presidents. He waged a successful campaign against the Seminole Indians in Florida in 1817–18. After he became president in 1828, he oversaw the Black Hawk War of 1832 (in which Lincoln served as a young captain), which resulted in the defeat of the Sac and Fox Indians of Wisconsin.

THE COMPARISON OF SIR ROBERT PEEL WITH ANDREW JACKSON

The sudden arrival at the White House of a representative of the frontier, in the form of Andrew Jackson, has no equivalent in British politics. Sir Robert Peel is the closest match because he was almost a contemporary and because he was the first prime minister from a non-aristocratic background.

Like Jackson, Peel was a radical departure from his predecessors as prime minister. He succeeded Lords Grey and Melbourne. As the son of a Lancashire cotton-spinner, he epitomized – as Jackson did in American public life – the end of the aristocratic laissez-faire and amateurish approach to legislation as practiced by people such as Lord Melbourne, whose "masterly inactivity" had been elevated to a public policy by Whig aristocrats as well as Tories.

In 1832, opposing popular demand for a wider franchise, Peel said, "No government can exist which does not control and restrain the popular sentiments." This was perhaps a comment on "Jacksonian" democracy (greater democracy for the common man) in the United States.

John Churchill, First Duke of Marlborough   Robert E. Lee

CHAPTER 13

John Churchill, First Duke of Marlborough and Robert E. Lee

―

John Churchill, First Duke of Marlborough

JOHN CHURCHILL'S FATHER, THE FIRST SIR WINSTON CHURCHILL (1620–88), had been a cavalier and supporter of King Charles I in the English civil war. On the defeat of the King's forces, he lost his property, but he had fortunately married Elizabeth Drake, fourth daughter of Lady Drake, who had a family house in Devon where they were able to sequester themselves with their five young children during the 11 years between the execution of King Charles I in 1649 and the restoration of King Charles II in 1660. This impoverished childhood marked John Churchill for life and made him, perhaps, more ambitious. His biographer and descendant Winston Churchill remarked that the conditions at Ash House "might well have aroused in his mind two prevailing impressions: first a hatred of poverty ... and secondly the need of hiding thoughts and feelings from those to whom their expression would be repugnant." Winston Churchill was referring to the fact that they were surrounded by parliamentarians who held different political beliefs. Indeed, John Churchill's grand-mother Lady Drake had supported the parliamentary cause.

With the Restoration, the first Sir Winston's fortunes improved, although he never had much money. Both John and, more impor-tantly, his sister, Arabella, were appointed to court. Arabella became a maid of honor to the Duchess of York, and John joined her a few months later as a page to James, Duke of York, the brother of King Charles II, who was later to become James II.

Churchill, who was then about 15 years old, often accompanied the Duke to inspect troops in the royal parks; and by 1667, he had obtained a commission in the King's own company, later called the Grenadier Guards. He served in Tangier at the age of 18 and stayed there for three years, receiving first-class training and field experience fighting against the Moors.

John Churchill was a handsome and appealing young man; back in London he attracted the attentions of one of the King's mistresses, Barbara Villiers, Duchess of Cleveland. There are several stories about his liaisons with this lovely, but dangerous, lady. According to one, he hid in the cupboard, but the King discovered him, and Churchill fell to his knees. "You are a rascal," said Charles, "but I forgive you because you do it to get your bread." Another version of this story has Churchill jumping out of the window. He was probably the father of the Duchess of Cleveland's daughter, Barbara, born in 1672, but by that year, he had gone to sea again and fought in the Royal Navy against the Dutch. He was soon credited with saving the life of the Duke of Monmouth, who was the illegitimate son of the King.

Churchill's early life alternated between scenes of martial ardor, both on land and at sea, and court life. He eventually returned to the court at St James's Palace. In 1675, he fell in love with Sarah Jennings, whom he married two years later. They had seven children.

Churchill was not merely a highly skilled and well-trained soldier, he also had rare skills as a diplomat. Together with his friend Sidney Godolphin, he went to The Hague in 1678 to negotiate a convention on the deployment of the English army in Flanders. He met William, Prince of Orange, and many other leading European statesmen, including King Louis XIV and many of his ministers. This was the end of the 17th century, the century of the wars of religion, and the struggle between southern Catholic Europe and northern Protestant Europe – Germany, the Netherlands and England – was a factor in every conflict and political intrigue. A crisis arose in England with the death of Charles II in 1685, and the succession of his Catholic brother, as James II. Now thirty-five and ennobled, having been close to King James II for over 20 years, Churchill was given a senior command in the army to quell the rebellion of the Duke of Monmouth, who was defeated at the Battle of Sedgemoor in July, 1685.

The "Glorious Revolution" of 1688 saw the Dutch prince William, married to James's daughter Princess Mary, land in the west country with a small force. Churchill switched sides at the critical moment from James to William and was later rewarded with the title Earl of Marlborough.

After the replacement of James II by William and Mary in 1689, one of Churchill's first duties was to take charge of the 8,000 British troops in the Low Countries, but during the next 10 years, he saw only three years' service in the field. His position at court had become weaker, and he was distrusted by King William and Queen Mary for his (and his wife's) closeness to Princess Anne, whose claim to the throne was stronger than William's. At the Battle of the Boyne in July, 1690, William III decisively defeated the forces of James II. Marlborough himself was then given a command in southern Ireland, where he learnt the significance of logistics to an army.

The deterioration of Marlborough's relationship with King William was brought to a head in 1692 when he was accused of treason and imprisoned in the Tower of London, where he spent five weeks. For several months, the Allies had been planning an attack on the French at Brest, and the French had somehow been alerted to this imminent assault. There was no evidence, but Marlborough's enemies claimed that he had alerted the enemy by betraying the Allied plans to James II, who was then living in France. Most historians give Marlborough the benefit of the doubt. (But his behavior in the 1688 crisis naturally led to doubts about his loyalty.)

In 1694, Queen Mary died and Princess Anne became the heir to the throne, which allowed Marlborough to draw closer to the center of power. King William III died in 1702 and she succeeded as Queen Anne. In the meantime, the War of the Spanish Succession began to dominate the European scene when King Charles II of Spain died without a natural heir and bequeathed his domains to the grandson of Louis XIV. If Spain and France combined into a single kingdom, it would drastically alter the European balance of power. Marlborough was given the task of negotiating a new coalition to oppose France and Spain and signed a treaty with the Dutch Republic and the Holy Roman Emperor Leopold I to do so.

Marlborough became commander of the combined allied forces in 1702 and captured four fortresses in the Low Countries. By the end of that year, Queen Anne had made him a duke. Unfortunately, his only surviving son and hope of founding a dynasty, John, died of smallpox at the age of 17, causing the Churchills great grief.

On August 13th, 1704, the Duke of Marlborough reached the peak of his fame with victory at the Battle of Blenheim. After marching 250 miles from the Low Countries with Prince Eugene of Savoy as his second-in-command, he delivered a crushing defeat on the French Army and the Elector of Bavaria. It has been described as one of the greatest examples of military tactics before Napoleon, and became a model for planning, logistics, and operational skill. Marlborough was now the foremost soldier of the age, one who had played a major part in changing the balance of power in Europe. The Queen lavished upon her favorite the royal manor of Woodstock. With an annual income of over £60,000 (approximately £6 million today), the Marlboroughs were not only powerful at court but extremely rich. However, the intimate friendship between Anne and the Duchess began to cool.

Despite frequent political attacks and maneuverings at Westminster, Marlborough continued to gain one victory after another during the next few years: Blenheim, Ramillies, Oudenarde, and Malplaquet, his four greatest victories, were achieved in 1704, 1707, 1708, and 1709, and left him undefeated on the European battlefield.

The Tories finally became dominant in London and Marlborough's enemies organized themselves to secure not only peace in Europe but the dismissal of the great captain-general on trumped-up charges of corruption. It was alleged that he had illegally received money from the bread and transport contractors in the Netherlands and 2.5% of the wages of the foreign troops in English pay, amounting to £280,000. Marlborough was able to refute all of this by producing a warrant signed by the Queen authorizing him to make the deduction. Nevertheless, Queen Anne wrote him a letter of dismissal: "I'm sorry for your own sake the reasons are become so public which makes it necessary for me to let you know you have render'd it impracticable for you to continue yet longer in my service."

Marlborough thought it best to leave England, and at the end of 1712 went into voluntary exile on the Continent, where he was shown respect and celebrated at the courts. In 1714, on the day Queen Anne died and was succeeded by the Elector of Hanover, King George I, Marlborough returned to England and to the influence and respect at court and favor under the House of Hanover. He was reappointed Captain-General and presided over the defeat of the 1715 Jacobite rising, directing matters from London because his health was declining.

In 1722, by now 72 years old, Marlborough had a second stroke. He died in the presence of his wife and two daughters. His great house, Blenheim Palace, lay uncompleted. His duchess, Sarah, survived until 1744.

Marlborough was one of history's greatest military commanders, bearing comparison with Wellington and Napoleon as well as the famed strategists of antiquity. He took great care of his men, and although his character has been impugned by some historians, his reputation, particularly after the 1933–8 four-volume biography written by his descendant Winston Churchill, has been rehabilitated. He was, undoubtedly, ruthlessly ambitious and relentless in the pursuit of wealth, power, and social advancement, but he was in tune with the spirit of his time.

Robert E. Lee

I felt like anything rather than rejoicing at the downfall of a foe who had fought so long and so valiantly.

[Ulysses S. Grant on the surrender of
General Robert E. Lee at Appomattox]

ROBERT E. LEE WAS BORN IN 1807, THE SON OF "LIGHT HORSE" Harry Lee, a Revolutionary War general and close companion of Washington. However, his father was a crook, who was cashiered from the Revolutionary Army. He had run up large debts, including one to George Washington, and was put into debtor's prison in 1809. Lee, his wife, Ann, and their five children then moved to a small house in Alexandria, Virginia. In 1812, Harry Lee was badly injured in a political riot in Baltimore and traveled to the West Indies. He would never return to the US, and died when Robert was only 11 years old. Left to raise (by now) six children in difficult circumstances, Ann and her family often paid extended visits to relatives and family friends.

Robert E. Lee's older half-brother, "Black Horse" Harry Lee, married a Virginia heiress. After she fell ill, he dosed her heavily with laudanum and then had an affair with her sister, who may have conceived a baby which was lost. Harry Lee was a disgrace to the family and motivated Robert E. Lee to be a man of honor in all things, including in his devotion to his native state of Virginia. For the rest of his life he fought to restore the family name by behaving with chivalry and nobility, to be beyond reproach in all his dealings.

Robert was sent to school and brought up as a devout Christian. When he was 17, his family asked that he be appointed to the United States Military Academy at West Point. He had to wait until 1825 to enter the Academy. He was an outstanding cadet and graduated second in his class, incurring no demerits, a rare distinction. He was commissioned in 1829 as a brevet second lieutenant in the Corps of Engineers. After his graduation in June, 1829, he returned to Virginia to find his mother on her deathbed; she died in July. In August, he was ordered to Georgia to build a fort on the Savannah River, and in 1831, he was posted to Fort Monroe in Hampton, Virginia.

Lee had been courting Mary Anna Randolph Custis, the great-granddaughter of Mrs. Washington by her first husband, George Custis. They married in 1831 at Arlington House, her parents' house overlooking the capital Custis had built for himself a few miles from Washington's own home. They would have seven children: three boys and four girls.

Lee distinguished himself in the Mexican–American War of 1846 as one of General Scott's chief aides in the march to Mexico City. Promoted to brevet major, he fought in four battles and was wounded at the Battle of Chapultepec. He was promoted to colonel, although he would remain a captain of engineers until his transfer to the cavalry in 1855. He also worked with Ulysses S. Grant during this war, and they both gained valuable military experience.

In 1852, Lee was appointed superintendent of the military academy at West Point and remained there until 1855, when he traveled to Texas as second-in-command of the Second Calvary regiment. In 1857 his father-in-law, George Washington Custis, died and, as executor of his will, Lee took on vast landholdings, hundreds of slaves and massive debts. Custis's will required that the slaves be "emancipated by my executors" within five years, but Lee found it difficult to manage the complicated estate, and they remained enslaved until 1863.

Was Lee, in fact, opposed to slavery? Douglas Freeman, his biographer, tried to set Lee's beliefs in a historical context: "people of Lee's class in the border states ... believed that slavery existed because God had willed it and they thought it would end when God so ruled." The time and means were not theirs to decide, conscious though they were of the ill effects of slavery on both races. Lee shared the convictions of his neighbors without ever having to come into direct contact with the worst evils of slavery. He never spent a great deal of time in any state south of Virginia until he went to Texas in 1856. He had never seen the behind-the-scenes operations of a cotton or rice plantation, and in Arlington, his slaves were notoriously well-treated.

In 1856 Lee had written to his wife:

> In this enlightened age, there are few I believe, but what I will acknowledge, that slavery as an institution, is a moral & political evil in any Country ... I think it is a greater evil to the white man than to the black race, & while my feelings are strongly enlisted in behalf of the latter, my sympathies are more strong for the former. The blacks are immeasurably better off here than in Africa, morally, socially & physically. The painful discipline they are undergoing, is necessary for their instruction as a race, & I hope it will prepare and lead them to better things. How long their subjugation may be necessary is known & ordered by a wise and Merciful Providence.

Lee served in the United States Army with distinction for nearly 20 years. The crucial period of his life came in the spring of 1861 with the secession of the Southern states. General Scott, commanding the Union Army, told President Lincoln that he wanted Lee for a high-ranking command. Lee was asked by one of his lieutenants if he intended to fight for the Confederacy or for the Union. He replied, "I shall never bear arms against the Union, but it may be necessary for me to carry a musket in the defense of my native state, Virginia, in which case I shall not prove recreant to my duty."

On April 18th, Lee was approached by Francis Blair on behalf of President Lincoln, who offered him a role as major-general to command the defense of Washington. He responded, "Mr. Blair, I look upon secession as anarchy. If I owned the four millions of slaves in the south, I would sacrifice them all to the Union, but how can I draw my sword upon Virginia, my native state?" He spent the next 48 hours thinking about the decision and then tendered his resignation from the US Army, writing to General Scott:

[My resignation] would have been presented at once, but for the struggle it has cost me to separate myself from a service to which I have devoted all the best years of my life & all the ability I possessed. During the whole of that time, more than 30 years, I have experienced nothing but kindness from my superiors, & the most cordial friendship from my companions. I shall carry with me to the grave the most grateful recollection of your kind consideration, and your name and fame will always be dear to me.

That same day he wrote to his sister, "Now we are in a state of war which will yield nothing." He was unable, he explained, "to raise my hand against my relatives, my children, my home. I have therefore resigned my commission in the Army, and save in defense of my native state, with the sincere hope that my poor services may never be needed, I hope I may never be called on to draw my sword." He rode over the Potomac Bridge for Richmond and three days later took command of the army of Northern Virginia.

Joining the Confederate army wasn't an easy decision for Lee. His wife, Mary, favored the Union, and while many of Lee's immediate family followed the Confederacy, over 40% of all Virginia officers remained loyal to the Union. Many families were divided. Nevertheless, once he had made the decision, he moved quickly to organize his forces.

In 1862, he led the Army of Northern Virginia against General George McClellan, who had advanced upon Richmond. Lee defeated McClellan in the Seven Days Battles. He defeated another Union army at the Second Battle of Bull Run. Within 90 days of taking command, he had moved the battle lines from six miles outside Richmond to only 20 miles from Washington, DC.

Lee invaded Maryland and moved north to Antietam Creek, near Sharpsburg. There, both sides suffered enormous losses, and Lee withdrew his battered army to Virginia. Lincoln used the Confederate reversal as an opportunity to make the Emancipation Proclamation, which put the Confederacy on the defensive.

Both Lee and his comrade "Stonewall" Jackson loved war and thought of it as a technical art to which they dedicated their lives. It was after the Battle of Fredericksburg in December, 1862, which caused 12,500 Union casualties and 5,000 Confederate casualties, that Lee reportedly said, "It is well that war is so terrible – we should grow too fond of it." At Fredericksburg, according to historian Michael Fellman, Lee had completely entered into the "spirit of war, where destructiveness took on its own beauty."

The critical moment of the war came during the summer of 1863, when Lee's victory at the Battle of Chancellorsville allowed him to advance into Pennsylvania, where he encountered Union forces under the command of General George Meade. Their battle in Gettysburg lasted three days and produced more casualties than any other action in the Civil War. The first day of the battle was controlled by the Confederates. The second day ended with the Confederates unable to break the Union position. On the third day, Lee decided to launch a massive frontal assault, known as Pickett's Charge, but was repulsed with heavy losses. The general rode out to meet his retreating army and proclaimed, "All this has been my fault." But Meade failed to follow up his victory with the destruction of Lee's army, which successfully escaped across the river. After Gettysburg, Lee tendered a letter of resignation to President Jefferson Davis, but Davis refused his request. Gettysburg was the high point of the Confederate tide, and they never recovered.

In 1864, the Union's new general-in-chief, Ulysses S. Grant, moved south in a war of attrition, pinning Lee against his capital, Richmond. By January, 1865, Lee had been promoted to general-in-chief of Confederate forces, but the South was running out of manpower, and the arming of slaves became necessary. Lee believed that "We should employ them without delay … [along with] gradual and general emancipation." By April Lee had abandoned Richmond and retreated west. He was surrounded and surrendered to Grant on April

9th at Appomattox Court House. He issued his Farewell Address to his army the following day. He stressed that the war was over and argued for reconciliation. "So far from engaging in a war to perpetuate slavery," he said, "I am rejoiced that slavery is abolished. I believe it will be greatly for the interests of the South."

Lee lived for five years after the war. He became a figure of respect and dignity and an icon to defeated Southerners. He was appointed president of Washington and Lee University in Lexington, Virginia, and served from 1865 until his death where he was much appreciated by the students. According to a professor there, "so kind, affable, and gentle was he toward them that all loved to approach him ... No student would have dared to violate General Lee's expressed wish or appeal." Lee told a colleague that the greatest mistake of his life was taking a military education.

Lee had been barred from the Proclamation of Amnesty to the rebels that President Andrew Johnson had made in May, 1865. Lee applied to Grant to be included and he also wrote to President Johnson, but he was not pardoned, nor was his citizenship restored until 1868. He was sympathetic to the freed slaves: "every one with whom I associate expresses kind feelings towards the freedmen. They wish to see them get on in the world and particularly to take up some occupation for a living, and turn their hands to some work." Lee also expressed his "willingness that blacks should be educated ... and that it would be better for both the blacks and for the whites," but he opposed allowing blacks to vote because he thought it would lead to demagoguery. He recommended that African Americans be deported from Virginia and resettled in Africa.

Since his death in 1870, Lee has become somewhat of a saint for Southerners. Fourteen years after his passing, he was described as

> a foe without hate; a friend without treachery; a soldier without cruelty; a victor without oppression, and a victim without murmuring. He was a public officer without vices; a private citizen without wrong; a neighbor without reproach;

a Christian without hypocrisy, and a man without guile. He was a Caesar, without his ambition; a Frederick, without his tyranny; Napoleon, without his selfishness, and Washington, without his reward.

His popularity spread to the North, and he has been commemorated in many ways and in many places throughout the United States. He may not have been the perfect man his popular image suggests, but he strove throughout his life to maintain a high ethical standard and reputation. In this respect, despite all the calumnies with which his name was associated during the Civil War, he has risen in the eye of history as a figure not of divisiveness, but of nobility.

THE COMPARISON OF JOHN CHURCHILL, FIRST DUKE OF MARLBOROUGH WITH ROBERT E. LEE

The worlds of European warfare in 1700 and the American Civil War of 1860s seem far apart, in technology and social norms. For instance, the machine gun made its debut in the US Civil War (but still took British generals by surprise in 1914–18). The Old South had some parallels with European aristocracy, but they can't be stretched too far: the court life of Louis XIV, of the Prince of Orange, of the Emperor in Vienna were very different from Robert E. Lee's life at Arlington before the war.

Marlborough lived in a far more sophisticated world of European diplomacy. Looking only at military achievement, Lee shines as one of the finest exemplars of military strategy in US history, while Marlborough, who proved himself in his series of victories against the French at Blenheim, Ramillies, Oudenaarde, and Malplaquet, would be without equal in British generalship until the Duke of Wellington a century later.

They were two of the finest soldiers of all time. With a scarcity of men and means, Lee proved himself a master of defensive warfare. On the offensive, he was bold, but Marlborough may have been his equal or superior.

Caring for and loved by his men, pious and private, Lee was free from Marlborough's more worldly temptations. His motivation seems to have been only for honor, while Marlborough's often seemed to have been for advancement. Both suffered their share of criticism but have since had their reputations restored.

Joseph Chamberlain   Theodore Roosevelt

CHAPTER 14

Joseph Chamberlain and Theodore Roosevelt

➤

Joseph Chamberlain

The day of small nations has long passed away. The day of Empires has come.

JOSEPH CHAMBERLAIN – FATHER OF PRIME MINISTER NEVILLE CHAM-berlain and Foreign Minister Austen Chamberlain – is little known today but was a dominant figure in British politics in the 1880s and 1890s.

Chamberlain was born in 1836 and came from a relatively humble lower-middle-class background. His family's trade was making shoes, and they did well supplying footwear to the armies of the Crimean War and the American Civil War. Joe left school when he was about 16 and joined the family business. He moved from London to Birmingham and was soon running one of the largest industrial businesses in England. It later became Guest, Keen & Nettlefolds (GKN) but in those days it supplied metal screws to the rapidly expanding manufacturing industry.

With his profound knowledge of labor and worker-employer relations, Chamberlain, though only 37, was well-equipped to become Mayor of Birmingham in 1873. With his dandified appearance, slicked-back hair, monocle, and smart clothes he was a distinctive figure in the late Victorian world, though his Birmingham accent gave away that he wasn't a part of the aristocracy.

When Chamberlain entered parliament in 1876, it was as a Liberal under Gladstone. He was a man of the people and promoted radical policies to help the poor and provide pensions and employment insurance; proposals that would not become political reality until Lloyd George enacted the "People's Budget" in 1909. During his tenure as Mayor of Birmingham, Chamberlain had instituted radical reforms in the way that the municipality organized water, electricity, and roads, but his municipal successes didn't translate into political success at a national level.

Chamberlain broke with Gladstone in the 1880s on the issue of Home Rule and became a Liberal Unionist, joining Lord Randolph Churchill and Lord Salisbury on the other side of the House. He was one of the first great figures to cross party lines. He was a dynamic force in the Liberal party and then the Unionist (later Conservative) party.

In 1895 Chamberlain became Colonial Secretary under Salisbury, but his family was criticized for supplying arms during the Boer War, a colonial and imperial expansion that Chamberlain so vividly and eloquently supported.

In 1903 at almost 70 years old, Chamberlain dramatically changed the political landscape by announcing his support of protectionism, in the form of imperial tariffs, to encourage free trade within the empire and to resist the importation of German and American products. This stance split the Conservative Party and encouraged the young Winston Churchill and his colleagues to join the Liberals in 1904.

He never achieved the high office that everyone expected he would. He was a prime-minister-in-waiting for perhaps 25 years but, in 1906, after the Unionists lost to the Liberals in a landslide, Chamberlain suffered a stroke and never fully recovered. He died in 1914, having changed the political landscape and paved the way for figures such as Lloyd George, Churchill, and the Liberal party of the early 20th century.

Theodore Roosevelt

Far better it is to dare mighty things, to win glorious triumphs, even though checkered by failure, than to take rank with those poor spirits who neither enjoy much nor suffer much, because they live in the gray twilight that knows not victory nor defeat.

There is a homely adage which runs, "Speak softly and carry a big stick; you will go far." If the American nation will speak softly and yet build and keep at a pitch of the highest training a thoroughly efficient navy, the Monroe Doctrine will go far.

THEODORE ROOSEVELT WAS BORN IN 1858 IN NEW YORK, JUST before the Civil War, the only son of an elderly father and a Southern mother. The Roosevelts were a wealthy family, but Teddy was weak and asthmatic as a boy and vowed to build up his strength. He later commented:

I was nervous and timid. Yet from reading of the people I admired, ranging from the soldiers at Valley Forge and Morgan's riflemen, to the heroes of my favorite stories, and from hearing of the feats performed by my Southern forebears and kinfolk, and from knowing my father, I had a great admiration for men who were fearless and who could hold their own in the world.

He was perhaps the first "body builder" to become a public figure. He set himself ambitious physical and mental challenges – he called it "the Strenuous Life" – with expeditions to Africa, Brazil, and the Rocky Mountains.

In 1884, his personal life was struck by tragedy when his mother and young wife died within hours of each other, leaving him with his infant daughter, Alice. He left her with his older sister, while he set out for the badlands of South Dakota. There, he raised thousands of head of cattle, only to be overwhelmed in 1886–7 by the worst winter of the century, when he lost half his capital and all his cattle in heavy snowdrifts.

Roosevelt became president of the Board of New York City Police Commissioners in 1895 and vowed to bust the crime and corruption that was characteristic of the city. As an ambitious young man, he quickly made enemies.

He was unusual in the rough and corrupt political world of New York at the time, coming, as he did, from an old Dutch family. As Lord Bryce commented, "The best men do not go with politics in America." And it is perhaps still true.

In 1898 Roosevelt joined the first US Volunteer Cavalry Regiment, known as the Rough Riders, and led them in the Cuban war. "Colonel Roosevelt" became a national figure and was selected as vice president by William McKinley in the 1900 election. When McKinley was assassinated soon after his inauguration, one observer complained, "that damned cowboy has become president" – and at the youngest-ever age of 42.

Roosevelt's presidency of 1901–1909 was marked by an energetic and radical attack on the great trusts epitomized by J.P. Morgan and John D. Rockefeller. Although it took several years and was not ultimately effective in curbing the excesses of capitalism, Roosevelt's policy succeeded in breaking up Standard oil as well as other major monopolies.

Roosevelt was nominated for the Nobel Peace Prize for his effort in bringing peace between Russia and Japan after the 1905 Russo-Japanese War, and he became an international figure. However, in a sense his career ended in failure because, after leaving the presidency to his trusted successor Taft, he was disappointed by Taft's inability to follow through on his policies. Roosevelt therefore stood again for President in 1912, as head of the "Bull Moose" or Progressive Party, splitting the Republican vote and allowing Woodrow Wilson to "steal" the presidency.

Roosevelt had written a number of books during his career: his military histories *The Winning of the West* and *History of the Naval*

War of 1812; and descriptions of his extraordinary adventures – *The Rough Riders* and *African Game Trails*. Perhaps most striking is *Through the Brazilian Wilderness*, the story of his expedition to the heart of the Amazon to find the headwaters of the Rio Duvida (River of Doubt) with his son Kermit and a group of Americans and Brazilians. Two men died during the expedition (Roosevelt himself almost died of a fever), and the physical challenges he overcame are extraordinary even today. One doubts whether any other public figure could have undertaken such an expedition with such energy.

Roosevelt is remembered as the father of the conservation movement in America – the preservation of Yellowstone National Park and many others are his legacy. He also paved the way for his cousin Franklin with his willingness to attack vested interests, including his own wealthy class of New England aristocrats, on behalf of the poorer classes in New York City and the nation.

THE COMPARISON OF JOSEPH CHAMBERLAIN WITH THEODORE ROOSEVELT

Joe Chamberlain was a wealthy and successful businessman who (like Baldwin and Hoover) failed in politics. Teddy Roosevelt was an aristocrat who nevertheless became a man of the people and attacked the trusts. Both men stood up for the working class. His "Progressive" policies on behalf of the people (like FDR later) and against the large corporations.

They were both radical, energetic, and enterprising, but their careers promised more than they delivered. Both were responsible for splitting their party: Chamberlain, twice – splitting the Liberals was not enough, he then had to split the Unionists. Roosevelt split the Republican vote in the 1912 presidential election, closing his political career.

Roosevelt's legacy is clearly the greater of the two. Except for founding the University of Birmingham (and to some extent in his municipal reform in the city of Birmingham, when he was mayor), Chamberlain left little in the way of legacy. He remains one of the might-have-beens of British political history.

William Gladstone

Woodrow Wilson

CHAPTER 15

William Gladstone and Woodrow Wilson

—

William Gladstone

Not for two centuries, since the historical strife of Anglicans and Puritans, had our island produced a ruler in whom the religious motive was paramount in the like degree. He was not only a political force but a moral force.

—Gladstone's official biographer, J. MORLEY (1903)

A sophistical rhetorician, inebriated with the exuberance of his own verbosity.   —BENJAMIN DISRAELI

WILLIAM GLADSTONE WAS BORN IN 1809 TO SCOTTISH PARENTS living in Liverpool, England. He was the fourth and youngest son of six children. His father, Sir John Gladstone, was a wealthy merchant who had made £750,000 from slaves, tobacco, and sugar. His mother, Lady Ann, was a Scottish Episcopalian on its extreme evangelical wing. Sir John was a Presbyterian who joined the Church of England before William was born, but whose beliefs also mirrored those of the evangelical wing.

John Gladstone, an MP, wanted one of his children to have a career in politics and decided it should be William. In 1821 he was sent to Eton, and he continued to Oxford University, where he achieved a double first in classics and mathematics in 1831. Though "a quintessential member of the rich upper middle class," he was also described as "Oxford on the surface, Liverpool beneath."

After graduation, he took a tour of Europe with his father, and upon return, stood for Parliament as a Tory. With help from the Duke of Newcastle, whose son was a friend, he was elected as MP for Newark in 1832 at the age of 23.

Gladstone was an arch Tory, and his maiden speech in 1833 demanded better terms of reparation for West Indian slave owners (like his father) whose slaves had been emancipated. He was an accomplished orator, dark-haired and handsome. He caught the eye of Prime Minister Robert Peel, who called him "a rising young man," and was briefly a whip in Peel's government, eventually becoming an under-secretary for war and the colonies under Lord Aberdeen.

Between 1835 and 1841, Gladstone opposed Lord Aberdeen. Although Gladstone prided himself on his writing, his works could be long and somewhat turgid. His first, *The State in Its Relations with the Church*, mainly detailed how Britain should protect and extend the influence of the Church of England.

Over the course of his sixty-one-year political career he was to move from an extremely conservative and traditional position to one which led him to be known as "the people's William." He became a radical liberal reformer with sympathies for the downtrodden, the poor, and those in foreign countries beneath the yoke of oppression.

In 1838, he made another Continental tour, and while in Rome, he met Catherine Glynne. In an uncharacteristically romantic gesture, he asked her to meet him by the Coliseum by moonlight. They were married in 1839 and would have eight children. Her family connected Gladstone to the Hawarden estate in North Wales, where he was to spend much of his life.

In 1841, Peel formed a government in which Gladstone was made Vice President of the Board of Trade. He was hard-working, handling the introduction of the income tax, which he struggled to abolish for the rest of his life. In 1843, he became President of the Board of Trade, a Cabinet-level post that made him master of the Royal Mint, second-in-command of British financial policy. This was becoming a sticky issue for the Tory Party as he and Peel began to move towards the repeal of protectionism, thereby opening markets for free trade.

In 1845, Gladstone joined a secret lay religious society called "The Engagement." Part of its mission was to convert prostitutes, which Gladstone did all his life. There is no evidence that he ever had a relationship with any of them, but in 1849, he began flagellating himself, often after he had met with a prostitute. He would meet the same woman on numerous occasions, and speak with them long into the night. The historian H.C.G. Matthew suggests that by 1854, he had spoken to perhaps 80 or 90 different women, of which only one was "saved."

Peel's government fell in 1846, and while Gladstone was in opposition, a family crisis arose: Oak Farm, a brick and iron works near Stourbridge partly owned by his wife's family, the Glynnes, was bankrupt. The Glynnes came very close to going under, and were forced to leave Hawarden Castle for some time, though they were provided with capital by John Gladstone. Gladstone claimed that the experience informed his time as chancellor.

In 1850–1 Gladstone took his family on a visit to Naples, where he directly experienced political oppression. It was an important milestone in his evolution from conservatism towards liberalism. In Naples he saw blatant injustice, "the negation of God erected into a system of Government." In the face of such evils he could not remain silent, and the Conservative orthodoxies that he had taken for granted, about the stability of Europe and the danger of revolution, could not restrain him. In 1851, he published his letters to Lord Aberdeen in which he attacked the Neapolitan Government, which caused an international sensation and marked him as a liberal sympathizer. He did, however, agree to become Chancellor of the Exchequer in Aberdeen's line-up of Peelites, Whigs, and liberals.

Gladstone's first budget was a defining moment in Victorian finance: he abolished 123 tariffs and reduced another 133. More than any other statesman, he defined the modern chancellor. He treated the annual financial report as a kind of "state of the union" of the British Isles, and his dispatch box continued to be used by Chancellors of the Exchequer for most of the twentieth century. His second budget was even more ambitious – he anticipated war and attempted to finance it without increasing the national debt. Instead, he raised the income tax, believing voters should know the real cost of war. At the same time, he helped lay the foundations of the modern, meritocratic system of university and civil service.

Gladstone's first budgets defined the Victorian age as one of free trade, and his work as chancellor under Palmerston sought to balance the budget and exert strict controls on expenditure (he made the Treasury reuse its envelopes, for instance). As he put it, "No Chancellor of the Exchequer is worth his salt who is not ready to save what are meant by candle-ends and cheese-parings in the cause of his country." Gladstone cemented free trade in 1860, with a reciprocal trade treaty with France and the abolition of every protective tariff except the shilling duty on corn.

Another of his innovations, which was to become a cornerstone of the financial stability of the working classes in the late Victorian and Edwardian ages, was the Post Office Savings Bank. The Post Office thereby became one of the great engines of social stability, allowing poor families to save in safety.

In 1865 Gladstone lost his Oxford seat. His politics had become too liberal for Oxford voters, but the loss was also a liberation for him; he announced to 6,000 people at the Free Trade Hall in Manchester: "At last, my friends, I am come among you, and I am come among you 'unmuzzled.'"

In 1868, Liberals returned with a majority of 112. Queen Victoria sent a telegram to Gladstone at Hawarden to announce the impending arrival of her secretary with a commission to form a government while Gladstone was felling trees at Hawarden. He paused long enough to remark, "My mission is to pacify Ireland," before he continued felling.

On Irish affairs, Gladstone's Irish Church Bill dis-endowed and dis-established the Anglican Church in Ireland (where three-quarters of the population was Catholic), granting its endowment instead to a poor-relief fund. The Irish Land Bill of 1870 attempted to recognize customary land relationships in Ireland and to reduce the power of landlords to evict tenants.

In 1871, Gladstone had three initiatives, all unpopular. The first was the Army Regulation Bill, which attempted to abolish promotion within the officer corps by purchase. When the Lords halted the bill, Gladstone went to the Queen and secured a Royal Warrant to abolish the practice. He was widely condemned in the Commons for being high-handed.

The second was to bring Queen Victoria back into public life. Gladstone had become convinced that the Queen had retired too much and that there had been a troubling growth in republican sentiment since the early death of the Prince Consort Albert in 1862. He convinced her to attend the service of thanksgiving at St Paul's to celebrate the recovery of the Prince of Wales from typhoid. But the Queen couldn't abide Gladstone and she remarked, "He addresses me as if I was at a public meeting."

Finally, Gladstone attempted to bring in a Licensing Bill to regulate alcohol. The Bill failed, only to be revived in 1872 in a more moderate form, which enraged the opposition and failed to satisfy its supporters. Brewers, a powerful and widespread industry, became die-hard opponents of the Government.

Gladstone's Irish policy was the most important to him, and he attempted to reform Irish universities by broadening Catholic attendance. The bill was defeated in 1873, and it was this that prompted his offer of resignation to the Queen. But when Benjamin Disraeli, his successor, declined to form a government, Gladstone resumed office. The Government limped along until 1874 when, in the election, the Liberals were smashed. Gladstone resigned and gave up leadership of the Liberal Party.

He appeared to be heading for retirement (he was then 65), but he had so come to hate Disraeli and everything he stood for, especially his pro-Turkish stance, that he began to prepare a return to politics. On September 6th, 1876, Gladstone published *The Bulgarian Horrors and the Question of the East*, which signaled a new kind of populist politics. An excerpt illustrates his rhetorical powers: "Let the Turks now carry away their abuses, in the only possible manner, namely, by carrying off themselves. Their Zaptiehs and their Mudirs, their Bimbashis and Yuzbashis, their Kaimakams and their Pashas, one and all, bag and baggage, shall, I hope, clear out from the province that they have desolated and profaned." Three days later, he spoke at Blackheath and began touring the northeast as a leader of moral outrage against the "unspeakable Turk" (word had reached Britain of Turkish massacres of Bulgarian Christians).

A Jingo mob broke the windows of Gladstone's London house in 1877, and military opinion was so powerfully against him that the Duke of Cambridge, the commander-in-chief, refused to shake his hand. There was deep unease in all political parties at Gladstone's barnstorming and his raw use of demagoguery to regain power.

Gladstone had been adopted as Liberal candidate for Mid-Lothian and in November, 1879, went to campaign in his new constituency. He gave 30 speeches and another 18 in 1880, which were heard by perhaps 90,000 people. Such an appeal to ordinary people by a leading statesman was unprecedented. He was uncomfortable in the drawing rooms of London society, but became wildly popular among ordinary voters and working people. The Liberals won a resounding election victory. When Gladstone formed his second government on April 23rd, 1880, his reputation for radicalism was secure in home affairs. However, in foreign affairs embarrassments were threatening to damage his liberal halo.

In 1881, Gladstone occupied Egypt where Arabi Pasha was leading a nationalistic movement against the interference of foreign powers, and in Sudan, General Gordon was ordered to evacuate the British when the Mahdi began a rebellion. Gordon was killed while Gladstone delayed the relief expedition. General Gordon was the epitome of the Christian hero, and Gladstone's failure to rescue him caused a popular outcry.

Meanwhile, Gladstone extended the franchise to create universal male household suffrage and a system of single-member constituencies. He advocated for, without success, devolved government for Ireland. In 1886 he resigned the premiership and began work on his autobiography. Nevertheless, in 1892, the Liberals won the general election and Gladstone was again asked to form a government. By now he was the oldest prime minister ever at the age of 84 (even Churchill only went on until he was 80 when he resigned in 1955. On February 17th, 1893, his Second Government of Ireland Bill was introduced, and it finally passed the Commons in early September after 82 sittings; the Lords sent it back, and Gladstone resigned for the final time.

Gladstone died at Hawarden on May 19th, 1898, and was buried in a ceremony noted for its civilian and religious overtones and its lack of military pomp and splendor. During his career, he challenged the definition of what a politician could be, riding the wave of the new democracy based on a much larger electorate and espousing a "bully pulpit" of leadership (as Teddy Roosevelt was later to call it). He introduced the idea that they could be Christian crusaders for good both at home and abroad.

~

Woodrow Wilson

It is not men that interest or disturb me primarily; it is ideas. Ideas live; men die.

I would never read a book if it were at all possible for me to talk half an hour with the man who wrote it.

Jefferson's Declaration of Independence is a practical document for the use of practical men. It is not a thesis for philosophers, but a whip for tyrants; it is not a theory of government but a program of action.

The Constitution of the United States is not a mere lawyers' document; it is a vehicle of life, and its spirit is always the spirit of the age.

THE IDEA OF WORLD GOVERNMENT AROSE AND BECAME WIDELY popular twice during the 20th century – both times in the year succeeding a world war. In 1945 there was universal revulsion from the terrible slaughter and genocide of the previous six years, and the United Nations was born. In 1919, for the first time, there was an idealistic vision of world government embodied in the League of Nations and inspired by one man, Woodrow Wilson.

Thomas Woodrow Wilson was born on December 28th, 1856, in Staunton, Virginia. He was the third child and first son of the Reverend Joseph Ruggles Wilson and Janet "Jessie" Woodrow, and he was known as "Tommy" throughout his youth.

The English-born daughter of a Presbyterian minister, Janet Woodrow came from a family with status in Presbyterian circles. Joseph Wilson was the son of Scotch-Irish immigrants and minister of the leading church in Staunton, the First Presbyterian Church. Though deeply religious, he was not a stern pastor. Witty and outgoing, he smoked, played billiards, and occasionally drank Scotch. He was a devoted and loving father.

Wilson's mother pampered and protected him. His older sisters also adored him, and his upbringing, surrounded by loving women, gave him a lifelong preference for female companionship. He inherited his mother's shyness – he always had to work to form personal relations with people outside his family and a small circle of close friends. His mother also instilled in him self-confidence and belief in his abilities.

At first the otherwise healthy Wilson did not appear very bright: he did not learn to read until he was nine years old and continued to be a slow reader and writer throughout his life. Whatever the cause, the handicap influenced his personality, and he developed a fierce concentration and near-photographic memory. He taught himself shorthand, which he used for note-taking and, later, for composing speeches.

Growing up in the South after a destructive Civil War, Wilson sympathized with the defeated, impoverished region of his childhood, and it inspired his interest in reform. He was a lifelong Democrat. He grew up with slaves (four lived in the house when he was born) and servants, and showed little interest in bettering the prospects of African-Americans. During his presidency, he would perpetuate racial segregation and other injustices.

Wilson entered Princeton in 1875 and experienced an intellectual awakening. He received good grades and remained in the top quarter of students. However, he often skipped class or shirked assignments in order to pursue independent projects. At first, this consisted of reading, but it later included participation in the Whig debating society and assignments as a writer and then managing editor of the student paper *The Princetonian*. He would use the publication as a platform to advocate for greater support for athletics and criticize Princeton's curriculum. At five foot eleven, he enjoyed playing baseball and became an avid football fan.

In 1878, during his junior year, he wrote an essay that marked his intellectual coming of age. Before writing the article, he had discovered the English editor, journalist, and writer Walter Bagehot. According to Wilson, Bagehot was his second most influential teacher after his father. In the essay, he addressed the failings of the existing political system. He pointed to a lack of meaningful debate and proposed that the US imitate Britain by appointing Cabinet members from Congress and allowing them to speak on the floor. He submitted a version of the essay to the *International Review*, and it was published in 1879.

After graduating from Princeton, he entered law school. He dropped the "Thomas" from his name and began going by his middle and last names only. He found the next four years, as a student and then practitioner of the law, dull. However, he gained respite from his related political activities: he continued to write essays while at school and, in 1883, decided to re-enter academic life, beginning graduate study at John Hopkins.

In 1884, he wrote *Congressional Government*, published in 1885 to great interest and acclaim. It has become a classic of American political analysis. He repeated his suggestion for maximizing debate in Congress through imitation of the British Cabinet. He also defended political parties as important elements in the workings of US government and accepted centralization as a governmental necessity. When he graduated with a PhD in politics and history, he was a rising academic star.

He received teaching appointments, first at Bryn Mawr College in Pennsylvania, then at Wesleyan University in Connecticut, and finally at his alma mater, Princeton. In 1885, he married Ellen Louise Axson, an artist, and the daughter of a minister from Rome, Georgia. They had three daughters: Margaret Woodrow, Jessie, and Eleanor.

During Wilson's academic career, he remained deeply interested in world affairs. As a professor, he thrived, giving lecture courses, to practice his oratory skills. In his lectures, he discussed the growing gaps between the wealthy and poor and emphasized the need for the government to wield federal power to rein in big business.

His primary weakness as a scholar was his dislike of solitary research. He disdained the act of accumulating facts and, for the most part, gained knowledge by direct, intuitive insight. However, his goal wasn't theoretical musing, but rather articulating contemporaneously relevant ideas and publicizing them. He published his views in popular magazines like *Harper's* and accepted numerous speaking invitations.

In 1902 the faculty unanimously elected him to become president of Princeton. He made significant changes and improvements to the institution. He endeavored to enliven the intellectual life of the undergraduates and introduced discussion sessions to the curriculum. He also helped to distance Princeton from its Presbyterian ties. He hired the first Jewish and Catholic professors in 1905 and 1909, respectively.

In 1906, he suffered a stroke that partially blinded him, and he experienced headaches and pain in his arms for the next year and a half. In 1909, Wilson was selected to become governor of New Jersey, and in 1910 he finally entered politics.

The bosses of the New Jersey Democratic Party supported his campaign. They hoped he would support their political agenda, but they may have discovered they had misjudged their man because he pursued progressive reforms and was able to put his political ideas into practice. He adopted a prime-ministerial model of governance by preparing legislation in advance and working through party caucuses, utilizing enforced party discipline.

As a result of Wilson's national prominence, he was selected as the Democratic candidate in the presidential election of 1912. He entered a tight race against Republican incumbent President Taft, former president Theodore Roosevelt, and Socialist Party nominee Eugene Debs. Wilson promised economic freedom, which was in contrast to Roosevelt's paternalism. He championed the people against special interests and promoted legislation that extended opportunity of the former and limited the power of the latter. He ultimately prevailed in becoming president because Teddy Roosevelt split the conservative vote.

During his first term, Wilson turned his ideology into legislation. He broke with 113 years of tradition by personally addressing a joint session of Congress and traveled to Capitol Hill more than any president before him. He described his leadership as the lead horse of a team rather than the coach driver.

Wilson's wife Ellen died of a kidney disorder in 1914 and Wilson sent through a period of depression. However, in 1915, he met and married a striking widow named Edith Bolling Galt. Edith would become a huge influence on Wilson and his politics: he consulted her on state matters and she read all important policy statements. Later, as her husband's health failed, she had unprecedented authority over matters of state.

In his second term, foreign affairs monopolized his time and energy. World War I had begun, and Wilson tried to maintain US neutrality. However, by 1917, when Germany instituted unrestricted submarine warfare in the Atlantic, he signed a proclamation of war.

When WWI ended, he attended the Paris Peace Conference. He was the first American president ever to travel overseas during his presidency, and none was ever in such a position of international popularity as when he stepped off the boat in France on December 13th, 1918. Europe lay in ruins. There was famine and disease throughout the continent, particularly in the defeated territories of Germany, Austria, and Hungary, and in Russia, the Bolshevik Revolution was still struggling to prevail in a civil war between the reds and the whites.

Backed by America's physical and financial resources, Wilson was regarded as a savior. The ex-professor, unworldly, and certainly idealistic, seemed to be a man who could save the world. At the heart of his ideals was his vision of the League of Nations and, in a sense, that was to be his only legacy, for it was soon apparent that Wilson's altruistic nature was no match for the nationalist passions and political subtlety of France's more realistic, or cynical premier of the time, George Clemenceau, and his European allies.

At the conference, Wilson pushed for the inclusion of his Fourteen Points. These included the re-establishment of invaded nations such as Belgium and Poland. Point 14 called for the formation of "a general association of nations ... under specific covenants for the purpose of affording mutual guarantees of political independence and territorial integrity to great and small states alike."

Clemenceau replied, "The good Lord had been content with only ten commandments." British Prime Minister Lloyd George, when asked about how he had done at the peace conference, said, "Not badly, considering I was seated between Jesus Christ and Napoleon."

Though the Treaty of Versailles no longer included most of his points, Wilson's plan for the League of Nations remained intact, but he returned home to resistance in November, 1919. Furthermore, he had a major stroke at a critical point in his national campaign to gain support for the treaty. The president lay near death and was permanently paralyzed on his left side. While incapacitated, Wilson's wife Edith imposed a self-described "stewardship" of the presidency, shielding him from outside visitors and becoming the sole conduit to the president. After his stroke, he was never again able to fulfill his duties as president.

Although Wilson was never able to convince congress to accept the League of Nations provision, he succeeded in passing the 18th (Prohibition) and 19th (Women's Vote) Amendments in 1919 and 1920. He signed his last acts of the 66th Congress before departing for his new home on S Street in Washington, DC. He died at the age of 68 on February 3rd, 1924, and thousands lined the streets as his funeral procession passed towards his final resting place at Washington National Cathedral.

In a League of Nations Address on September 25th, 1919, he said: "I can predict with absolute certainty that within another generation there will be another world war if the nations of the world do not concert the method by which to prevent it." Although he didn't live to see his prediction come to pass, he had envisioned the importance of an organization of united nations.

THE COMPARISON OF WILLIAM GLADSTONE WITH WOODROW WILSON

When he was 16 years old, Woodrow Wilson had a portrait of William Gladstone on the wall of his room and told his mother, "There is the greatest statesman in the world." So Gladstone was his inspiration as Lincoln had been to LG.

Both from Presbyterian stock, William Gladstone and Woodrow Wilson share a scholarly Christian idealism. Gladstone's *The State in its Relations to the Church* set the tone of his political life, which was dominated by the tortured issues of his faith. Wilson came from an equally intense religious background, although he only published works of a political character.

Gladstone and Wilson were open-minded and tolerant regarding the faiths of others. Gladstone worked for Home Rule for predominantly Catholic Ireland, and Wilson opened Princeton to Jewish and Catholic lecturers.

In an address at Sioux Falls in 1919, Wilson said, "Sometimes people call me an idealist. Well, that is the way I know I am an American. America is the only idealistic nation in the world." Wilson had the vision to found the League of Nations. Gladstone had a similar approach to foreign policy, and his and Wilson's idealism commanded a great following. However, Wilson's hope of pacifying Europe failed, blocked by the power politics of the Empire of the Republic leaders in the Senate; like Gladstone, he expected foreign statesmen to behave as Christian gentlemen, and just like Gladstone he was deeply disappointed. Gladstone, though a more practiced politician, also came to grief with his foreign policy: he could not resolve matters in Ireland on the question of Home Rule, and his rival Disraeli outmaneuvered him in the Balkans with his realpolitik.

Lord Morley said, "As a matter of historical fact, most of those who have held the place of Prime Minister in the House of Commons have hardly been orators at all, any more than Washington and Jefferson were orators. The exception to this rule may be William Pitt the Elder and the Younger, Charles James Fox, Gladstone, Lloyd George, and Churchill." Wilson, on the other hand, lacked Gladstone's eloquence and popular and domestic appeal so failed to gain approval for his League of Nations in his home legislature. Gladstone, thought a more practiced politician than Wilson, was also criticized for his idealistic foreign policy. He couldn't resolve matters in Ireland on the question of Home Rule, and in the Balkans, his rival Disraeli outmaneuvered him with his "realpolitik."

Their careers are examples of the need to be pragmatic and realistic in foreign affairs, as much as in domestic reform. It is nevertheless arguable that each man left a greater legacy because of their stubborn idealism.

Benjamin Disraeli

Thomas Jefferson

CHAPTER 16

Benjamin Disraeli and Thomas Jefferson

―

Benjamin Disraeli

A Jew at the head of a phalanx of country gentlemen was an unusual sight in English politics.   —WINSTON CHURCHILL

There are three kinds of lies: lies, damned lies, and statistics.

Youth is a blunder; Manhood a struggle; Old Age a regret.

DESPITE THE FACT THAT BENJAMIN DISRAELI DIED AS THE FIRST Earl of Beaconsfield, he was by no means an aristocrat by birth. He was born to a Sephardic Jewish family with a commercial background. Although he often romanticized his origins, his father's family and his grandparents immigrated from Italy to England in 1748. He was one of five children, and when Disraeli was 12, his father, never having had a deep or conventional faith, decided to leave the synagogue and have his children baptized into the Church of England. His father's decision dramatically affected Benjamin's career prospects. Britain was not as anti-Semitic as perhaps France or Germany were at the time, but it was impossible for a practicing Jew to become a Member of Parliament without taking an oath of allegiance on the truth of the Christian faith.

Disraeli was educated privately and, when 17, articled as a clerk to a firm of solicitors in London. He was a romantic, Byronic figure ill-suited to the law. He made a tour of Germany in his twenties with his father and decided to leave the profession. In London, he went to work promoting South American mining companies and lost a great deal of money by speculation. He tried to start a newspaper, called the *Representative*, which was supported by the famous British publisher John Murray, who lost £7,000 in the debacle of this short-lived enterprise. Disraeli's reputation suffered from these early setbacks.

When he was about 26, he traveled to the Middle East with his prospective brother-in-law, William Meredith, who died of smallpox in Cairo during the trip. Disraeli's vision of himself and of the world was substantially changed by this expedition, and the journey encouraged his interest in the East and in the values of different cultures. It was a formative experience and influenced several of his novels – during his lifetime, he published no less than 18, one unfinished. Many of them were romantic visions of his own role in the Empire; the other major subject of his writing was England and its classes.

Disraeli's politics were driven by his rebellious streak and his ambition. He decided to become a Tory although he was quite radical in terms of supporting democratic reforms. In 1834, he had an affair with the wife of Sir Francis Sykes, and in 1835 fought his first by-election against the Irish MP, Donald O'Connell, who attacked him viciously because of his Jewish origins. The most important outcome of this argument was that Disraeli's name became widely known, and he was soon taken up by the aristocratic group in Parliament and the London salons.

Elected to Parliament in 1837, Disraeli made his maiden speech, following Daniel O'Connell, whose speech he criticized. He was shouted down by O'Connell's supporters and responded, "You silence me now, but you will hear me in the future." In 1839 he married Mary Anne Lewis, the widow of his friend Wyndham Lewis. She was 12 years older than Disraeli and had a substantial income of £5,000 a year ($1 million today). She said later, "Dizzy married me for my money; but if he had the chance again, he would marry me for love." He said, "She is an excellent creature, but she never can remember which came first, the Greeks or the Romans." They were happily married until she died in 1872.

When Sir Robert Peel became Prime Minister in 1841, Disraeli hoped to win office but was ultimately disappointed. He was always at odds with the conservative agricultural and aristocratic interests of the Tory party and forged links with people such as John Bright, a leading radical and Lancashire manufacturer. He became a sharp critic of Peel and attacked him in 1846 over the repeal of the Corn Laws, which split the Tory Party. Peel resigned.

Disraeli spent most of his life in opposition to his peers, and he outshone them with his blistering oratory. In 1847 Lionel de Rothschild was elected Member of Parliament for the City of London when the motion to allow a reform of the rules allowing Jews to become MPs came before the House of Commons. Disraeli spoke in favor of this measure, arguing that Christianity was completed Judaism, and he asked the house, "Where is your Christianity if you do not believe in their Judaism?" Radicals generally admired this view, but the establishment didn't like his position, and the rest of his party voted against the motion.

Disraeli's fortunes began to improve not only with his marriage but also with the loan of £25,000 from the Bentinck family of the Duke of Portland, who lent him money to buy Hughenden Manor in Buckinghamshire. Finally when Lord Derby became Prime Minister in 1851, Disraeli managed to hold office briefly as Chancellor of the Exchequer. His great rivalry with William Gladstone began at that time. But Gladstone won a majority and formed a government, so Disraeli was again out of power for the next few years. When the Indian mutiny broke out in 1857, Disraeli was involved in the select committee to replace the British East India Company with direct government rule. In 1858, Disraeli tried to get Gladstone, still nominally a Tory, to join him in the government, and wrote him a letter asking him to place the good of the party above personal animosity. "Every man performs his office, and there is a power greater than ourselves that disposes of all this." Gladstone refused but denied that personal feelings played a role in his decision.

In 1867 Disraeli passed the Reform Act, which extended the right to vote from only about 112,000 to nearly a million by enfranchising male householders and lodgers who paid at least £10 for their rooms, which eliminated rotten boroughs. The right wing of the Tory Party, especially the future Lord Salisbury, spoke against the bill, accusing Disraeli of "a political betrayal which has no parallel in our Parliamentary annals." Disraeli, however, became a hero to the rest of his party for his "marvelous parliamentary skill."

In the following year, at the age of 68, Disraeli finally became Prime Minister. He visited Queen Victoria at her summer residence on the Isle of Wight, and she wrote to her daughter, the Prussian Princess Victoria, "Mr. Disraeli is Prime Minister! A proud thing for a man 'risen from the people' to have obtained!" Disraeli declared, "I have climbed to the top of the greasy pole." However, his first term in office was only about 10 months; he only managed to pass a small amount of legislation but was soon replaced by Gladstone. During his time in opposition for the next four years, he wrote a new novel, *Lothair* – the first time a former prime minister had done so – and it became a bestseller. Soon thereafter, he compared the Liberal front bench to a "range of exhausted volcanoes. Not a flame flickers on a single pallid crest. But the situation is still dangerous. There are occasional earthquakes and ever and again the dark rumbling of the sea." Gladstone, he said, dominated the scene and "alternated between a menace and a sigh."

When he had left 10 Downing Street, Disraeli had asked the Queen to give his wife the title of Lady Beaconsfield, but the 80-year-old peeress was now suffering from stomach cancer, and soon died. Although Disraeli lived for almost another decade, he was never reconciled to her loss.

In 1874 Disraeli formed a second government, and this time, after holding office for six years with a cabinet of six peers and six commoners, he was elevated to House of Lords as the Earl of Beaconsfield. By 1876, he was able to write of the Commons: "I am quite tired of that place." When asked by a friend how he liked the Lords, he replied, "I am dead; dead but in the Elysian fields," an apt description of the upper house of peers even to this day.

Apart from his democratic reform bills, Disraeli's greatest influence on history was in foreign affairs. He was fascinated by the Middle East and in 1875 managed to acquire a 50 percent interest in the Suez Canal. Eighty percent of the ships using the canal were British, and it was a critical link in its commerce with India. On the acquisition, Disraeli said to the Queen, "It is settled; you have it, madam." The Suez Canal purchase has been described as "the greatest romance of Mr. Disraeli's romantic career," and it became a focus of British foreign policy. A later foreign secretary, Lord Curzon, described it as "the determining influence of every considerable movement of British power to the east and south of the Mediterranean."

Disraeli took pains to please the queen. "Everybody likes flattery," he said, "and, when you come to royalty, you should lay it on with a trowel." He knew that the Queen longed to have an imperial title and so he managed to pass a bill making her Empress of India, but it was hardly a popular move, and he was attacked in the House of Commons.

In 1876, a crisis arose in Bulgaria when the Christians revolted against the Ottoman empire. Gladstone penned a pamphlet attacking so-called atrocities committed by the Turks in Bulgaria, and the Russians invaded Bulgaria. Disraeli managed to avoid declaring war and traveled with Lord Salisbury to the Congress of Berlin in 1878 to negotiate the new settlement in Eastern Europe with the German chancellor, Bismarck, who famously commented, "Der alte Jude, das ist der Mann!" (The old Jew that is the man). The Treaty of Berlin was signed in July, and Disraeli returned home to a hero's welcome. Foreshadowing Chamberlain in 1938, he said, "Lord Salisbury and I have brought you back peace – but a peace I hope with honor." The Queen offered him a dukedom, which he turned down, although he accepted the Order of the Garter.

Whenever he was out of power, as he was after 1880, Disraeli returned to writing literature. He completed a novel called *Endymion* in 1880; and when he died in 1881, he was working on a novel called *Falconet*. The queen wanted to visit him, but he declined saying, "She would only ask me to take a message to Albert." His popularity with the working classes was evident on a card he received, signed "A Workman," which said "Don't die yet, we can't do without you."

Considering his mercurial temperament and changing political opinions, it's surprising that, since his death in 1881, Disraeli has come to be considered a leading influence on the modern Conservative party. It was, in fact, not Disraeli, but Lord Randolph Churchill who invented the term "Tory democracy," although it was Disraeli who made it an essential part of Conservative policy and philosophy. As leader of the Tory Party, he presided over the reorganization of their electoral machine and the Primrose League, which (named after his favorite flower) had broad influence for 50 years after his death. Historians have said of Disraeli's romantic impulse to Empire and foreign affairs: "To the mystical Tory concepts of Throne, Church, Aristocracy and People, Disraeli added Empire." In contrast to Gladstone, who, his biographer Philip Magnus claims, "never understood that high moral principles, in their application to foreign policy, are often more destructive of political stability than motives of national self-interest," Disraeli had a strictly realistic view of British power.

Personally, Disraeli's was complex and somewhat enigmatic. One of his contemporaries wrote, "Could I only satisfy myself that Disraeli believed all that he said, I should be more happy: his historical views are quite mine, but does he believe them?" Disraeli remains the only British Prime Minister of Jewish birth and origin. As an outsider and a Jew, many of his fellow Tory party members doubted the depth of his sincerity and loyalty, but there was nothing in his career to indicate that he was anything less than patriotic. He fascinated and divided contemporary opinion and was seen by many, including members of his own party, as an adventurer and a charlatan; by others, as a far-sighted and patriotic statesman.

—

Thomas Jefferson

Science is my passion, politics my duty.

... a little rebellion now and then is a good thing, and as necessary in the political world as storms in the physical ... It is a medicine necessary for the sound health of government.

—To James Madison, 30 January 1787

The spirit of resistance to government is so valuable on certain occasions, that I wish it to be always kept alive. It will often be exercised when wrong, but better so than not to be exercised at all. —To Abigail Adams, 22 February 1787

And what country can preserve its liberties, if its rulers are not warned from time to time that this people preserve the spirit of resistance? Let them take arms.

—To William Smith, 13 November 1787

I sincerely believe that banking establishments are more dangerous than standing armies, and that the principle of spending money to be paid by posterity, under the name of funding, is but swindling futurity on a large scale.

THOMAS JEFFERSON WAS BORN IN 1743 IN VIRGINIA TO A FAMILY of substantial plantation owners. His father, Peter, died when he was about 14 years old and left him two large estates and about 60 slaves. Despite his aristocratic background and education at William & Mary College in Virginia, Jefferson became a radical thinker at an early age. He had read deeply in the classics, in contemporary English literature, and political thought; he told Alexander Hamilton that the three greatest men who ever lived were Newton, Locke and Bacon. Jefferson decided that he would be a polymath and a thinker and would stand against the established church and ideology. He swore "eternal hostility against every form of tyranny over the mind of man," and held the conviction that human intelligence can unlock not only the treasure house of the past but also the secrets of the universe. He was deeply read in French as well as English political writing: Montesquieu, the eighteenth-century encyclopedist Diderot, and Voltaire. Jefferson never followed a conventional Christian faith and was a deist who believed that the universe was created by a higher power, but left to run itself. Because of his inheritance, he also became deeply interested in agriculture, science, climate, and his plantations. He was also passionate about architecture and deeply influenced by the most fashionable architect in England at the time, Palladio, whose work was a model for Jefferson's home in Monticello. It was nevertheless an original, eccentric, and idiosyncratic building, which spoke more of Jefferson himself than of Palladio. Jefferson began building in 1768, and construction continued for his entire life.

Jefferson started to practice law when he turned 24 and continued for about seven years. He took the case of a young slave, Samuel Howell, the grandson of a white woman and a black man who had sued to be freed. Jefferson made the argument that "everyone comes into the world with a right to his own person and using it at his own will . . . This is what is called personal liberty, and is given him by the author of nature, because it is necessary for his own sustenance." After this radical statement, Jefferson was immediately cut off by the judge and lost the case.

In 1772 he married his third cousin, the twenty-three-year-old Martha Wayles Skelton. They had a very happy marriage, but she died ten years later, having given birth to six children, only two of whom survived into adulthood: Patsy, who lived the longest and was a companion to Jefferson, and Mary, who died at 26. In 1773, Jefferson inherited 135 slaves and 11,000 acres from his father-in-law, as well as debts that took years to pay off. He was distraught after his wife's death and promised to never marry again. There seems little doubt, however, that he had a relationship with Sally Hemings, who was a half-sister of his wife's, Sally Hemings bore five children to Jefferson, was with him in France in the 1780s, and only agreed to return to the United States (since slavery had been abolished in France) on the condition that their children would be freed when they turned 21. Jefferson kept this promise. When he died, Sally Hemings left Monticello with her three sons, who were counted as free whites in the next census.

Later, Jefferson was described as the pen of the revolution, as Washington was its sword and Patrick Henry its tongue, but none of the three was pre-eminent as yet, Jefferson least of all. He was about 30 years old when he wrote *A Summary View of the Rights of British America*, which was printed in 1774 in Philadelphia, also appeared in England, and greatly contributed to his reputation.

Jefferson was asked to draft the Declaration of Independence of 1776. He believed that the relationship between the American colonies and the Mother Country should be the same as that of Scotland and England between 1603 and the 1707 – both should have the same executive, but no other political connection. This was a radical view that few others agreed with. The principal of bowing to external taxation by Parliament was generally conceded in Virginia until Jefferson took this radical stand against it, although Benjamin Franklin had contested it in the 1760s. Jefferson's concept was essentially that of a Commonwealth. He was one of the first Americans to anticipate the British Empire of self-governing states. Jefferson claimed that the colonists in America were free and had a natural right to emigrate and establish laws and regulations of their own. He didn't recognize that the British government or Parliament had made any contribution to the economies of the American colonies. He asserted that the exercise of free trade was a natural right of the colonists. "It is neither our wish," he wrote, "nor our interest to separate from England."

The Declaration is one of Jefferson's major achievements. "All men are created equal" is said to be "one of the best-known sentences in the English language," containing "the most potent and consequential words in American history."

Jefferson was elected governor of Virginia and served for about two years during the Revolutionary War. He was heavily criticized for leaving the capital under the threat of British troops in 1781. It was during this time that he published his first book, in response to questions from a French diplomat. It was called *Notes on the State of Virginia*. It contained history, politics, law, ethnography, and extensive notes on the geography of rivers, lakes, and mountains. It also describes Jefferson's opinion about what constitutes a good society, which he believed was incarnated in Virginia. He wrote about slavery, miscegenation, and his belief that blacks and whites could not live together as free people in one society because of lingering resentments over slavery, writing "We have the wolf by the ears and we can neither hold him, nor safely let him go. Justice is in one scale, and self-preservation in the other." He feared that abolition would lead to the "extermination of the one or the other race." He also expressed the view that "Those who labor in the earth are the chosen people of God, if ever he had chosen a people.".

Jefferson's writing on the State of Virginia, his authorship of the Declaration of Independence, and his scholarly and creative interests are key to his character. His vision of the westward expansion of the American colonies began to be outlined in *Notes on the State of Virginia*. These notes inspire the same sense of freedom and individual liberty that is embodied in the Declaration of Independence. And Monticello, his great architectural creation, looks west over the Blue Mountains.

Two years after his wife, Martha, died in 1784, Jefferson continued to be depressed, but he was sent by Congress to Europe to join Benjamin Franklin and John Adams as ministers to Paris to negotiate commercial agreements with England, Spain, and France. He taught himself Spanish and French, and settled down in Paris after Franklin returned to America. When the French Foreign Minister, the Count de Vergennes, met Jefferson, he said, "You replace Monsieur Franklin, I hear." Jefferson replied, "I succeed him. No man can replace him." That same year Lafayette, who had just returned from America, broke the news to Jefferson that his daughter Lucy had died of whooping cough. He sent for his youngest surviving child, Polly, then aged 9, and she came over with Sally Hemings.

Jefferson visited England in 1786, five years after the surrender at Yorktown and three years after the treaty between England and America. He explored England and Wales – his family was supposed to have come from the foothills of Mount Snowdon. But he didn't like the cold, he didn't like the food, and he found the English rude and formal. Together with John Adams, he tried to achieve a treaty settling the Revolutionary War debts and restoring loyalist property, but when he went to attend the King's morning levee on March 17th, something made Jefferson feel that the King was being rude to him. Public rudeness wasn't normally associated with George III, whose affability, courtesy, and ability to put any man at ease were celebrated, but after Versailles, Jefferson may have been put off by the unexpected formality of the situation. The King might have just had very little to say to him. The negotiations went badly, and Jefferson was unable to settle their pre-war debts.

After living in a boarding house in London for two months, Jefferson was convinced that the nation "hates us, their ministers hate us, and their King, more than all other men." He had a very dark and prejudiced picture of the country, of its aristocracy, and even though he admitted that the laboring class in England was treated much better than in France, he wrote, "I considered the British as our natural enemies, and as the only nation on earth who wished us ill from the bottom of their souls." All this was unique to Jefferson and certainly not reflected by John Adams, John Jay, or any other Founding Fathers who acted as ministers in London. Jefferson certainly enjoyed going to the theatre and watched many of Shakespeare's plays; he went to the British Museum and the Tower of London. In April, 1786 he and John Adams set out to see Windsor Castle and various country estates, such as Chiswick House (an inspiration for Monticello), Pope's garden at Twickenham, Hampton Court and, of course, Shakespeare's birthplace, Stratford-on-Avon. Coming back from Stratford, they stopped at the poet William Shenstone's house, Hagley Park, and then Blenheim Palace and the Civil War battlefields of Edge Hill and Worcester.

Jefferson loved English history and tradition, but had a deep-seated resentment of the English aristocracy. He wished it otherwise, writing to Adams, "Were [the English people] under a government which should treat us with justice and equity, I should myself feel with great strength the ties that bind us together, of origin, language, laws and manners; and I am persuaded the two people would become, in future, as it was with the ancient Greeks, among whom it was reproachful for Greek to be found fighting against Greek in a foreign army."

Jefferson was also obsessed with the potential turn toward monarchy in America.

> I was much an enemy of monarchies before I came to Europe.
> I am ten thousand times more so since I have seen what they
> are. There is scarcely an evil known in these countries which
> may not be traced to their king as its source, nor a good which
> is not derived from the small fibers of republicanism among
> them. I can further say, with safety, there is not a crowned
> head in Europe whose talents or merits would entitle him to
> be elected vestryman by the people of any parish in America.

However extreme and prejudiced Jefferson's view of European monarchy and aristocracy, he nevertheless represents a strong strand in American republicanism that continues to this day. The irony was that in his admiration for things French, Jefferson missed a more extreme divide between rich and poor, between the aristocracy and the laborers of France than existed at any time in England, which was more informal and open to social mobility because of the impact of the Industrial Revolution.

Jefferson returned to Paris and fell in love with Maria Cosway, who was, however, married. After six weeks of passionate romance, she returned to England, but they maintained a correspondence thereafter.

He became a regular companion of Lafayette and met many of the important people in France in the three years before the revolution of 1789. Many of the would-be revolutionaries met at his residence in Paris, the Hotel de Langeac. He left France in September, 1789, just after the Storming of the Bastille, convinced that the revolution was a splendid thing to have happened. He said, "What signify a few lives lost in a century or two? The tree of liberty must from time to time be refreshed with the blood of patriots and tyrants. It is its natural manure." A chilling comment that might have been made by Hitler, Mao, or Stalin in the 20th century.

Upon returning to America, he became Secretary of State to George Washington, and he was constantly at odds with Alexander Hamilton, the Secretary of the Treasury. Hamilton took a more robust attitude to central government, whereas Jefferson and the Republicans stood for state's rights and democracy. Hamilton's party, the Federalists, were accused by Jefferson of Royalism, and of "panting after . . . crowns, coronets and mitres," a somewhat misleading allegation. Although Hamilton had previously collaborated with James Madison and John Jay on writing *The Federalist Papers*, Madison now joined Jefferson in organizing the Republican Party. Washington was furious with Jefferson's political maneuverings and never spoke to him after he left office in 1793.

At a private dinner in New York in 1790, Jefferson agreed with Hamilton and Madison that the capital should be moved to a new site on the Potomac River, and that the Federal Government would assume the war debts of the 13 states. There was no doubt that Hamilton's influence over Washington was greater than that of Jefferson. Jefferson's support of the French alienated the first president and many of the Founding Fathers, who were more conservative in their views. Jefferson was also deeply opposed to British interests, whereas Hamilton brought peace and trade with Britain with the Jay Treaty of 1794. In the 1796 election, Jefferson came second to John Adams and served as vice president for four years. He took little part in the rulings of the Senate, but wrote his Parliamentary Pocket Book on procedure and law in Parliament.

Jefferson was elected president in 1800, with his runner-up, Aaron Burr, becoming vice president; but Congress was dominated by Federalists. Despite being a Virginian aristocrat by birth and upbringing, Jefferson managed to portray himself as the "People's President." Unlike

Washington, he eschewed formal etiquette and arrived in plain clothes on horseback without a guard for his inauguration. His two key appointments were James Madison, as Secretary of State, and the Swiss-born Albert Gallatin, as Secretary of the Treasury. Gallatin reduced taxes and repealed many of Alexander Hamilton's financial policies.

In 1802 Jefferson founded the West Point Military Academy. The decisive act of his presidency was the $15 million Louisiana Purchase in 1803, which more than doubled the territory under United States control. Immediately afterwards, Jefferson dispatched Lewis and Clark to explore, map, and document the new territory. With 45 men, guided by a Native American, Sacagawea, they took two years to reach the Pacific Ocean and returned with much scientific knowledge. But despite his interest in Native Americans, Jefferson recommended forcibly relocating the Cherokee and Shawnee tribes that had fought for the British in the revolution, believing that assimilation or removal to the west was best for them.

In 1803, Anthony Merry arrived in Washington as the first British Ambassador to the United States. When Merry, dressed in full diplomatic uniform, came to present his credentials, he found a president given to wearing two vests, one red and threadbare and the other described as "grey-colored" and "hairy," with an old brown coat over the top. Jefferson's favorite stockings were yarn and his favorite shoes a pair of slip-ons. He was known to cross his legs and dangle a shoe off his toes while he was seated. Both his breeches and his linen were described as soiled, and he seems to have placed little importance on combing his hair.

Merry's secretary was sure that Jefferson, who had attended the most sophisticated salons of Paris, knew better but was chasing popularity by dressing like the masses. He was also living in what was essentially a rural setting, and wasn't about to make an exception to his dress, especially not for a minister from Britain. Jefferson was similarly relaxed when it came to dinner parties. When it was the time to sit, he turned to the woman who was serving as hostess for him and led her into dinner. Merry and his wife, unaware of this disregard for rank and precedence, were shocked when Jefferson escorted Dolley Madison to the table rather than Elizabeth Merry. Not long after, the Merrys were dismayed to hear about a party at the president's house attended by Napoleon's brother Jerome Bonaparte and his new wife, the former Elizabeth Patterson of Baltimore. Rather than escorting a cabinet member's wife into dinner, the president had offered his arm to Madame Bonaparte. Jefferson's actions suggest that he took some delight at disconcerting the Merrys, but he might simply have been delighting in Madame Bonaparte, who was gorgeous and wore transparent dresses.

After Vice President Burr mortally wounded Alexander Hamilton in July, 1804, Jefferson replaced him with George Clinton on the 1804 ticket. Burr immediately left for the west, plotting to separate the newly acquired western territories from the United States and capture New Orleans. A spy reported Burr's activities, and Jefferson sought to have him arrested and charged with treason. However, Chief Justice John Marshall couldn't find any evidence to convict Burr of treason and acquitted him, to Jefferson's fury.

Jefferson was reelected in 1804, but his popularity suffered in his second term because of wars in Europe. In 1806, he had to deal with the first Barbary War with Muslim pirates in Libya. The American Navy had their first successful overseas action. Jefferson failed in an attempt to buy Florida from Spain for $2 million and enacted an embargo against British trade that led to the War of 1812.

In old age, Jefferson described slavery as a "fire bell in the night." Knowing that it would become the great issue dividing the nation, he hoped to stop its spread into the western territories, and made several attempts to free his slaves.

Jefferson died in 1826. He wrote the epigraph for his tombstone:

HERE WAS BURIED THOMAS JEFFERSON
AUTHOR OF THE DECLARATION OF AMERICAN INDEPENDENCE
OF THE STATUTE OF VIRGINIA FOR RELIGIOUS FREEDOM
AND FATHER OF THE UNIVERSITY OF VIRGINIA

As the inscription suggests, in his mind his presidency was not his life's greatest achievement. He was prouder of his scientific and scholarly accomplishments and his defense of human rights and religious freedom.

Jefferson's life is a combination of his extraordinary literary and scientific eminence and his political naiveté. He failed to accomplish many of his goals as president, but he had a seminal influence on the future of America.

THE COMPARISON OF BENJAMIN DISRAELI WITH THOMAS JEFFERSON

Perhaps the most incongruous pairing in this book is that of Benjamin Disraeli and Thomas Jefferson. Jefferson stands alone among American presidents as a polymath – philosopher, architect, naturalist, linguist and follower of so many other scholarly pursuits. Benjamin Disraeli was Britain's only novelist prime minister – like Jefferson, therefore: a writer, a romantic and an idealist.

Both Thomas Jefferson and Benjamin Disraeli preferred to retreat to their country houses to write rather than occupy their seats of power. Disraeli had been an unsuccessful speculator – a gambler – in his youth, and the money he made from his books was essential to keep him solvent. But – more significantly – it was the men's imaginative and literary character that inspired their public policies and achievements. It is apparent from their literary output how important their books became to their political careers, and their writing is key to understanding their policies and political achievements.

One was a man with a vision of the east and the other the west. Both favored democratic reform and in giving more power to the people. They achieved little during their time in office, but their influence endures today. Perhaps Disraeli's greatest political achievement was the establishment of the modern Conservative party. Similarly, Jefferson became a founder of the Democratic party.

Jefferson was an insider, a Virginian aristocrat rebelling against the Mother Country. Disraeli was an outsider, a middle-class Jewish convert who longed to become part of the aristocracy. Incongruous as it appears, this Plutarchian parallel is of two men who were writers and thinkers before they were political leaders.

David Lloyd George   Franklin Delano Roosevelt

CHAPTER 17

David Lloyd George and Franklin Delano Roosevelt

—

David Lloyd George

You Cannot cross a chasm with two small steps—you have to make a leap.

A fully equipped DUKE costs as much to keep up as two Dreadnoughts, and Dukes are just as great a terror and they last longer.

D AVID LLOYD GEORGE'S UNCLE RICHARD LLOYD WAS THE VIL-lage cobbler in the small village of Llanystumdwy, north Wales. He was self-educated, and taught himself Greek, Latin, and French in order to homeschool his two nephews, David and William, so that they might pass the very difficult solicitor's exams (which they both successfully did). By his cobbler's bench, Richard Lloyd had a notebook in which he would write down thoughts and Biblical quotations. He was the unpaid preacher of the local Baptist church, and taught David to preach and read the lesson in the chapel from the age of about 15. Although David later confessed he had lost his faith in God at about the age of 12, he revered his uncle and did not want to hurt him, so he dutifully went to chapel twice every Sunday.

In 1888, when David Lloyd George was 25, he married Margaret Owen, who was a Methodist, and whose parents had a sheep farm of considerable acreage near Criccieth. In fact, she was proud of her descent from the ancient princes of Gwynedd of over 800 years ago. Well-to-do by Welsh standards, they looked down on Lloyd George. However, he proved himself by winning the Llanfrothen Burial Case that year. This established the right of non-conformists to be buried according to their own rites in parish burial grounds, and made him a household name in Wales. He was duly elected as the as Liberal MP for Caernarvon Boroughs two years later.

Lloyd George and Margaret had five children: Richard, Mair (who tragically died of appendicitis at the age of 17) Gwilym, Olwen, and Megan. Gwilym and Megan continued in politics after their father's death, one as a Conservative and the other as a fiery and radical Labour member.

At the beginning of his career, Lloyd George spoke mainly on Welsh issues but, with the arrival of the Boer War in 1899, he became a national figure by standing strongly against the war. He accused the military of inefficiency and waste, and the Chamberlain family company of profiteering. When he spoke in 1901 at Birmingham Town Hall, he had to escape a Chamberlainite mob by borrowing a policeman's uniform. When the Liberals formed a cabinet in 1905, Lloyd George was appointed President of the Board of Trade under Henry Campbell Bannerman, and two years later became Chancellor of the Exchequer under Herbert Henry Asquith.

Lloyd George's great triumph was the People's Budget of 1909, in which he introduced old-age pensions and sickness and unemployment benefits. To pay for this incipient welfare state, he increased taxes on income, tobacco, and alcohol. He also introduced a tax on land, which caused an uproar in the House of Lords, who threw out the bill. Lloyd George was vindicated by the election of 1910, after which the Parliament Act of 1911 reduced the veto power of the House of Lords (especially on financial bills), and he succeeded in passing his National Insurance Act.

Lloyd George formed a close friendship and alliance with Winston Churchill at this time. They disagreed about the level of naval spending when Churchill went to the Admiralty in 1911, but remained close allies for many years afterwards. Churchill defended

Lloyd George during the Marconi Scandal of 1913, which nearly finished his career and, in turn, Lloyd George brought Churchill back into the cabinet when he became prime minister in 1917.

During the First World War, Lloyd George's relations with his generals, particularly Robertson and Haig, were difficult and strained. As a man of the people, he always sought to reduce casualties, particularly the terrible shelling and machine-gun deaths that happened at the Battle of the Somme and afterwards at Passchendaele in 1917. He introduced a small war cabinet of five members, which met daily, and he brought a new energy and determination to the prosecution of the war. Against the advice of the navy he introduced convoys to secure Britain's food supply. Though at first he welcomed the Russian Revolution and wanted to protect the Russian royal family, but the King's adviser vetoed this and the family was executed by the Bolsheviks in 1918.

Lloyd George was an important figure behind the Balfour Declaration of 1917 and supported the eventual creation of Israel. He was also a key figure, after the hostilities of 1920, in the creation of the Republic of Ireland in 1921.

Lloyd George's post-war government, in which the Conservatives had about 400 seats and the Liberals only about 100, was in some ways a most successful reforming coalition government. John Maynard Keynes wrote of him: "How can I convey any just impression of this extraordinary figure of our time, this siren, this goat-footed bard, this half-human visitor to our age from the hag-ridden magic and enchanted woods of Celtic antiquity?"

Many saw him as a Welsh wizard – unreliable, but brilliant, mercurial – yet he was, as Baldwin described him, "a dynamic force" who transformed Britain, the way in which the war was run, and, in the process, almost destroyed the Tory party. But his genius was undeniable. Although he had little knowledge of foreign policy, his success at Versailles was in trying to prevent the French revanchism or heavy reparation demands against Germany and, balance that against Woodrow Wilson's Fourteen Points.

Lloyd George had a good relationship with Woodrow Wilson despite his doubts about Wilson's impracticality, and visited him in Washington in 1923 just before Wilson died. Coming from religious backgrounds they were both "children of the manse" and this helped them understand each other.

During his coalition government, Lloyd George gave votes to women for the first time – the Suffragettes had made this a primary issue before the First World War; he raised the age at which a student could leave school to 14; he expanded government housing; he extended national insurance to almost 11 million additional workers, including farm laborers; he enacted legislation for the blind and doubled old-age pensions; and he tried to fulfill his pledge to make Britain "a country fit for heroes to live in." But there were, of course, immense social and economic problems from the rapid demobilization of almost six million men from the army in 1918–19, and there was a deep slump in 1921 with a wave of strikes. In addition, Conservative opposition – to the independence of Ireland and to Lloyd George's granting of honors – grew, and he was voted out by the Tories in 1922. Lloyd George never held power again despite being highly visible in the political world of London.

In 1929, he collaborated with John Maynard Keynes in writing *We Can Conquer Unemployment*, which sets out many of the policies that Franklin Roosevelt introduced to the United States in his New Deal four years later. Lloyd George's life in the 20 years after he left power was in some ways unfulfilled, although he wrote his war memoirs and a book about the peace conference. He also traveled extensively to the United States in 1923. Lloyd George was the first British statesman to be fascinated by the United States, perhaps because of his admiration of Lincoln. He went to Nazi Germany in 1936, where he met Hitler and, impressed by him, called him "the George Washington of Germany," a gross misjudgment, which came back to haunt him and his standing among historians. But, to be fair, in 1936, few foresaw the excesses of Nazism.

When World War Two began, Lloyd George was thought to be

a defeatist. Perhaps instead he was being realistic about Britain's chances. He refused his friend Winston Churchill's invitation to join the war cabinet in the summer, primarily because he didn't want to serve with Neville Chamberlain and Halifax, "The Guilty Men," the appeasers and architects of the disastrous situation, that had been created by their lack of rearmament in the 1930s.

His wife Margaret died suddenly in 1941, and Lloyd George was heartbroken. Two years later, he married his long-term mistress and secretary, Frances Stevenson. This caused much ill feeling in the family. Lloyd George had a reputation for having an eye for pretty women, which almost ruined him in 1911, but, thanks to the loyalty of his wife, his career survived.

Lloyd George died in 1945; I was born in 1952, but I heard much about my great-grandfather from my father, who said that "there was an aura of magic about him and a thrill of excitement of going to see him. He had a beguiling voice and the most wonderful gurgling laugh and twinkling pale blue eyes, his magnificently leonine head with its flowing mane of white hair created an amazing image for a small boy, and he loved children; and he was always pleased to have us about." His attraction for children was as nothing compared with the effect he had on women. "With an attractive woman, he was as much to be trusted as a Bengal Tiger with a gazelle," as my grandfather said. Yet the only person whom he deeply loved all his life was his wife Maggie, his bedrock. She was rooted in Wales and took care of his constituency of Caernarvon Boroughs; they shared a matchless serenity coupled with an impish sense of humor.

—

Franklin Delano Roosevelt

Let me assert my firm belief that the only thing we have to fear is fear itself – nameless, unreasoning, unjustified terror which paralyzes needed efforts to convert retreat into advance.

Be sincere, be brief; be seated.　　　—[On public speaking]

Presidents do make mistakes, but the immortal Dante tells us that divine justice weighs the sins of the cold-blooded and the sins of the warm-hearted in different scales.

FRANKLIN DELANO ROOSEVELT WAS ONE OF AMERICA'S ORIGINAL aristocrats. Although not a Virginian, he was part of the Knickerbocker Society described by Henry James and Edith Wharton. The Van Rensselaers, the Schuylers, the Astors, the Belmonts, the Vanderbilts and the like were part of this exclusive society, what was called "the 400" in New York in the mid-nineteenth century. It is remarkable that – having emerged from this rarified aristocratic climate on the Hudson River, having been to Groton and Harvard, having inherited millions of dollars from the Delano family, which had been a China trader – Roosevelt rebelled against all this privilege, power and wealth and became a committed or apparently committed social reformer.

Roosevelt was the only child of an elderly father and a doting mother. He had a beautiful home at Hyde Park and was educated at prestigious schools. His mother, Sarah Delano Roosevelt, was utterly devoted to him. He was an only child and was taken to Europe every summer, traveling in private railway cars through England, Germany, and France. Roosevelt's greatest interest was the sea: his library contained over 2,000 books about US naval history and 200 fully rigged ship's models, so it was appropriate that his first office in the government was Secretary for the Navy.

Roosevelt became Secretary of the Navy when he was in his thirties. He was clearly a rising star of the Democratic Party under President Wilson, and Wilson's heir apparent. In 1905 he married Teddy Roosevelt's niece, Eleanor, reinforcing his name-recognition by making the link with his fifth cousin. Although he was never close to Teddy Roosevelt, who presided over their wedding, he was able to achieve national recognition thanks to the aura of his name.

The newlyweds moved into Springwood, Roosevelt's family's estate. They had six children, all of whom lived long lives, except for Franklin Jr. On the whole, his marriage was successful, but he had affairs, including one with Lucy Mercer, Eleanor's social secretary. Eleanor discovered letters revealing the affair, and Roosevelt promised never to see Lucy again. But Franklin didn't keep his promise and saw Lucy regularly after 1941, and she was with him on the day he died.

After commanding the Navy through World War One, Roosevelt was chosen as vice-presidential candidate in 1920 for Governor James Cox of Ohio. They were decisively defeated by Harding and Coolidge, but Roosevelt used the opportunity to burnish his public image.

Then, in August, 1921, tragedy struck and changed Roosevelt's life and his character. At the age of 40, he was struck down by polio, which crippled him. He was never able to walk properly again. With magnificent courage and persistence, he overcame this handicap, and he became more compassionate, concerned, and sympathetic to those who suffered hardships. With the help of his wife, Eleanor, who became his eyes and ears, he was able to acquire a much broader knowledge of the conditions in which working-class Americans lived. His visits to Warm Springs, Georgia brought him into contact with a range of people from all classes who had only their need for a cure from the polio in common.

In a remarkable show of resolve, Roosevelt managed to return to political life. Using customized leg braces, he was able to walk for short distances but used a wheelchair in private. He was never seen in public in his wheelchair.

In 1929, as governor of New York, he introduced progressive

measures to counter the Great Depression. By March, 1933, when he took office as president, the nation's situation was dire – unemployment had reached 25 percent. Many were starving or living on the streets, and the American economy was in a deep slump. Roosevelt believed that the malaise was purely psychological. "The only thing we have to fear is fear itself . . . I pledge myself to a new deal for the American people." Many of his measures had been initiated by Herbert Hoover, who was unfairly blackened as being heartless and passive in the face of the depression. Nevertheless, Roosevelt won the presidency by a landslide and in the first 100 days of his administration, introduced an extraordinary amount of legislation. He closed the banks and reorganized the financial system. He signed the Glass-Steagall Act and created the Federal Deposit Insurance Corporation. The new administration primarily focused on unemployment, and the civilian conservation corps hired 250,000 unemployed young men to work on local projects. The administration also gave the Federal Trade Commission broader reach, expanded the Hoover Agency and the Reconstruction Finance Corporation, and set up the AAA for agriculture.

Roosevelt devalued the dollar by raising the price of gold from $20 to $35 an ounce to counter the deflation that was paralyzing the economy. He tried to keep his promise to reduce the federal deficit, and he finally repealed prohibition, which may, in itself, have strengthened the economy. Government spending actually only increased from 8% of GNP under Hoover to about 10.2% by 1936. The national debt had doubled during the previous administration, but it was still around 40% of GDP when the Second World War started. Unemployment fell from 25% to about 14% in the first four years of Roosevelt's presidency, but was only truly resolved with the outbreak of war in 1941, when it fell to 2%. Income taxes were raised when the war began, reaching a marginal tax rate of 91% – because of wartime expenditure – on salaries over $25,000 (or about $400,000 today).

In Roosevelt's second term he was opposed by the Supreme Court, which he tried to pack with his own appointments. There was

continuous Republican opposition in Congress to his domestic proposals, but by the late 1930s, Roosevelt was focusing on foreign policy and preparing the United States for war.

Americans were deeply isolationist in the late 1930s, but Roosevelt
was prepared to defy this mood, saying, "America should become the
Arsenal of Democracy." He signed the Lend-Lease Bill to support
Britain in September, 1940. It wasn't entirely a selfless action; in exchange for giving Britain 50 used destroyers, the US received base
rights in Bermuda and Newfoundland. In his biography of FDR, Conrad Black argues that he provoked war by cutting Japan off from its
oil supplies and by extending American naval patrols into the mid-
Atlantic, where they were bound to be attacked by U-boats. Nevertheless it came as a shock to everyone when the Japanese attacked the
American fleet at Pearl Harbor on December 7th, 1941, "a day that
will live in infamy" as FDR said. Roosevelt immediately agreed to
Churchill's proposal that Europe would come first and the Pacific theater of war would be secondary. With the extraordinarily rapid pace
of rearmament, the Americans were able to encompass both theaters
of war successfully.

With the Soviet advance against the Nazis in 1943, it became
apparent that a long-term political strategy about the future of Europe
was needed. Roosevelt was determined to dismantle the British Empire, especially in India, and had many arguments with Winston
Churchill. Roosevelt died in Warm Springs on April 12th, 1945, when
he was only 62. Winston Churchill paid tribute to him:

> I conceived an admiration for him as a statesman, a man of
> affairs, and a war leader. I felt the utmost confidence in his
> upright, inspiriting character and outlook, and a personal re-
> gard – affection I must say – for him beyond my power to ex-
> press today. His love of his own country, his respect for its
> constitution, his power of gauging the tides and currents of
> its mobile public opinion, were always evident, but added to
> these [was] . . . that generous heart which was always stirred

to anger and to action by spectacles of aggression and oppression by the strong against the weak. It is indeed a loss, a bitter loss to humanity, that his mighty [heart] is stilled forever.

President Roosevelt's affliction lay heavily upon him. It was a marvel that he bore up against it through all the many years of tumult and storm. Not one man in ten millions, stricken and crippled as he was, would have attempted to plunge into a life of physical and mental exertion and of hard, ceaseless political controversy. Not one in ten millions would have tried, not one in a generation would have succeeded, not only in entering this sphere, not only in acting vehemently in it, but in becoming indisputable master of the scene . . . [through an] extraordinary effort of the spirit over the flesh, of will-power over physical infirmity.

There is no doubt that the president foresaw the great dangers closing in upon the pre-war world with far more prescience than most well-informed people on either side of the Atlantic . . . There was never a moment's doubt . . . upon which side his sympathies lay . . . He and . . . vast numbers of his countryman . . . felt the Blitz of the stern winter of 1940–41 . . . as much as any of us did, and perhaps more indeed, for imagination is often more torturing than reality. There is no doubt that the bearing of the British, and above all of the Londoners, kindled fires in American bosoms far harder to quench than the conflagrations from which we were suffering . . .

He devised the extraordinary measure of assistance called Lend-Lease, which will stand forth as the most unselfish and unsordid financial act of any country in all history. [Following the] act of treachery and greed [of Japan] both our countries were in arms [together].

[After recounting the progress of the war] At Yalta I noticed that the President was ailing. His captivating smile, his gay and charming manner, had not deserted him, but his face had a transparency, an air of purification, and often there was a far-away look in his eyes. When I took my leave of him in Alexandria harbor I must confess that I had an indefinable sense of fear that his health and his strength were on the ebb. But nothing altered his inflexible sense of duty. To the end he faced his innumerable tasks unflinching . . .

What an enviable death was his! He had brought the country through the worst of its perils and the heaviest of its toils. Victory had cast its sure and steady beam upon him.

In the days of peace he had broadened and stabilized the foundation of American life and union. In war he had raised the strength and might, and glory of the great Republic to a height never attained by any nation in history . . .

All this was no more than worldly power and grandeur, had it not been that the causes of human freedom and social justice, to which so much of his life had been given, added a luster [to him and his achievements] which will long be discernible among men . . .

For us it remains only to say that in Franklin Roosevelt there died the greatest American friend we have ever known, and the greatest champion of freedom who has ever brought help and comfort from the New World to the Old.

THE COMPARISON OF DAVID LLOYD GEORGE WITH FRANKLIN DELANO ROOSEVELT

From contrasting backgrounds, David Lloyd George and Franklin Delano Roosevelt found their way into politics by way of the law. Both were charismatic figures of inspiration, though Roosevelt was not such a natural orator. Perhaps, just as Roosevelt's polio transformed him into a man of compassion and a social reformer, so, too, did Lloyd George's tragic loss of his daughter Mary in 1908 transform him into a man more determined to help the poor, the sick, the old, and the unemployed.

In times of hardship, both leaders worked for the good of the common man against vested interests: "These unhappy times call for the building of plans that rest upon the forgotten, the unorganized but the indispensable units of economic power, for plans that build from the bottom up and not from the top down, that put their faith once more in the *forgotten man* at the bottom of the economic pyramid," Roosevelt said in a 1932 radio speech, but it might equally have been spoken by Lloyd George.

In 1911 during the Agadir Crisis, Lloyd George evolved from being a pacifist to being an international statesman, saying: "Peace at that price would be a humiliation intolerable for a great country like ours to endure." Likewise Pearl Harbor pushed Roosevelt to move from isolationism to global involvement. In one of his fireside chats of 1942, he said:

> This generation of Americans has come to realize, with a present and personal realization, that there is something larger and more important than the life of any individual or of any individual group – something for which a man will sacrifice, and gladly sacrifice, not only his pleasures, not only his goods, not only his associations with those he loves, but his life itself. In time of crisis when the future is in the balance, we come to understand, with full recognition and devotion, what this Nation is, and what we owe to it.

Men of peace who inherited wars, they were able to lead their countries to victory, and then to leading roles in the post-war order.

Constitutionally, Roosevelt irrevocably altered the relationship between Americans and the government by centralizing unprecedented levels of power, especially in the hands of the president. While he conversed widely to gain advice and knowledge, he kept the decision-making process firmly in his own hands. The same is true of Lloyd George. As historian Robert Blake put it, "No one has come closer to presidential government on the American model than Lloyd George."

CHAPTER 18

Stanley Baldwin and Herbert Hoover

Stanley Baldwin

S TANLEY BALDWIN WAS BORN WELL-TO-DO (HE WAS THE FIRST COUSIN of Rudyard Kipling). The family owned an iron-and-steel business. Stanley did not enjoy his school days at Harrow, saying "all the king's horses and all the king's men have drawn me into the company of school masters, and in relation to them I once had every qualification as a passive resister." Although he continued on to Cambridge University, he didn't shine academically and left school with a third-class degree in history. Left with few options, he joined the family business. His father sent him for one term to the future University of Birmingham as preparation. Baldwin became an extremely wealthy man when he inherited £200,000 (£20 million today) and a directorship of the Great Western Railway after his father died in 1908.

Baldwin was elected to Parliament when he was 40 years old, succeeding his father. He didn't make much of an impression as a young Conservative MP, but became Parliament Private Secretary to the leader of the party, Andrew Bonar Law, during the First World War. In 1917, he became Financial Secretary to the Treasury in Lloyd George's administration. He wrote to *The Times* promoting the idea that wealthy Englishmen should make donations to repay the growing war debt, and he set an example by giving the Treasury one-fifth of his fortune.

By 1921 Baldwin had been promoted to the Cabinet as President of the Board of Trade and supported Lloyd George's coalition. However, at the famous meeting at the Carlton Club in October, 1922, he

Stanley Baldwin

Herbert Hoover

announced that he would no longer support Lloyd George's coalition. He described the Prime Minister as a "dynamic force" who had destroyed the Liberal Party and would in turn destroy the Conservative Party. This speech persuaded Conservative MPs to end the coalition, and as a result, Baldwin's mentor, Andrew Bonar Law, became Prime Minister and promoted Baldwin to Chancellor of the Exchequer. In the election that November, the Conservatives returned with a large majority.

In 1923 Bonar Law was diagnosed with cancer and retired. It was thought that Lord Curzon, the Foreign Secretary, who had the most experience and qualification, having been viceroy of India as a young man, would succeed as Prime Minister. But senior ministers of King George V advised him not to appoint a Prime Minister from the House of Lords, so the king called for Baldwin. His first term of office lasted only eight months, but he had become established in the public mind as a "safe pair of hands."

The Labour Party briefly formed a minority government under Ramsay MacDonald, but by the end of 1924 the Conservatives were back in office with a landslide majority of 223. Britain had flirted with the idea of a socialist government and clearly didn't feel comfortable with the idea, especially after the Labour Party negotiated a commercial treaty with the new Soviet government, and the Zinoviev letter was published, causing a tremendous backlash. In a speech during the campaign, Baldwin said: "It makes my blood boil to read of the way which Mr. Zinoviev is speaking of the Prime Minister [MacDonald] today. Though one time there went up a cry, 'Hands off Russia,' I think it's time somebody said to Russia, 'Hands off England.'" This was typical of Baldwin's simple appeals to patriotism and common sense.

From 1924 to 1929, Baldwin was able to call on some of the most gifted members of the previous Lloyd George coalition, in particular, Winston Churchill, who became Chancellor of the Exchequer; Austen Chamberlain, the Foreign Secretary; and Arthur Balfour as Lord President. However, the period was marked by the return to the gold standard, which Churchill enacted in 1925, and the General Strike the following year. For the first time Baldwin was faced with a major crisis in the economy and protests by the working classes. He was neither sympathetic to or capable of finding a solution to the growing problem of unemployment. He did, however, pass a Pensions Act in 1925 that guaranteed humanitarian welfare for the unemployed, which the Tory party accepted.

By 1929 the government had lost popular support and Labour once again held the majority. Baldwin managed to survive as leader of the Conservatives in opposition, and he was instrumental in organizing political fundraising for the party.

In 1931 Baldwin returned to government as part of a coalition under the Labour leader Ramsay MacDonald. Although his title was only Lord President of the Council, Baldwin was the real power behind the throne. By 1935 he had again become Prime Minister and had to cope with the growing power of Nazi Germany, the USSR, and Italy, which was Fascist under Mussolini.

Baldwin's policies made it clear that he would not or could not rise to the challenge of rearmament, and he famously remarked that "the Bomber will always get through," so he clearly understood that Britain needed to build an air force. In practice, however, he did little and was unwilling to make the necessary expenditures at a time when most British people were averse to the idea of another war so soon after the "war to end all wars." In 1933, for instance, the Oxford University Union had voted that "This House would not fight for King and country." Public opinion was pacifist.

In the election of 1935 Baldwin said he would support the League of Nations and modernize Britain's defenses, but he continued to refuse to embrace rearmament. To the British people he said, "I give you my word that there will be no great armaments." He concentrated instead on housing, unemployment, and particular areas of economic depression. By that point, Churchill was regularly making speeches to raise awareness of the growing threat of Nazism, and to prepare Britain for war by rebuilding the air force. (Churchill was probably the only

British statesman who had already read *Mein Kampf* and understood Hitler's true intentions, his anti-semitic views, and the threat of war for *Lebenstraum*. Baldwin denied there was a threat and said that the Luftwaffe was only half the size of the RAF, but figures suggested otherwise. Churchill attacked the government as being "decided only to be undecided, resolved to be irresolute, adamant for drift, solid for fluidity, all-powerful to be impotent. So we go on, preparing more months and years – precious, perhaps vital, to the greatness of Britain – for the locusts to eat." Baldwin responded only to the strong pacifist feeling in the country, which he lacked the courage to go against.

In 1936 a crisis arose with the abdication of King Edward VIII. Only Churchill and Lloyd George supported the King's desire to marry Wallis Simpson. Baldwin was against the marriage and had a large majority supporting him as he tried to persuade the King to abdicate. Some of the protestors in the crowd cried "God save the King from Baldwin! Flog Baldwin! Flog him! We want Edward."

In 1937 Baldwin resigned as Prime Minister, handing over the position to Neville Chamberlain, who continued the policy of appeasement. Baldwin's reputation soon began to suffer, and with the crisis of 1940 and Churchill's ascent to power, a book called *Guilty Men* accused Baldwin and Chamberlain of being responsible for Britain's unpreparedness in that terrible year. His popularity continued to decline when he refused to give up the iron gates of his estate for the war in 1942. "Here [said the *Daily Mirror*] was an old stupid politician who had tricked the nation into complacency about rearmament for fear of losing an election."

After Baldwin's death, Churchill said, "I wish Stanley Baldwin no ill but it would be much better had he never lived." This was uncharacteristically belligerent and ungenerous on the part of Churchill, who was notable for his magnanimity about political opponents. Churchill believed that Baldwin rather than Chamberlain would be blamed by generations for the policies that led to the most unnecessary war in history, but Churchill also said that "he was the most formidable politician I ever encountered in public life."

Recently historians have begun to treat Baldwin more considerately. He is now seen as having done more than most and perhaps as much as possible in the context of Britain in the 1930s, but the fact remains that it wasn't enough to deter the aggressors. He is now being rediscovered as a moderate and inclusive Conservative, part of a "one-nation" tradition stemming from Disraeli in the 19th century.

—

Herbert Hoover

HERBERT HOOVER WAS BORN IN 1874 TO A QUAKER FAMILY BUT was orphaned at the age of nine and raised by his grandmother and then his uncle. He had lofty Christian ideals and a strong work ethic. He was successful in school and was one of the first students to enter Stanford University in 1891, working his way through college and graduating in 1895 with a degree in Geology. Soon thereafter, he departed for Western Australia, where he worked at a London-based gold-mining company, but the conditions were harsh on the edge of the Great Victoria Desert. He served as a geologist and mining engineer, and searched the Western Australian goldfields for investment opportunities. He was appointed as a mine manager at the early age of 23 and led a major program of expansion for the Sons of Gwalia gold mine, bringing in Italian immigrants in order to counter the Australian unions. Hoover was a well-known patriot and was nicknamed "H. C." or "Hail Columbia" by his Australian friends. A British friend in London later called him the "star-spangled Hoover" because of his intense patriotism.

By 1899, Hoover was already successful, and he married his Stanford sweetheart, Lou Henry, and moved to China. They had two sons. Both Hoover and his wife learned Mandarin and later used it as a private language in the White House when they wanted to confound eavesdroppers. Hoover made many recommendations to improve the lot of the Chinese worker, including ending the practice of long-term servitude contracts and instituting reforms for workers based on merit.

Hoover and his wife were trapped in Tianjin in June, 1900, for almost a month due to the Boxer Rebellion. Mrs. Hoover worked in a hospital and Herbert guided the US Marines. By 1901 he was a partner in Bewick, Moreing & Company (of London) earning a salary of $12,500 and a 20% share of profits. The company eventually controlled almost 50% of the gold production in Western Australia. He also became a director of the Chinese Engineering and Mining Corporation and shipped many Chinese workers to the South African mines, a contentious issue that was debated in the British Parliament. In 1905 he founded the Zinc Corporation, which mined the zinc that had been left behind at Broken Hill after the lead and silver had been removed, which later proved very profitable.

From 1908 to 1914 he was an independent mining consultant and traveled worldwide to offices in London and San Francisco. He also had a very successful venture in Burma, where he developed silver, lead, and zinc. This, the Namtu Bawdwin Mine, became the chief source of his fortune.

By 1914 Hoover had an estimated fortune of $4 million (almost $500 million today). He was quoted as saying, "If a man has not made a million dollars by the time he is forty, he is not worth much." He was known throughout the mining world as a doctor of sick mines. He was very successful not only as an investor and financier but as an organizer.

When the First World War broke out in 1914, Hoover changed his life. He helped organize the return of around 120,000 Americans from Europe and led 500 volunteers who distributed food, clothing, steamship tickets, and cash. "I did not realize it at the time," he said, "but on August 3rd, 1914, my business career was over forever. I was on the slippery road to public life." He liked to say that the difference between dictatorship and democracy was simple: dictators organize from the top down, democracies from the bottom up.

He started the Commission for Relief in Belgium, working 14

hours a day (based in London), distributing over two million tons of food to nine million war victims. Hoover crossed the North Sea 40 times to meet with the German authorities to persuade them to allow food shipments. Although Britain was reluctant to support the Commission, Hoover was generally admired and recognized as a hero for his humanitarian efforts.

When the United States entered the war in April 1917, President Woodrow Wilson appointed Hoover to the head of the US Food Administration. Hoover was convinced from his work in Belgium that centralization of authority was essential to any relief effort. "Food will win the war," he used to say. He established meatless Mondays, wheatless Wednesdays, and said, "when in doubt, eat potatoes."

After the war, Hoover provided aid to Germany as well as to famine-stricken areas of Russia. When he was criticized for his Russian relief efforts by the Republican Senator Henry Cabot Lodge, he retorted, "Twenty million people are starving. Whatever their politics, they shall be fed!" Even so, over six million people died in the Russian famine. Maxim Gorky wrote to him: "Your help will enter history as a unique, gigantic achievement, worthy of the greatest glory, which will long remain in the memory of million of Russians whom you have saved from death." By this time he had become famous and *The New York Times* named him one of the "Ten Most Important Living Americans."

Hoover rejected Democratic overtures to run for president in 1921. He registered as a Republican and supported Warren G. Harding, who would win the election and appoint Hoover Secretary of Commerce. Washington wags referred to Hoover as the "Secretary of Commerce and Under-Secretary of Everything Else!" He had extraordinary energy and was willing to become involved in every economic issue. He tried to build voluntary partnerships between government and business, so-called "associationalism," which focused on eliminating waste and increasing efficiency in business and industry. He promoted international trade by opening commerce offices overseas and was eager to promote Hollywood films. His campaign to "Own your Own Home" promoted ownership of single-family dwellings. Hoover held frequent radio conferences and reorganized this fast-growing sector (there were over 732 radio stations by 1927). He also contributed to major projects in navigation, irrigation, electricity, and flood control.

When Coolidge succeeded Harding in 1923, Hoover continued his role in the Commerce Department. He helped organize national highways and traffic control, and when the Great Mississippi Flood of 1927 displaced 1.5 million people, it was Hoover who mobilized local state authorities.

In 1928 Hoover was the front-runner as presidential candidate for the Republican Party. He still supported Prohibition; as a Quaker he called it "an experiment noble in purpose." He won a landslide victory with 58% of the vote because of his national reputation and the booming economy. The prosperity, however, did not last long and, when the stock market crashed in October, 1929, just eight months after he took office, he could not find an answer to the economic challenge of his time. Before the crash he had said, "We in America today are nearer to the final triumph over poverty than ever before in the history of any country." Well-meaning, high-minded, and a believer in self-reliance instead of government intervention, Hoover had ambitious plans to reform the government and encourage public-private cooperation.

Hoover set aside three million acres of national parks and 2.5 million acres of national forests. He advocated for tax reduction for low-income Americans and closed certain tax loopholes used by the wealthy. He also doubled the number of veterans' hospital facilities, wrote a Children's Charter that advocated protection of every child regardless of race or gender, and created an antitrust division in the Justice Department. He required that airmail carriers adopt stricter safety measures and improve service. He reorganized the Bureau of Indian Affairs, and instituted prison reform.

Hoover was a strong supporter of civil rights: his vice president, Charles Curtis, was from the Kaw tribe in Kansas and the first Native American to hold that office. Hoover's humanitarian and Quaker principles, along with his vice president, gave special meaning to his Indian policies.

When the Great Depression began to overtake every other issue during his presidency, Hoover was unable to deliver inspiring leadership or effective policies to combat it. But there was more continuity between Hoover's and Roosevelt's policies than is generally realized. He initiated many public-works programs, including the Hoover Dam, and got an extra $100 million from Congress for the Federal Farm Board lending. He established a National Wool Marketing Corporation. He advocated strong labor laws and tried to reform the banking sector. He was, however, a firm believer in balanced budgets and was unwilling to increase the deficit to fund welfare programs.

His greatest mistake occurred in June, 1930, when, against the advice of many economists, he signed into law the Smoot-Hawley Tariff Act. The Act sought to encourage the purchase of American-made products by increasing the cost of imported goods and raised tariffs on thousands of imported items. Unfortunately it spread the economic depression worldwide, and many nations retaliated by raising their tariffs on imports from the US. Internationally, trade spiraled downward until 1933. It was a terrible lesson and a trade war began that ended in the Second World War.

By 1932, unemployment had reached nearly 25% and 5,000 banks had failed. Hundreds of thousands of Americans found themselves homeless and began congregating in shanty towns called Hoovervilles. That year, Congress enacted the Revenue Act, which was the largest peacetime tax increase in history, but it only increased problems.

Franklin Roosevelt criticized Hoover and said that he was spending too much, increasing national debt, raising tariffs, and blocking trade, as well as placing millions on the government dole. Ironically he criticized Hoover for thinking "that we ought to center control of everything in Washington as rapidly as possible," and Roosevelt's running mate, John Nance Garner, accused Hoover of "leading the country down the path of socialism."

Four months before the 1932 election, Hoover sent US Army forces to clear out veterans who were camped outside Washington. General Douglas MacArthur, who was leading the mission, believed he was fighting a communist revolution and cleared out the camp with military force, injuring hundreds of civilians. It was a disaster for Hoover and deeply damaged his humanitarian image, and in the eyes of voters, he appeared cold and unfeeling. Although he didn't want to run again, he felt it was his duty to continue with the economic policies he had enacted.

There were several attempts to kill Hoover by disgruntled citizens during the campaign. He lost by a large majority and his reputation took a long time to recover.

He was against US involvement in the Second World War and foresaw that Stalin would impose communism in Eastern Europe. After 1945 he became friends with Truman and initiated a program of food supplies to Europe, especially to Germany, as he had after the First World War. Hoover lived to the age of 90 and is commemorated at his birthplace in Iowa and at the Hoover Institution at Stanford University, where the Hoover Tower still stands.

THE COMPARISON OF STANLEY BALDWIN WITH HERBERT HOOVER

Stanley Baldwin and Herbert Hoover were wealthy, successful, and well-meaning businessmen who failed as political leaders. Baldwin inherited his family's iron and steel business, and Hoover had made a fortune by the age of 40. Baldwin was a patriot who donated a fifth of his fortune to the Treasury, while Hoover was known for his patriotism and humanitarian efforts.

Each was judged by the electorate to be a "safe pair of hands." Baldwin spoke of "safety first" and downplayed the threat of war and German rearmament. He was what the public thought they wanted. Hoover's reputation crumbled in the face of the Depression because he lacked warmth and empathy; he talked of efficiency, of balancing the budget and self-help. During these crises, both Baldwin and Hoover were overshadowed by the rivals who criticized and eventually surpassed them. However, the reputations and legacies of Baldwin and Hoover stand higher now than when they left office.

Neville Chamberlain   James Buchanan

CHAPTER 19

Neville Chamberlain and James Buchanan

——

Neville Chamberlain

> However much we may sympathize with a small nation con-
> fronted by a big and powerful neighbour, we cannot in all
> circumstances undertake to involve the whole British Empire
> in a war simply on her account.

NEVILLE CHAMBERLAIN CAME FROM A WEALTHY AND DISTIN-
guished family of Birmingham manufacturers. His father,
Joe Chamberlain, had been a masterful colonial secretary
in the 1890s, responsible for the infamous Jameson Raid in South
Africa in 1895, which was propelled by Rand gold and diamond
magnates who sought political control of the Transvaal. Joe's oldest
son and Neville's half-brother, Austen Chamberlain, had been a distinguished minister and chancellor in the Tory cabinet.

Neville was thought to be the "less promising" second son and
was dispatched to manage the family's sisal plantations in the West
Indies. In this, as in so many aspects of his life, he was unlucky –
the crop failed. He returned to England with a fierce determination
to succeed in politics. He was a loyal follower of Stanley Baldwin,
and was appointed Chancellor of the Exchequer. Chamberlain saw
the need for a balanced budget and also the need to rebuild the
Royal Air Force.

However, the austere uptight penny-pinching chancellor lacked vision. The man he hated above all was the ebullient Winston Churchill who, though out of office throughout the 1930s (Baldwin was said to be afraid of "Winston's hundred-horsepower brain"), continued, in speech after speech, to drive home the dangers of being unprepared for war with Germany. But since Churchill had been wrong about the gold standard in 1925, wrong about Indian self-government in 1931, and wrong about the Abdication in 1936, why should he be right about the much more important question of defense and the peril of Nazism?

To the complacent upper-class Conservative cabinet of Baldwin, Chamberlain, Halifax, Hoare, Inskip, and company, it was a rude challenge that they preferred to sidestep; besides, the country did not want war. Since the 1914–18 "war to end all wars" and the 1933 Oxford Union motion that "this House would not fight for king and country," there was an undercurrent of pacifism in England. Baldwin, prime minister for much of the 1930s, faithfully reflected public opinion.

Chamberlain was austere, cold, and calculating, with little interest in, or knowledge of, his fellow man. In his attempt to help the poor, he abolished the Poor Law Boards. In 1938, as Prime Minister, Chamberlain passed the Factories Act, which limited the working hours of women and children. He had firsthand knowledge of manufacturing and industry from his upbringing in Birmingham. Most of his domestic policies were successful, but despite this, he had a very poor relationship with the Labour opposition. The Labour leader Attlee complained that Chamberlain "always treated us like dirt." Chamberlain himself had written in 1927: "More and more do I feel an utter contempt for their lamentable stupidity."

Not only would his strained relationship with the Labour Party play a major role in his downfall in 1940, but his lack of social grace made him unlikable even to his fellow Tories. In the late '30s, his parliamentary private secretary, Lord Douglas (later prime minister as Sir Alec Douglas-Home), escorted him to the smoking room of the

Commons to socialize with his colleagues, but the visit ended in an embarrassing silence.

It was in his foreign policy, however, that this lack of human imagination and sympathy cost Chamberlain most dearly. He negotiated with the Irish Prime Minister Eamon de Valera to secure economic ties and the use of the three Treaty Ports in the event of war. Chamberlain naively accepted Valera's verbal assurances, but Britain was badly let down when the Irish denied the Royal Navy access during the critical Battle of the Atlantic in 1940.

In 1937, Chamberlain opened talks with Mussolini, and bypassed his foreign secretary, Antony Eden, who was aghast at the idea of Britain recognizing the Italian conquest of Ethiopia and resigned in 1938. That March, Germany surprised the world by its "Anschluss" with Austria. At last, Chamberlain told the Commons, "It is perfectly evident that force is the only argument that Germany understands." At this stage, he still had strong support both in Parliament and among the British people (60 percent approval).

German aggression in Sudetenland, or northwestern Czechoslovakia, became the next *casus belli* and the object of talks with Hitler. Hitler gave a wildly demagogic speech in Nuremberg in order to prepare the Nazis for an invasion. Chamberlain flew (for the first time in his life) to Munich to meet the Fuhrer. At the third meeting of the two leaders (later described by Churchill as "a curate going to tea with a tiger"!), Hitler announced he would invade Czechoslovakia on October 1st. Chamberlain had Hitler sign the Munich Agreement paper of three paragraphs "symbolic of the desire of our two peoples never to go to war again." (After lunch the Fuhrer told his foreign minister Ribbentrop, "Don't take it seriously. That piece of paper is of no significance whatever.")

Chamberlain returned to London, triumphantly waving the paper at Heston Aerodrome and saying it was "Peace with honor" or (as it was called) "Peace in our time." The king summoned him to Buckingham Palace to congratulate him. There was popular support, and, in Parliament, only a handful of Conservative MPs abstained, including Churchill, who told the House, "England has been offered a choice between war and shame. She has chosen shame and will get war."

How prophetic Churchill was. Within six months Hitler invaded Czechoslovakia, and Chamberlain belatedly began to rearm British forces, especially the Royal Air Force. He issued a guarantee to Poland but was reluctant to seek a military alliance with Stalin, whom he distrusted. Churchill, Lloyd George, and even some of the Conservative cabinet saw that Hitler could be deterred only by an alliance with Russia and France. But Chamberlain was too late again. In August, 1939, the Soviet-German pact was announced. Hitler had no fear of Chamberlain (he did, however, fear Churchill). "Our enemies are small worms," he said. "I saw them in Munich."

When Hitler invaded Poland, Britain declared war. Chamberlain brought Churchill back (after 10 years in "the wilderness") as First Lord of the Admiralty. Chamberlain was still equivocating at the debate on the day following the Nazi invasion.

In declaring war, Chamberlain said, "We have a clear conscience; we have done all that any country could do to establish peace." He had forgotten Teddy Roosevelt's dictum "Speak softly, but carry a big stick." England had no big stick, nor much of an air force to counter the Luftwaffe. She was not ready for war. Her diplomacy was weak because of her military weakness. To the House of Commons, Chamberlain said, "Everything that I have hoped for, everything that I have believed in, during my public life, has crashed into ruins."

Chamberlain's fatal flaws of arrogance and aloofness had left his country in the most perilous situation in its entire history. Only the courage and leadership of Churchill in 1940 was able to save Britain.

Chamberlain lived for only another year and died of cancer in November, 1940. "Few men can have known such a reversal of fortune in so short a time," he wrote of himself.

"Neville Chamberlain acted with perfect sincerity according to his lights . . . and strove to save the world from the awful devastating struggle in which we are now engaged," said Churchill after his death. But in *The Gathering Storm*, Churchill depicted him as well-meaning but weak, blind to the threat posed by Hitler and oblivious to the fact that Hitler could (arguably) have been removed from power by a coalition of European states.

James Buchanan

What is right and what is practicable are two different things.

GENERALLY SEEN AS AMERICA'S WORST PRESIDENT, JAMES BUCHANAN was born in 1791 to Scottish-Irish parents in Mercersburg, Pennsylvania. He was another log-cabin president. He graduated from Dickinson College and had a successful legal career in Lancaster, PA, by the age of 30. He then served as congressman, senator, and secretary of state under President James Polk (1844–8), during which time the war with Mexico broke out, and the northwest boundary of the Oregon territory was under dispute with Great Britain.

When he was 29, Buchanan became engaged to a young woman named Anne Coleman, but she wrote him a letter of dismissal after gossips gave her false reports of his supposed philandering. Before he could set the matter straight, Anne became ill and died. The tragedy stayed with him all his life, and he was never interested in another woman. He would become the only bachelor to hold the office of president in 220 years.

Buchanan was elected president in 1856 with only 45 percent of the vote, having won the Democratic nomination with the help of the pro-slavery Stephen A. Douglas, the senator who had defeated Abraham Lincoln. Buchanan appointed four slaveholding Southerners to his cabinet, and even his Northern cabinet ministers favored the appeasement of the South.

Contrary to the popular misconception of his being weak, James Buchanan dominated his cabinet, who shared his politics and narrow vision and believed that their opponents, especially Northern abolitionists, were wrong and even fanatical. They believed that civil war could be averted.

It is something of a mystery why Buchanan was such a sympathizer with the South. He was clearly a "trimmer," meaning a politician who, over the course of a long career, often changed his position to account for public opinion or political realities. In 1824, for instance, he supported Henry Clay for president, but switched to the winning ticket of Andrew Jackson in 1828. He stood both as a federalist and later as a Democrat. He also changed his mind several times about the Oregon boundary.

Perhaps the real explanation for his policy of appeasement was simply a social rather than a moral issue. He was a bachelor, but enjoyed social life and had many close friendships, especially with Southern colleagues who often left their wives at home down South. His closest friendship was with his long-time roommate, senator, later vice president, William King of Alabama. Other close friends were Howell Colt of Georgia and Jefferson Davis (later President of the Confederacy). Buchanan was also the patriarch and financial supporter of a large number of orphaned cousins, nieces, and nephews, so he could understand the Southern defense of slavery as a paternalistic institution.

He became wealthy (he amassed a $300,000 fortune from his legal work) and cherished his "plantation" at Lancaster. He had a conservative respect for property that blinded him to the greater moral issue of slavery. By 1857, he thoroughly identified with the South and with its fears and ambitions. Although he occasionally expressed a dislike for slavery – and certainly never owned slaves himself – he never opposed its expansion. He once said that slavery could not be remedied "without the introduction of evils infinitely greater." He thought that emancipation would turn slaves into masters and said, "Who could for a moment indulge in the horrible idea of abolishing slavery by the massacre of the high-minded, and the chivalrous race of men in the south? . . . for my own part, I would without hesitation buckle on my knapsack and march in defense of their cause."

Nowadays we think of property as being land, houses, and other investments. One hundred and fifty years ago, property also included other human beings. (This was true not only in America but in Brazil, Tsarist Russia, and several other nations.) It is, therefore, not easy for readers in the 21st century to imagine the mentality of slave-owners or even their sympathizers, such as James Buchanan.

In his inaugural address of 1857, President Buchanan had to face the looming issue of the day: whether slavery should be allowed to expand territorially – in particular, in Kansas, where a minority at Lecompton had written a pro-slavery state constitution (subsequently rejected by popular vote). Buchanan was well aware of the Dred Scott case pending before the Supreme Court, which involved a slave who had sued for his freedom in Missouri after living with his owner in Illinois and Wisconsin. The court announced two basic principles: that no Negro could be a citizen, and that slaves were property protected by the Constitution in all states. This ruling invalidated the Missouri Compromise (permitting slavery only in specific states) and caused uproar in the North.

During Buchanan's four-year administration, the issue of slavery continued to dominate the country. Harriet Beecher Stowe's *Uncle Tom's Cabin* was published in 1852 and widely read. Runaway slaves were a constant news item. Then, in October, 1859, John Brown invaded Harper's Ferry, Virginia, with 22 men, intending to arm the slaves and rouse them to revolt. The governor of Virginia had him hanged, and he became a martyr for the Abolitionists. Buchanan, on the other hand, was horrified by Brown's actions, and considered him one of the authors of the Civil War.

By this time it seems clear that Buchanan, cocooned in his circle of Southern sympathizers, had lost touch with the fast-changing mood of the country, especially the North. This becomes apparent in his influence over the Democratic Party in 1860, when he prevented moderates from putting forward his hated rival, Stephen Douglas. Their convention was held in Charleston and nominated Vice President John Breckenridge of Kentucky, who was endorsed by the president. The party split between Southern and Northern democrats. The Republicans met in Chicago and rejected the frontrunner William Seward, turning, in a surprise choice, to the moderate Abraham Lincoln, who had spoken only for a containment of slavery and a hope for its ultimate extinction. Lincoln's subsequent triumph is history.

James Buchanan died in 1868, only three years after the end of the Civil War, still embittered and bewildered by the tremendous historical changes in which he had played a minor, but important, role. He had excelled in his earlier career – as a lawyer, as minister to Great Britain and as Secretary of State. When finally he had "greatness thrust upon him," he could not rise to the great challenge of his age.

THE COMPARISON OF NEVILLE CHAMBERLAIN WITH JAMES BUCHANAN

Neville Chamberlain is infamous for his policy of appeasing Hitler and Mussolini, and James Buchanan failed to grapple with the threat of secession by the South. The terrible charge of "appeasement" hangs over both these misunderstood, tragic, figures.

Buchanan was a successful man and had a deep and conservative respect for property. Like Chamberlain, another businessman, his narrow vision couldn't conceive of greater moral issues. Chamberlain had the horror of Bolshevism, and Buchanan faced the possible chaos of emancipation – which Lincoln and Churchill, with their broader human sympathies, and higher moral vision, could embrace.

It was in 1858, during Buchanan's presidency, that Abraham Lincoln and Senator Stephen Douglas held their famous debates in which Lincoln declared that "a house divided against itself cannot stand [as Jesus said in St Mathew's Gospel]. I believe this government cannot endure permanently half-slave and half-free . . . It will become all one thing or all the other." Like Chamberlain, Buchanan was willing to defer, to postpone, to appease in the hope of avoiding inevitable war. Their personal flaws led to national tragedies.

Winston Churchill

Abraham Lincoln

CHAPTER 20

Winston Churchill and Abraham Lincoln

~

Winston Churchill

The statesman declares his mind before the end and submits himself to be tested by those who have believed in him. The politician is silent when he ought to have spoken.

—DEMOSTHENES

There never was a Churchill from John Duke of Marlborough down, that had either morals or principles.

—[Gladstone on Lord Randolph]

Courage is rightly esteemed as the first of human qualities because, as has been said, it is the quality which guarantees all others.

Even though large tracts of Europe and many old and famous States have fallen or may fall into the grip of the Gestapo and all the odious apparatus of Nazi rule, we shall not flag or fail. We shall go on to the end. We shall fight in France, we shall fight on the seas and oceans, we shall fight with growing confidence and growing strength in the air, we shall defend our island, whatever the cost may be. We shall fight in the fields and in the streets, we shall fight in the hills; we shall never surrender.

The empires of the future are the empires of the mind.

CHURCHILL'S LIFE BEGAN IN 1874 AT THE LARGEST PRIVATE HOME in Britain, Blenheim Palace, the seat of his grandfather, the Duke of Marlborough. He was born prematurely – as he said, he was always in a hurry – at seven months. Perhaps Lord Randolph and Jennie Jerome had been in a hurry to get married, too.

Churchill was brought up in the typical upper-class Victorian manner: sent away to boarding school as a young boy and then to Harrow. He had an unusual relationship with both of his parents. His mother was American, and he described her as "the evening star" whom he adored from afar. He longed for his father's companionship, respect, and attention, but got little of it as his father's illness (syphilis) altered his personality and sapped his energy during Winston's teenage years. He wrote cruelly to Winston about losing his watch and about entering Sandhurst (which Winston was happy about), predicting he would become "a public-school wastrel." Churchill was determined to prove his father wrong, to be a success in life, and to achieve greatness. In his 1947 essay, "A Dream," he describes how his father appears in his painting studio and asks him, "What has happened in the last half century?" and Churchill describes all the wars and revolutions and extraordinary events of the 20th century. His father looks at him rather sadly and says, "Well, I suppose you were just a painter," and before Winston can correct his impression, his father's spirit fades from the scene. So, in his boyhood, his only emotional constant was his nanny, "Woomany," Mrs. Elizabeth Everest. She was also Churchill's only contact with ordinary people; he stayed with her and her brother on the south coast and heard sea stories and experienced the life of working people.

It was only in 1895, when Winston arrived in India at 21 years old, that he set out – as his biographer, Randolph Churchill, wrote – "to become his own university," to read the great historians, Gibbon and Macaulay, and educate himself in the records of parliamentary debate. That year Churchill also made his first visit to America – on his way to the Cuban War. Sixty years later, he was asked by Adlai

Stevenson when he had learned his famous style of oratory, and to Stevenson's surprise, Churchill replied, "Here in America from Bourke Cockran, who taught me how to use the human voice, how to play on the vocal cords as an organ." When he was young, Churchill had had a lisp; he trained himself to speak with wonderful, slow rotundity, and began to acquire the vocabulary, turn of phrase, and eloquence that he became known for. (He used to practice on the phrase "The Spanish ships I cannot see, for they are not in sight.")

When he was first seeking election to Parliament, in 1899, Churchill approached a voter in the street to ask for his support. "Vote for you?" said the man, "I'd rather vote for the devil." "I quite understand," said Churchill, "but since that person is not running this time, perhaps I could count on your support." He did not get elected. He returned to India and, having experienced action in Cuba, was determined to seek military glory wherever it could be found. Thus, during the years 1895–1900 Churchill was successively on the front in Afghanistan and writing about it – *The Story of the Malakand Field Force*; then in the Sudan, where he took part in the last great cavalry charge of the British Empire, beautifully described in *The River War* and *My Early Life*; and finally, in South Africa, where he participated in the Boer War, was captured by the Boers, imprisoned in Pretoria, escaped, and became a household name overnight.

He had published three books by the age of 25 and had had plenty of military experience. With his newfound fame, he was able not only to embark on a lucrative speaking tour in the United States and Canada (he made about 10,000 pounds or at least a million dollars in today's currency) but also finally to get elected to Parliament in 1900. He took his seat on the Conservative benches at the age of 26, and was to remain in Parliament for nearly 60 years, serving in virtually every ministerial office. He made his maiden speech four days after entering Parliament, on February 18th, 1901, and found himself opposite the young Liberal radical member for Caernarvon Boroughs, David Lloyd George. Within two or three years they became close friends and allies, and it was not a complete surprise to the Tory Party when, in 1904, Churchill, who had bitterly criticized the Protectionist policies of Balfour, crossed the floor to become a Liberal. This is one of the reasons why Churchill was so distrusted and hated by the Tories until he finally achieved greatness as prime minister during the Second World War nearly 40 years later.

Churchill joined with Lloyd George in making the social reforms of 1909–11. By 1910, Churchill was Home Secretary, and in 1911, he became First Lord of the Admiralty, in which office he achieved perhaps his greatest success as a young minister by modernizing the Royal Navy – converting the battleships from coal to oil. In the process, Britain had to acquire a controlling interest in Anglo-Iranian Oil (which became BP). When the First World War broke out in August 1914, the fleet was ready – Churchill had already deployed it in the North Sea in anticipation of the German declaration of war.

Churchill's chronic desire to be on the front line once again came to the fore: he went to Antwerp to fight with the young naval troops and asked Asquith, the Prime Minister, if he could give up his seat in the Cabinet for a front-line regimental command. The request was greeted with "Homeric laughter" in the Cabinet room. Unfortunately, Churchill's great strategic idea was to break through in the Dardanelles in Turkey. In 1915, this operation failed with heavy casualties, and British forces had to retreat. Churchill's reputation was permanently damaged by this debacle, and he had to resign, returning to the front line with the Grenadier Guards and then the Royal Scots Fusiliers, with whom he stayed in the trenches for six months, an extraordinary act of courage for the volunteer 42-year-old Cabinet Minister.

Churchill seems to have had extraordinary luck throughout his life. Nothing typifies this more than when, during this time, he was called to see the commanding general one afternoon. He left his bunker with his batman and shortly afterwards heard a shell behind them. Thinking nothing of it, they went on to find the general unavailable. Churchill was in a foul mood for the waste of the afternoon, but returned to discover that two minutes after he left, a shell had scored a direct hit on his trench.

After his own miserable childhood, Churchill was determined to create a happy family life, which he did with his beloved wife, Clementine, to whom he was married for nearly 60 years. They had five children: Randolph, Sarah, Diana, Mary, and Marigold, who died in 1922 at the age of three.

In 1923, Churchill lost his seat, as well as his appendix, and changed parties again. He was out of office for nearly two years until, to his amazement, he was offered the second post in the government – Chancellor of the Exchequer – by Stanley Baldwin. For five years Churchill was an outstanding chancellor, although his return to the gold standard in 1925 may have led to the General Strike of 1926. (Economics was never his strong suit.)

The ten years between 1929 and 1938, Churchill's wilderness years, were perhaps the years when his character emerged fully and his confidence in his own judgment and vision of the future became a dominant theme. He was against the establishment on the question of India. He was against the Conservative leadership on the question of rearmament, and he was, once again, in opposition to Baldwin and Chamberlain in 1936 over the abdication of King Edward VIII.

Churchill was a Nobel Prize-winning writer. He published over five million words. His six volumes on the Second World War alone total over two million words. In *Thoughts and Adventures* (1932) he writes:

Almost the chief mystery of life is what makes one do things. Let the reader look back over the path he has travelled and examine searchingly and faithfully the reasons, impressions, motives, occasions which led him to this or that decisive step in his career. Sometimes he will find that people who impressed him least, influenced him most. Small people, casual remarks, and little things very often shape our lives more powerfully than the deliberate, solemn advice of great people at critical moments . . . But usually in our brief hazardous existence some trifle, some accident, some quite unexpected and irrelevant fact has laid the board in such a way as to determine the move we make ... In a broad view, large principles, a good heart, high aims, a firm faith, we may find some charts and a compass for our voyage. Still, as we lean over the stern of the ship and watch the swirling eddies in our wake, the most rigid and resolute of us must feel how many currents are playing their part in the movements of the vessel that bears us onwards.

He then mentions his father Lord Randolph, the American Representative Bourke Cockran and his political mentor Lloyd George as having been great influences on his life.

Churchill was immensely proud of his Marlborough ancestry and wrote biographies of his father Lord Randolph and of the first duke, John Churchill;. He loved the English language, had absorbed the classics, and wrote *A History of the English-Speaking Peoples*. He also immersed himself in English history and was deeply aware of the balance of power in Europe. He reflected on the political questions of his time in the light of history; just as Marlborough had stood against Louis XIV, and Sir Francis Drake had stood against Philip II of Spain and the Armada, he would stand against Hitler. In his speeches, this historical awareness is apparent. It was critical to him in his conviction, in his leadership, and in the guidance he gave to his contemporaries in explaining the direction of his policy. Nothing separates Churchill more from his contemporaries both in Britain and America in the 1930s than his understanding of Nazism. In 1932, Churchill had already read an English translation of Hitler's book, *Mein Kampf*, and he understood that the Nazis were bent on European conquest and the reversal of the Treaty of Versailles. He understood that Hitler was deeply anti-Semitic – indeed, fanatically so. He understood also that Hitler would very likely look for *Lebensraum* or living space for the Germans in the East and would probably attack the communist totalitarian dictatorship of the Soviet Union under Stalin.

In a BBC broadcast in 1939, he said, "I cannot forecast to you the action of Russia. It is a riddle wrapped in a mystery inside an enigma; but perhaps there is a key. That key is Russian national interest. It cannot be in accordance with the interest or the safety of Russia that Germany should plant itself upon the shores of the Black Sea, or that it should overrun the Balkans or subjugate the Slavonic peoples of southeastern Europe." Once again Churchill was thinking ahead, and he was right. He could see, as he had said of Lloyd George, two fields ahead. Churchill saw so far ahead that sometimes he was five or ten years ahead of his fellow politicians. He spoke eloquently about the Iron Curtain that descended across Europe in 1946 – again, well ahead of most American and British statesmen of the time.

Churchill had been despised by the Tories ever since he had crossed the floor in 1904 to become a Liberal. He was considered a maverick. In May, 1940, Chamberlain lost the confidence of the Tories, a coalition with Liberals and Labour was proposed, and everyone (including the King) hoped and expected Lord Halifax to succeed. But he was a peer, sitting in the House of Lords, so Churchill was chosen as a compromise candidate. His contemporary Rab Butler commented, "This half-breed American and his gang have taken power."

On the same day, May 10th, 1940, the Nazi blitzkrieg rolled through Holland and Belgium into France; and Britain was threatened with invasion. Churchill had taken office at the most perilous moment in Britain's modern history – "by a miracle of deliverance," as he rightly called it. He gathered his 25 ministers together and revealed that he had reflected "whether it was part of my duty to consider entering into negotiations with That Man." He ran through the consequences of such a devil's bargain – right down to becoming a Nazi slave state, saying, "I am convinced that every man of you would rise up and tear me down from my place if I were for one moment to contemplate parley or surrender. If this long island story of ours is to end at last, let it end only when each one of us lies choking in his own blood upon the ground."

By the end of May, the BEF (Britain Expeditionary Force) of 300,000 men had been rescued from Dunkirk, so the island was not left entirely defenseless. A second miracle occurred in September when the RAF managed to repel the Luftwaffe (who outnumbered them three to one) to maintain control of British airspace. It still seemed as if Britain was doomed. Only Churchill believed that, against all odds, we could win and had faith that America would (as in 1917) eventually join the war and tip the balance of power.

Churchill had a close relationship with Franklin Roosevelt throughout the Second World War. It was, in some ways, a one-sided relationship. Churchill said that he had courted Roosevelt as if he were his mistress, knowing that he needed to seduce him to become an Ally. Roosevelt, like Wilson during the First World War, refrained from declaring war for as long as possible, knowing his countrymen's isolationist tendencies. It was only under pressure that he agreed to the Lend-Lease deal, which gave Britain 50 used destroyers in exchange for leasing bases in Newfoundland, Bermuda, and Trinidad to the U.S. for 99 years.. After Pearl Harbor, Churchill traveled to Washington and for three weeks, addressed Congress and he eventually persuaded Roosevelt and his military staff that it was important to put Europe first and the Pacific second in the war strategy.

Churchill wanted to lead, to take the initiative, and to fight it out to the end. "In war, resolution; in defeat, defiance; in victory, magnanimity; in peace, goodwill." That was his approach in both world wars. It was the 18 months between May, 1940, and December, 1941, that made him perhaps the greatest British leader ever and one of the greatest men in history. It was his resolute actions and speeches – above all, in the dark days of Dunkirk and the Blitz – that confirmed his greatness. As Kennedy later said, Churchill "mobilized the English language and sent it into battle." Because of the lack of rearmament policy by his predecessors in the 1930s, the reality on the ground was grim. Britain was short of aircraft, she was short of destroyers, she was short of food, and the Battle of the Atlantic assumed as great an importance in that period as the Battle of Britain had in the summer and autumn of 1940 when he said, "Never in the field of human conflict was so much owed by so many to so few."

In June, 1940, Churchill flew to France three or four times to see the faltering French leaders Petain, Reynaud and, eventually, de Gaulle, whom he was able to bring to London and support as the leader of the Free French. He was so dismayed by the defeatism of the French politicians that he took the extraordinary step of offering the French population a united citizenship with Britain, perhaps a pre-vision of the European Union to come.

This was the MP Harold Nicolson's diary entry for November 5th, 1940:

> The Prime Minister makes a statement after Question Time. He is rather grim. He brings home to the House as never be-fore the gravity of our shipping losses and the danger of our position in the Eastern Mediterranean. It has a good effect. By putting the grim side foremost he impresses us with his ability to face the worst. He rubs the palms of his hands with five fingers extended up and down the front of his coat, searching for the right phrase, indicating cautious selection, conveying almost medicinal poise. If Chamberlain had spoken glum words such as these the impression would have been one of despair and lack of confidence. Churchill can say them and we all feel, 'Thank God that we have a man like that!' I have never admired him more. Thereafter he slouches into the smoking-room and reads the Evening News intently, as if it were the only source of information available to him.

There would be many shocks and setbacks, such as the sinking of the battleship *Prince of Wales* and battle cruiser *Repulse*, and the surren-der of Singapore, but as the tide turned, first in North Africa, then Europe and Southeast Asia, Churchill looked ahead and began to plan how the Allies would deal with the Soviet Union after the war. He saw the need to support Greece in 1945 before the communists took over. He tried, but failed, to persuade Roosevelt to stand up to Stalin at Yalta on the question on Poland.

The Conservatives lost the election of 1945, but Churchill returned to lead the country in 1951 before retiring in 1955. He died in January, 1965. I was 12 years old, and I remember we were all taken down to watch the train bearing Churchill's body. Many people in Britain remember that day 50 years ago, just as people in America remember what they were doing on the day that Kennedy was assassinated. Churchill's funeral was a moment of deep national mourning for the passing not only of our greatest statesman, but of an era of British greatness.

Abraham Lincoln

George Washington was a great American, but Abraham Lincoln belongs to the common people of every land. They love that haggard face with the sad and tender eyes.

[David Lloyd George]

Nobody has ever expected me to be President. In my poor lean, lank face, nobody has ever seen that any cabbages were sprouting out.

Whenever I hear anyone arguing for slavery, I feel a strong impulse to see it tried on him personally.

Perhaps a man's character is like a tree and his reputation like its shadow. The shadow is what we think of it; the tree is the real thing.

It has been said of the world's history hitherto that might makes right. It is for us and for our time to reverse the maxim, and to say that right makes might.

My best friend is the man who'll get me a book I ain't read.

If you once forfeit the confidence of your fellow citizens, you can never regain their respect and esteem. It is true that you may fool all the people some of the time; you can even fool some of the people all the time; but you can't fool all of the people all the time.

Assassination has never changed the history of the world.

—DISRAELI about Lincoln, 1865

He was one of those rare men whom you do not associate with any particular creed or party or even country. He belongs to the human race in every clime and age.

—DAVID LLOYD GEORGE

L ITTLE IS KNOWN ABOUT ABRAHAM LINCOLN'S ANCESTRY. JOHN Buchan wrote *The Path of the King*, a romance about Lincoln's mother that imagined her family was descended from Viking kings. In 1860, Lincoln's campaign biographer, John Locke Scripps, asked him to share his early life: "Why, Scripps," Lincoln replied, "it is a great piece of folly to attempt to make anything out of my early life. It can all be condensed into a single sentence . . . you will find in Gray's 'Elegy,' 'the short and simple annals of the poor'."

Lincoln did not have a close relationship with his father, Thomas, who, after the death of his mother, left for several months, leaving he and his twelve-year-old sister to look after themselves in a remote region of Kentucky. Lincoln described it as "a wild region" where "the panther's scream filled the night with fear, [and] bears preyed on the swine." When his father finally returned with his new stepmother, Sarah Bush Johnston, she found them living like animals, wild, ragged, and dirty. However, Lincoln responded to her maternal love and, recognizing that he was a boy of uncommon natural talents, she encouraged him to read and learn. His ambition would, as one biographer remarked, require a herculean feat of self-creation. His command of the English language and extraordinary gift of oratory came from an ability, acquired when very young, to tell stories. The Lincoln farm, which sat along Knob Creek on the Cumberland Trail, attracted many pioneers, peddlers, and preachers, and every night,

Thomas Lincoln would exchange stories with his visitors and neighbors while his young son sat in the corner listening to every word. Abraham developed a talent for mimicry and an uncanny memory for stories inherited from his father. Even though he was only 10 years old, he would listen to the story, memorize it, and then try to retell it in his own words to his schoolboy friends. Throughout his political career, this great talent for storytelling would be a key component of his success. What he had in the way of education, he had to learn from the King James Bible, *The Pilgrim's Progress, Aesop's Fables*, and poetry, such as Thomas Gray or Byron and, of course, Shakespeare, whom he became familiar with through William Scott's *Lessons in Elocution*. He started reading law books, including the Statutes of Indiana, which contained the Declaration of Independence and the Constitution – these he memorized and knew perhaps more thoroughly than any president has ever known them. Repeatedly reading the Bible and Shakespeare implanted rhythms and poetry in his mind that would come to fruition in his great speeches. He has been described as the only poet president. He also borrowed Parson Weems's *Life of Washington* from a nearby farmer and read it by candlelight in his log cabin. Leaving the book between the cabin logs, it got severely damaged by rain, and he had to do two days' work pulling corn in order to repay the farmer.

With his deep love of learning and desire for more education, he was resentful of his father's decision to hire him out at the age of 15 to do various jobs for his neighbors. At the age of 22 he left home and traveled from Indiana to New Salem, Illinois, a small but growing town with 25 families, three general stores, and a tavern. He worked as a flatboatman, clerk, merchant, postmaster, surveyor, and storekeeper. He engaged in a systematic regime of self-improvement, mastering the principles of English grammar at night after the store was closed, carrying Shakespeare's plays while he walked the streets, devouring newspapers, and studying geometry and trigonometry while qualifying as a surveyor.

At the age of 25 Lincoln decided to study law. Most young men were apprenticed to practicing lawyers while they read the law, but Lincoln simply borrowed law books from a friend and, reading Blackstone's Commentaries and Chitty's pleadings, set out to learn on his own. Although he didn't have a mentor or partner to talk about his studies with, he had extraordinary concentration, memory, and reasoning skills. He read and reread his books until he understood them. In 1855 he told a law student seeking advice, "Get the books and read and study them. It doesn't matter whether the reading is done in a small town or a large city, by yourself or with others. The books, and your capacity for understanding them, are the same in all places. Always bear in mind that your own resolution to succeed is more important than any other one thing."

At this time, Lincoln's natural melancholy was further deepened by the loss of his sister, Sarah, in childbirth. As he tried to make a life for himself in New Salem, he fell in love with a girl named Ann Rutledge, but she died of typhoid at only 22. One of his neighbors said that she had never seen a man mourn for a companion more than Lincoln did. He couldn't be reconciled, he said, to have the snow, rains, and storms beat on her grave. It was feared that he would go mad, and he did run a little off the track, having lost the three women he had loved most, but he wasn't crazy. He was simply very sad. But, he also had a deep resilience. As Tolstoy said, "Only those people who are capable of loving strongly can also suffer great sorrow, but this same necessity of loving serves to counteract their grief and heal them." Lincoln's neighbor Mrs. Hill asked him whether he believed in an afterlife. "I'm afraid there isn't," he replied sorrowfully. "It isn't a pleasant thing to think that when we die that is the last of us." To the end of his life he was haunted by the finality of death and the fleeting nature of earthly accomplishments.

In 1837, almost two years after Ann's death, now aged 28, Lincoln left New Salem for the thriving western township of Springfield, Illinois. He wandered into the general store to see if he could buy a bed and some sheets. Joshua Speed, the young owner of the store, said it would cost him about $17. Lincoln asked for credit. Speed looked at the tall shambling figure in front of him: "I never saw a sadder face," he recalled, saying to Lincoln: "You seem to be so much pained at contracting so small a debt; I think I can suggest a plan by which you can avoid the debt and attain your end. I have a large room with a double bed upstairs, which you are very welcome to share with me." Lincoln's face was transformed. Beaming with pleasure, he exclaimed, "Well, Speed, I am moved." Speed had been raised on a Southern plantation with 70 slaves, and had received an excellent education in Kentucky, but had been determined to make his own way in life to the west, investing in real estate and becoming the owner of the general store. For nearly four years, Lincoln and Speed shared the same room and developed a close friendship. Both of them were ambitious to improve themselves and raise their status in the world. This was Lincoln's first close friendship.

Lincoln had tried to enter the state legislature at the age of 23, but wasn't elected until two years later, 1825. He was always popular because of his storytelling and always got plenty of votes from his neighbors and friends. He stood honestly on questions of principle, such as slavery. In Illinois in the 1830s there was strong popular feeling against the abolitionists. By a vote of 77 to 6, the Illinois State Assembly resolved to disapprove of the formation of the abolition societies and uphold sacred the right of property and slaves. Lincoln was among the six dissenting voices. He said that the institution of slavery was founded on both injustice and bad policy. He believed that if slavery wasn't wrong, then nothing was wrong, and he couldn't remember a time when he didn't think and feel this way. Having been born in the slave state of Kentucky, his parents, nevertheless, had been against slavery and had moved to the free state of Indiana partly because of this. Lincoln didn't believe that the Constitution gave Congress the power to interfere with slavery in the states where it was already established, but he also believed it shouldn't be established in new states as the population spread west.

Lincoln stood 6'5" tall, and had shaggy black hair, a rumpled appearance, and a deeply lined and gravely melancholy face. He was awkward in the presence of women. "Oh, boys, how clean those girls look," he would say, bursting into a ball with his heavy boots on. He didn't know what to do with his hands or his long legs and wasn't ever at ease talking with women. He had, however, a deep longing for love, and after he recovered from the loss of Ann Rutledge, he proposed to Mary Owens, who declined. Eventually, he became engaged to Mary Todd who came from a well-to-do Southern family. They seemed to be opposites at first sight: she, vivacious and talkative; he, serious and silent. She was short and he was tall. They did, however, share intellectual interests and liked to discuss politics and poetry. They had both lost their mothers at an early age. Mary, however, had an emotional temperament and was somewhat unbalanced, a trait that emerged fully after her husband's assassination.

They broke-off their engagement in 1841, perhaps because of objections from her family and perhaps because of other suitors such as Stephen Douglas, later the Democratic senator for Illinois. Mainly, their engagement ended because of Lincoln's self-doubt that he could make any woman happy. He was apprehensive about his ability to please and support a wife and doubtful about marriage itself. He probably feared that a wife and family would undermine his concentration and was worried that he wouldn't be able to provide the wealth and luxury that Mary was accustomed to. He drafted a letter to her, ending the engagement, but Joshua Speed refused to deliver it. He then went to see Mary and tried to break off the engagement in person.

This, coupled with the departure of his best friend to Kentucky, caused Lincoln to descend into a melancholy period of what Churchill called the "black dog," a feeling of hopelessness, listlessness, and thoughts of death and suicide. "I am now the most miserable man living. If what I feel were equally distributed to the whole human family, there would not be one cheerful face on the earth. Whether I shall ever be better, I cannot tell. I awfully forebode that I shall not. To remain as I am is impossible. I must die or be better, it appears to me." He consulted various doctors about his depression. Lincoln told Speed that he was more than willing to die but "that he had done nothing to make any human being remember that he had lived and that to connect his name with the events transpiring in his day and generation and so impress himself upon them as to link himself with something that would redound to the interests of his fellow man was what he desired to live for." Even in his deepest depression, the strength of Lincoln's desire to write his name in history kept him going. Lincoln seemed to believe that a person's worth is tied to the way others, both contemporary and future generations, perceive him. With resilience, conviction, and sheer strength of will and character, he gradually re-covered from his depression, deciding that he had to avoid being idle and engage in business and the conversation of friends. He returned to his law practice and his duties in the legislature.

Encouraged by the accounts of Joshua Speed's marriage in Ken-tucky, Lincoln finally took the plunge and renewed his commitment to Mary Todd. They were married in 1842. "Nothing new here," Lin-coln wrote to another friend, "except my marrying, which is, to me, a matter of profound wonder." Nine months later, a son, Robert Todd, was born to the Lincolns, followed three years later by a second son, Edward.

Lincoln was elected to Congress in 1846 when he was 38 years old. In January, 1848, he made his first speech, in which he strongly attacked the president, James Polk, about the Mexican War. Lincoln's belief was unpopular at the time because the American people were eager to expand into the west and claim Mexican territory, such as New Mexico, Arizona, Nevada and California.

Lincoln left politics after two years as a congressman in Wash-ington. He had missed his family terribly but had advanced his polit-ical career and made connections. He had visited Massachusetts and met William Seward and made speeches in support of President Zachary Taylor, but in 1850 he resumed his Springfield law practice, which was flourishing and giving him a steady income. In his *Book of Heroes*, Paul Johnson quotes a letter, in which Lincoln returned $10 to a client, having said that $15 was enough for the job.

One day his law partner William Herndon found him so deeply absorbed in study that "he scarcely looked up when I entered. He was surrounded by a quantity of blank paper, heavy sheets, compass, rule, pencils, bottles of ink, and a profusion of stationery." Lincoln was apparently struggling with a calculation of some magnitude and when Herndon asked what he was doing, he announced that he was trying to solve the difficult problem of squaring the circle. He had spent almost two days on this task posed by Greek mathematicians 4,000 years ago. In addition to geometry, Lincoln's solitary studies allowed him to explore astronomy, political economy, and philosophy, subjects that his fellow lawyers had had the opportunity to discover in college. He even applied for, and gained, a patent for a method of lifting boats over shoals and bars by means of inflatable chambers. It never made him money, but it illustrates his extraordinary mind – looking at the world in a fresh way.

In February 1850, the Lincolns suffered a terrible loss when their three-year-old son Eddie died from tuberculosis. Mary was inconsolable and refused to eat. Lincoln was the only person who could reach her. She found some solace in her belief in the afterlife, and although Lincoln didn't share her faith, he was grateful for the comfort that it gave her. She soon became pregnant again and had a third son, Willy, in 1850, and a fourth son, Thomas, in 1853; but the death of Eddie left an indelible scar on Mary Lincoln, deepening her mood swings and increasing her fears. She began to behave erratically with hysterical outbursts. She apparently chased Lincoln through the yard with a knife and a broomstick and smashed his head with a chunk of wood. Lincoln remained calm. He developed what one of his neighbors called a "protective deafness," which undoubtedly exasperated Mary. He would lose himself in thought, quietly leave the room, or take the children for a walk. If her hysteria continued, he would go to the state library or his office, where he would occasionally stay until the emotional storm had subsided. Had his marriage been happier, perhaps Lincoln would have been satisfied as a country lawyer. But Lincoln was driven by ambition. Whether or not his wife drove him from the house he wanted to succeed and make his name in the world.

In 1852, Harriet Beecher Stowe's *Uncle Tom's Cabin* was published. Three hundred thousand copies were sold in the United States and it aroused great compassion for the slaves. In 1854, the passage of the Kansas Nebraska Act – allowing those two new states to decide by popular sovereignty if they wished to become free or slave states – was a clarion call to the anti-slavery movement and resulted in the formation of the Republican Party and Lincoln's pathway to the presidency six years later. Lincoln delivered his first great anti-slavery speech in Springfield that October. He had heard Stephen Douglas speak the day before in favor of the Kansas Nebraska Act. In his speech he returned to the Founding Fathers and powerfully recounted how slavery had grown within the country despite the warnings of Jefferson and others of the dangers of this expansion. At the time of the Constitution, Lincoln said, "the plain, unmistakable spirit of that age toward slavery was hostility to the principle and toleration only by necessity since slavery was already woven into the fabric of American society." Noting that neither the word slaver nor slavery was ever mentioned in the Constitution, Lincoln claimed that the Founding Fathers concealed it. (In fact, Jefferson had included a reference to slavery in the first draft of the Declaration of Independence.) Lincoln's final point was: "No man is good enough to govern another man without that other's consent. I say this is the leading principle, the sheet anchor of American Republicanism."

In 1858 Lincoln ran for senator of Illinois against the "Little Giant," Stephen Douglas, who had also courted Mary Todd 20 years earlier. Lincoln's speeches in the debates with Douglas focused on the principle that a house divided against itself cannot stand: "I believe this government cannot endure permanently half slave and half free. I do not expect the house to fall, but I do expect it will cease to be divided. It will become all one thing or all the other." Lincoln lost the race for the senate, but gained a national reputation, and two years later he became the dark-horse candidate for the presidency. William

Seward was the favorite to be nominated. Other contenders – Salmon Chase, Henry Bates, and Edwin Stanton – would all become members of Lincoln's cabinet. All three had the advantages of an East Coast education, of money and influence. In the course of the 1860 campaign, Lincoln was invited to New York to speak at Cooper Union, where he made one of his greatest speeches, finishing with the pledge, "Let us have faith that right makes might; and in that faith, let us to the end dare to do our duty."

The Republican National Convention was held in May, 1860, in Chicago. Lincoln had carefully prepared for the situation in which there was a strong movement to support Seward. Lincoln had earned widespread respect and admiration and, with the goal of becoming everyone's second choice, had been careful not to alienate any of the other candidates. In fact, he had always been generous to his opponents and conceded to them and had never taken any umbrage or offense at being treated as an uneducated Westerner. A long-armed ape, as Stanton had called him, he was able to overcome all the hostility and political rivalry of the convention. It was hardly doubted that Seward would become the candidate. In the first ballot, he was well ahead at 173; Lincoln at 102; Chase at 49; and Bates at 48. By the third ballot, however, Lincoln had reached 231, and then there was a final vote, which nominated Lincoln.

In the meantime, the Democratic Party had splintered between the North and the South, greatly enhancing Lincoln's prospects of victory. But he was still ridiculed by much of the press, especially in the South. His formidable rival, Stephen Douglas, was nominated by the Northern Democrats, and John Breckinridge of Kentucky by the South. In those days candidates did not campaign or go on speaking tours, so Lincoln stayed at home in his small frame house in Springfield and received visitors. He moved quickly after he had been elected, appointing Seward as Secretary of State and bringing other rivals into the cabinet. A cabinet of great talent and experience was severely needed as the country was rapidly deteriorating into crisis.

On December 20th, 1860, just a few weeks after the election,

South Carolina elected to secede from the Union. Within the next few weeks, Mississippi, Louisiana, Florida, Alabama, Georgia, and Texas followed suit. On February 11th, 1861, Lincoln left Springfield, Illinois, and made a short speech from the platform of his private railway carriage:

> My friends, no one, not in my situation, can appreciate my feeling of sadness at this parting. To this place, and to the kindness of these people, I owe everything. Here I have lived a quarter of a century and have passed from a young to an old man. Here my children have been born, and one is buried. I now leave not knowing when or whether I may return, with a task before me greater than that which rested upon Washington. I hope in your prayers you will commend me. I bid you an affectionate farewell.

He would never return to Springfield. In a sinister foreshadowing of events four years later, there was a plot to assassinate Lincoln on his way to take office as president during a stop in Baltimore. He had to be smuggled into Washington overnight. (Supposedly dressed as a Scotsman.)

In his inaugural speech, Lincoln had written a moving appeal to the South: "I am loth to close. We are not enemies, but friends. We must not be enemies. Though passion may have strained, it must not break our bonds of affection. The mystic cords of memory, stretching from every battlefield and patriot grave to every living heart and hearth stone, all over this broad land will yet swell the chorus of the Union when again touched, as surely they will be, by the better angels of our nature."

The Civil War divided families; Lincoln's brother-in-law, Benjamin Hardin Helm, from Kentucky, had married Mary Todd's half-sister, Emily. He was staying with the Lincolns at the White House two weeks after Fort Sumter was surrendered. Lincoln offered to appoint him major and paymaster in the Union Army. Helm was a friend of Robert E. Lee's, and, unable to sleep, he said the next day, "I am going home. I will answer you from there. You have been very generous to me, Mr. Lincoln, generous beyond anything I have ever known. I have no claim on you. I opposed your candidacy and did what I could to prevent your election." When he reached Kentucky and spoke to his friends, he realized he had to decline Lincoln's offer and side with his native South, which he did and received a commission as a brigadier-general in the Confederate Army.

In all his decisions, Lincoln faithfully followed the Constitution. He was deeply attached to the idea of the Union that George Washington had outlined in his Farewell Address: "It is of infinite moment that you should properly estimate the immense value of your national union to your collective and individual happiness. That you should cherish a cordial, habitual, and immoveable attachment to it, accustoming yourselves to think and speak of it as of the palladium of your political safety and prosperity." Washington had also advised vigilance against "the first dawning of every attempt to alienate any portion of our country from the rest or to enfeeble the sacred ties which now link together the various parts." It was with this in mind that Abraham Lincoln summoned the Army to defend the Union.

In July, 1861, the Union Army was decisively defeated at the First Battle of Bull Run, only 30 miles from the capital. It was a major setback for the new president, whose situation was precarious. He appointed George McClellan general-in-chief. McClellan was only 34 but seemed to be the best man suited for the task of heading the Union armies. McClellan, however, proved to be arrogant, indecisive, and unwilling to offer battle to the Confederates. Lincoln spent the next three years searching for a victorious general.

Churchill wrote of this time: "Through his office flowed a stream of politicians, newspaper editors, and other men of influence . . . Lincoln treated all his visitors with patience and firmness. His homely humour stood him good stead. A sense of irony helped to lighten his burdens. At tense moments, a dry joke relieved his feelings. At the same time his spirit was sustained by a deepening belief in Providence. When the toll of war rose steeply and plans went wrong, he appealed for strength in his inmost thoughts to a power higher than man's. Strength was certainly given him. It is sometimes necessary at the summit of authority to bear with the intrigues of disloyal colleagues, to remain calm when others panic, and to withstand misguided popular outcries. As the war drew on, Lincoln became more and more gaunt, and the furrows on his cheeks and brow bit deep. Fortitude was written on his countenance," Churchill wrote of Lincoln; and surely writing in 1950, he was reflecting on his own wartime experience. The loneliness of power, the capacity to face defeats and setbacks with courage and to inspire the nation with calm, resolute leadership.

Besides the worries of the war, Lincoln was afflicted with personal loss. Two of his closest friends, Colonels Edward Baker and Elmer Ellsworth, were both killed in the early weeks of the war. Then in February, 1862, tragedy struck when his 11-year-old son Willy died of typhoid in the White House. Both parents were convulsed with grief and their other son, Tad, was also very ill. Lincoln's life was marked by continuous tragedy, and, in the series of photographs taken during his four years in the White House, it's obvious how he aged: his face became lined with sorrow.

Lincoln's problems with generals continued as McClellan became increasingly insubordinate. Eventually, he would stand against Lincoln in the election of 1864. Lincoln replaced him, first with Ambrose Burnside, then with Joseph Hooker, before he found a winning team in Ulysses S. Grant and William T. Sherman. When warned that Grant drank too much, Lincoln was supposed to have replied, "Tell me which brand of whiskey he drinks and I'll send it to all my other generals."

The defining moment of Lincoln's career and centerpiece of his legacy was the Emancipation Proclamation of 1863. Everything in his life had led to this. His proclamation had military as well as humanitarian reasons because the slaves who were working for and assisting the Confederate Army would be turned towards the Union cause. In July, 1862, Seward persuaded Lincoln to wait for public opinion to catch up with the enormous prospect of freeing 3½ million slaves, about a third of the population of the South. Some cabinet members still believed that deportation to Liberia was the only way to treat freed slaves. This, of course, was impractical, but many feared it would be difficult for whites and blacks to peacefully live together, and that there was such a large educational and social gap that it would be several generations before African Americans could be fully integrated into national life.

Lincoln was attacked by Horace Greeley in the *New York Tribune* for his slow pace in emancipating the slaves. He replied:

> My paramount object in this struggle is to save the Union and is not either to save or destroy slavery. If I could save the Union without freeing any slave, I would do it; and if I could save it by freeing all the slaves, I would do it; and if I could do it by freeing some and leaving others alone, I would also do that. What I do about slavery, and the colored race, I do because it helps to save the Union. And what I forbear I forbear because I do not believe it would help to save the Union. I shall do less whenever I shall believe what I am doing hurts the cause and I shall do more whenever I shall believe doing more will help the cause.

Lincoln's attitude disappointed the abolitionists.

Meanwhile, the Confederates moved north. McClellan was hesitant and discouraged, and Lincoln went to the front to visit the Union soldiers. On January 1st, 1863, he signed the Emancipation Proclamation. "I never in my life felt more certain that I was doing right than I do in signing this paper," he said. "If my name ever goes into history, it will be for this act; and my whole soul is in it." "Fellow citizens," Lincoln said to Congress, "we cannot escape history. We of this Congress and this Administration will be remembered in spite of ourselves. No personal significance or insignificance can spare one or another of us. The fiery trial through which we pass will light us down in honor or dishonor to the latest generation." (Like Churchill's comment that "this was the finest hour.")

Lincoln saw the strategic, as well as the moral, significance of his emancipation proclamation. Concerning its timing, he understood that if it had been issued six months earlier it would not have been supported by the public. If the question of slavery, as opposed to war, had been placed before the American people in 1861, Walt Whitman said, "The former would have triumphantly carried the day in the north." In other words, the north would not fight to end slavery, but it would fight to preserve the Union. Sounding like Tolstoy, Lincoln explained, "A man watches his pear tree day after day, impatient for the ripening of the fruit. Let him attempt to force the process, and he may spoil both fruit and tree; but let him patiently wait and the ripe pear at length falls into his lap."

After the momentous Battle of Gettysburg in the summer of 1863, Lincoln went to the battlefield for the consecration of the cemetery. Edward Everett, the former President of Harvard, spoke for two hours and then Lincoln spoke for two minutes. He had thought deeply of what he had wanted to say, particularly as it regarded the Declaration of Independence and the justification for the war in terms of democracy. He declared that the nation was born not in 1789, but in 1776, "conceived in Liberty, and dedicated to the proposition that all men are created equal," and that "government of the people, by the people, for the people, shall not perish from the earth."

Comfortably re-elected in November, 1864, Lincoln gave his last speech, his inaugural, on March 4th, 1865. "Both read the same Bible and pray to the same God. Each invokes his aid against the other. It may seem strange that any men should ask a just God's assistance in wringing their bread from the sweat of other men's faces, but let us judge not, that we be not judged. The prayers of both cannot be answered; that of neither has been answered fully. The Almighty has his own purposes." This was a constant theme of Lincoln's; but "With malice toward none, with charity for all, with firmness in the right as God gives us to see the right let us strive on to finish the work we are in; to bind up the nation's wounds; to care for him who shall have borne the battle, and for his widow and his orphan. To do all which may achieve a just and a lasting peace among ourselves and with all nations." In this second inaugural speech, Lincoln's religious faith is evident as well as his political judgment. Reading a transcript of the second inaugural in London, the American Minister, Charles Francis Adams, who had dismissed Lincoln as an ignorant Midwesterner, said, "That rail splitting lawyer is one of the wonders of the day. The inaugural strikes me in its grand simplicity and directness as being for all time a historical keynote of this war." And the London *Spectator* called the address the noblest that any American president had yet uttered to an American congress.

As the war drew to an end in April, 1865, with Lee's surrender at Appomattox, Lincoln, at 56, was already an old man. Despite his good humor, his face showed his sorrow. His expression was of unspeakable sadness and all-sufficing strength. Lincoln made his historic journey to Richmond on April 4th, and was surrounded by freed black laborers shouting, "Here is the great messiah." "Don't kneel to me," he responded. "That is not right; you must kneel to God only and thank him for the liberty you will hereafter enjoy."

On his own American tour of 1923, David Lloyd George singled out the two messages Lincoln wanted to communicate in that postwar period (messages that Lloyd George himself had heard): "Trust the Common people" and "Reconcile the vanquished."

There was concern about Lincoln's life as he toured the fallen Southern capital, but ironically it was in Washington itself, watching a new play called *Our American Cousin* at Ford's Theatre on Good Friday, April 14th, that Lincoln was shot and killed by John Wilkes Booth. There is a kind of awful inevitability about Lincoln's assassination, the sacrifice he made as the last soldier to die in the Civil War, only 10 days after the surrender at Appomattox. There were many premonitions of the murder, and Lincoln had had a dream only two or three days before in which he saw his coffin in the White House. As Lloyd George said: "In the Civil War in America, there were millions of men who were prepared to sacrifice their lives to wage successful war but there was only one man who was prepared to risk his career to make a successful peace and he was shot down."

The tribute of his Secretary of War, Edwin Stanton, still stands, "Now he belongs to the ages."

THE COMPARISON OF SIR WINSTON CHURCHILL WITH ABRAHAM LINCOLN

Winston Churchill and Abraham Lincoln are the two greatest leaders produced by Britain and America in the past 200 years. They led their respective nations through great wars to preserve democracy, freedom, and progress.

On the face of it, two men could scarcely have had more different backgrounds and personalities. Churchill was aristocratic, militaristic, impetuous, and bombastic. Lincoln, the rugged Midwesterner who had made it from log cabin to White House, was a lawyer, with powers of quiet persuasion and rocklike integrity.

Both their childhoods seem deprived of love, except for that of Lincoln's stepmother and Churchill's nanny. Both men suffered personal tragedy in their own families: Churchill's daughter Marigold died in 1922 at the age of three, and two of Lincoln's sons died in boyhood. Both men were dogged by a tendency to depression, or "Black Dog," but had the resilience to overcome it.

Lincoln was only 56 when he died. He had achieved the presidency at the age of 52 and had been a congressman for only two years without any other political experience. Churchill was 65 and old enough to receive an old-age pension when he became prime minister in May, 1940. He had been elected to Parliament at the age of 25 and continued to serve in various positions until he was 50. So, in complete contrast to Lincoln, Churchill had wide-ranging and long experience as a national politician and as a minister.

Both Churchill and Lincoln came to power almost by accident, as compromise candidates in the face of a national emergency requiring unusual strength of character. Like Lincoln, Churchill was a dark horse; no one expected him to succeed but fate had chosen him. Like

Lincoln, he was the man of the hour capable of saving the nation. As Churchill wrote, "[Lincoln's] spirit was sustained by a deepening belief in Providence. When the toll of war rose steeply and plans went wrong he appealed for strength in his inmost thoughts to a power higher than man's. Strength was certainly given him." Both leaders had an unconventional religious faith, although neither belonged to any church. Lincoln, however, was in some ways the most deeply religious of all presidents. He said, "I claim not to have controlled events but confess plainly that events have controlled me . . . the Almighty has his own purposes." Churchill surprised everybody when the Korean War broke out in 1951 when he said to his fellow Conservative MPs, "Well, the old man has been good to me because, if I had been Prime Minister when this happened, I would have been accused of being a warmonger." When one of the MPs asked, "Excuse me, sir, who is the old man?" Churchill replied, "Why, God Almighty, of course, the old man upstairs." In his writings, Churchill revealed that he believed in providence: in the way he was saved in the First World War; in the luck he had throughout his military adventures; in 1940 he said, "All my life had been a preparation for this hour." He felt a profound sense of relief that he had finally been put in charge of the war effort. So, both men humbly recognized the hand of God in their lives and in their elevation to supreme power in the critical moment in their country's history.

Both men were essentially self-educated and had absorbed the English classics. They loved language and wrought it into something wholly original with the genius of their expression.

Both had a sense of history, and their speeches are pervaded with historical awareness. Such sense of history was critical to both of them in their conviction, in their leadership, and in the guidance they gave to their contemporaries in explaining the direction of their policies.

Both were wonderful orators, but their styles were very different. Lincoln's Gettysburg Address (only 280 words) took two minutes to read and could hardly be heard. Its influence only came after it was published and widely circulated. Churchill's wartime radio addresses were heard at home and abroad (even on hidden receivers throughout Nazi-occupied Europe). He was, like Lincoln, a master of memorable phrase-making: "I have nothing to offer but blood, toil, tears, and sweat"; "Never in the field of human conflict was so much owed by so many to so few" (of the RAF in the Battle of Britain); "now this is not the end. It is not even the beginning of the end. But it is, perhaps, the end of the beginning."

Lincoln's message to Congress in 1862 sounds uncannily like Churchill's address to the House of Commons in 1940. "Fellow citizens," Lincoln said, "We cannot escape history. We of this Congress and this Administration will be remembered in spite of ourselves. No personal significance or insignificance can spare one or another of us. The fiery trial through which we pass will light us down in honor or dishonor to the latest generation." In comparison, Churchill's' words were: "The Battle of Britain will shortly begin. Upon this battle depends the survival of Christian civilization. Upon it depends our own British life and the long continuity of our institutions and our empire. Let us, therefore, brace ourselves to our duties, and so bear ourselves that if the British Empire and its Commonwealth last for 1,000 years, men will still say, 'this was their finest hour.'"

Churchill wrote that Lincoln's "popularity with the troops stood high. They put their trust in him . . . They had a sense . . . of his natural resolution and generosity of character." Both leaders would go to the front with their soldiers. Lincoln visited the wounded in Washington Hospital; Churchill visited the people of east London during the Blitz. Lincoln was a compassionate man who felt a deep sense of empathy with the many mothers and wives he wrote to about the loss of their sons and husbands in the Civil War. Churchill wept when he saw the destruction of the bombing and the casualties in Egypt.

Both men could see the big picture: Lincoln understood that it wasn't simply the Civil War that mattered, it was also the New World's relationship with the Old. At the beginning of the Civil War, England and France supported the South. Two agents of the South were stopped by a Union frigate and taken prisoner, but Lincoln had them released to avoid a fight with Britain. In the meantime, the French had landed 35,000 troops in Mexico where Napoleon III was planning a series of Catholic colonies. Lincoln resisted the Union leaders' push to drive the French out of Mexico, but warned Napoleon that his invasion would not be tolerated if the French colluded with the Confederates. It was his Emancipation Proclamation that won public support in Europe, especially in Britain, because it gave the Union the moral high ground. So, too, in the Second World War, Churchill had the unenviable task of being allied to both the Soviet Union and the United States. In 1941 when Germany invaded Russia he remarked, "If Hitler invaded hell, I would at least make a favorable reference to the devil in the House of Commons." He was a lifelong opponent of communism. Nevertheless, he recognized the importance of supporting Stalin. He realized that Stalin was unlikely to be a reliable long-term friend, and he saw the dangers of the impending Soviet domination of Eastern Europe and that Stalin's promises about Poland couldn't be trusted. He saw farther and deeper than his contemporaries and perhaps this reveals a difference between Churchill and Lincoln: Churchill was ahead of public opinion, while Lincoln tended to be perfectly in tune with it.

Both drew on an inexhaustible and rich mine of wisdom, reflection and insight, which still inspires us today. Hence the value of studying the lives and character of these two great statesmen, of reading their speeches and writings.

Perhaps a final comparison between Churchill and Lincoln may be with regard to their funerals. In 1865, Lincoln's body lay in the capital and was taken on a long train journey, the reverse of his journey of 1861 from Springfield to Washington. A century later, in 1965, when Churchill died, he too lay in state, in Westminster Hall, where over 300,000 people passed by his coffin. After the state funeral in St Paul's Cathedral, he traveled first by boat up the Thames and then by train back to his birthplace at Blenheim in Oxfordshire.

Clement Attlee

Harry S. Truman

CHAPTER 21

Clement Attlee and Harry S. Truman

Clement Attlee

A sheep in sheep's clothing.	—WINSTON CHURCHILL
A monologue is not a decision.	—ATTLEE to CHURCHILL

CLEMENT ATTLEE WAS PERHAPS THE MOST UNDERESTIMATED MAN of the twentieth century. He was the original "quiet man," who emerged from the shadows to become leader of the Labour Party in the 1930s. He was Deputy Prime Minister under Winston Churchill during the Second World War, and then, between 1945 and 1951, leader of the most radical reformist government of the century. It changed Britain into a social welfare state, nationalized her major industries, and withdrew Britain from India as well as her colonies in the East.

Attlee was born in Putney, the seventh of eight children. His father was an upper middle class country solicitor. Clem was sent to Haileybury College, a traditional public boarding school that prepared boys to serve in the Indian civil service. He went on to University College Oxford and trained as a lawyer. Between 1906 and 1909 he worked in London's East End as manager of Haileybury House, a charitable club for working-class boys in Stepney, which was run by his old school. He had been a Conservative as a young man, but the poverty and deprivation he saw while working in the East End changed his view of the world. He decided that private charity would never be sufficient to alleviate poverty, and he became a fully fledged supporter of socialism. He joined the Labour party in 1908 and worked briefly as a secretary to Beatrice Webb. In 1911 he was employed by the British government to explain the National Insurance Act that David Lloyd George had just passed, and later became a lecturer at the London School of Economics, and an army officer when the First World War broke out. His elder brother Tom was a conscientious objector, but Attlee himself served in the South Lancashire Regiment. He saw action at Gallipoli, where he fought bravely.

Attlee was wounded in Mesopotamia. Sent home with the rank of major, he was known as Major Attlee for many years afterwards. He married Violet Miller in 1922, and they had four children, three girls and a boy. He became mayor of Stepney in the East End in 1919 and forced slum landlords to keep their properties in habitable condition. He set out many of the principles of his political philosophy in his first book, *The Social Worker*:

> In a civilized community . . . there will be some persons who will be unable at some period of their lives to look after themselves, and the question of what is to happen to them may be solved in three ways – they may be neglected, they may be cared for by the organized community . . . or they may be left to the goodwill of individuals in the community . . . A right established by law, such as . . . an old-age pension, is less galling than an allowance made by a rich man to a poor one, dependent on his view of the recipient's character and terminable at his caprice.

He strongly supported the Poplar Rates Rebellion of 1921 and in 1922 became a Member of Parliament for the constituency of Limehouse in Stepney. Although he worked with Ramsay MacDonald, he later became disillusioned with him and moved to the left. By this time he had joined the Shadow Cabinet and, in 1931, became Postmaster General. Because he held one of the safest working-class Labour seats in the country, he was one of the few leaders of the Labour Party to survive the 1931 election and acted as leader of the party in 1933. Attlee was officially elected leader of the Party in 1935. Although they initially opposed rearmament, by 1937, with the rising threat from Nazi Germany, they abandoned their pacifist position and opposed Chamberlain's policy of appeasement. In 1938 Attlee spoke against the Munich Agreement:

> We cannot . . . feel that peace has been established . . . We have felt humiliation. This has not been a victory for reason and humanity. It has been a victory for brute force . . . We have seen today a gallant, civilized and democratic people betrayed and handed over to a ruthless despotism . . . We have seen the cause of democracy . . . in our view, the cause of civilization and humanity, receive a terrible defeat . . . it is a tremendous victory for Herr Hitler . . . he has achieved a dominating position in Europe which Germany failed to win after four years of war [1914–18].

When war broke out in September, 1939, Attlee remained as leader of the opposition. In May, 1940, unwilling to serve under Chamberlain, the Labour party entered a coalition government led by Winston Churchill. Attlee was the only minister who served at Churchill's side throughout the war, initially as Lord Privy Seal, then in 1942 as Britain's first Deputy Prime Minister. Attlee supported Churchill throughout the war and proved to be a loyal ally.

After the defeat of Germany, Attlee was willing to continue the coalition government, but the Labour Party demurred and an election was held. To everybody's surprise, there was a landslide victory for Labour, attributable, some believe, to the votes of soldiers who expected social change after five years of war. At home, the Beveridge Report of 1942 had called for full employment and a welfare state. This was Attlee's mandate for change.

Attlee's key reform was the creation of the National Health Service, the first publicly funded healthcare system in the world, which offered treatment free of charge. In the beginning, it was a great success, treating 8.5 million dental patients and dispensing more than five million pairs of eyeglasses during its first year of operation. There was an enormous improvement in the general health of the working classes, and cases of diphtheria, pneumonia, and tuberculosis were significantly reduced. Although today there are many debates about the funding and organization of the NHS, there is still general national and popular support from all parties in Britain for the continuance of this remarkable creation. Spending on health increased from about 2.1% to 3.6% of GDP, or about £11 billion during the Attlee administration.

Attlee also set about creating a "cradle to grave" welfare state, with social security, national insurance, flat-rate pensions, and sickness, unemployment, and funeral benefits. There was an enormous increase in the construction of council housing. A torrent of legislation ensued for workers' rights and the nationalization of major industries such as steel, coal mining, railways, canals, cable and wireless, as well as the Bank of England. Many of these were the great state companies – British Airways, British Petroleum, British Gas, etc. – that were supposed to be denationalized in the 1980s by Margaret Thatcher. Despite the hopes of the left, nationalization didn't work well and failed to give workers greater say in the management of these industries.

Attlee's main problem was that the war had left Britain nearly bankrupt, with a large debt to the United States to repay. Many of Britain's overseas investments had been used to pay for the war, and by 1949 it was necessary to devalue the pound from $4.80 to $2.80 (the largest devaluation for sterling in history). Although he had sought good relations with Stalin at the end of the war, Attlee was resolutely anti-communist. By 1947 he recognized that Stalin's ruthless occupation of Eastern Europe would leave no room for compromise. He moved quickly to implement British decolonization and appointed Lord Mountbatten as Viceroy of India, and by August 1947, both India and Pakistan had become independent. They were followed by Burma, Ceylon, and Palestine, where the state of Israel was founded in May, 1948. By 1950 the electorate was exhausted by post-war austerity, and Labour's majority was reduced to five seats. They then lost the 1951 election, which was followed by 13 years of Conservative rule. Attlee continued as leader of the opposition until 1955 when he retired at the age of 72. Subsequently he was given a peerage and became Earl Attlee. Today he is regarded as perhaps the greatest Labour leader ever. "A modest man, but then he has so much to be modest about," is often said about him. Attlee himself wrote a limerick:

> Few thought he was even a starter.
> There were many who thought themselves smarter.
> But he finished PM,
> CH and OM,
> An earl and a Knight of the Garter.

[Prime Minister, Companion of Honour, and Order of Merit – three rare and difficult-to-achieve honors.]

Attlee changed the character of Britain with the creation of the welfare state and the National Health Service, and by nationalizing many of the country's largest industries. Attlee died in 1967.

Harry S. Truman

The buck stops here.

If you can't stand the heat, get out of the kitchen.

CURIOUSLY, THE "S" IN HARRY S. TRUMAN STANDS FOR NOTHING at all. It was a compromise made by Harry Truman's mother after he was born in Missouri, in 1884. One grandfather's middle name was Shippe and the other's first name was Solomon, so why not please both by simply using the letter "S"? It was the kind of homespun practicality that Truman would carry with him for his entire life. His father, John, was a farmer and cattle dealer, while his mother, Martha, looked after her four children. The Truman family was respectably middle class. As well as doing hard farm work, Harry grew up playing the piano and reading the classics, but politics was his early passion, and he read everything he could on US presidents and even served as a page at the 1900 Democratic Convention in Kansas City.

After graduating from high school in 1910, the diminutive and deceptively mild young Truman took a series of clerical jobs and, as America entered World War One in 1918, joined the army, despite having such poor eyesight that he had to memorize the eye chart to pass the entrance exam. Sent to France as a captain in an artillery regiment, he proved to be a tough officer and good leader. After the war, he allied himself with the notorious Kansas City political boss Tom Prendergast. In the 1920s, he was elected to a judgeship, and in 1934, he became a senator for Missouri. A strong supporter of President Franklin Roosevelt's New Deal program, Truman had close ties with the Roosevelt administration, which helped him get re-elected to the Senate in 1940, despite the conviction of Prendergast on income-tax-evasion charges.

By 1940, Truman was seen by most as a party politician, about as honest as most of them, and a man who toed the Democratic line and did what he was told. The real Harry Truman had yet to emerge on to the public stage.

Truman's rise from a workmanlike senator to president occurred in a matter of five short years. As the election year of 1944 began, Franklin Roosevelt, unhappy with his vice president, Henry Wallace, chose Truman to be his new running mate. Truman, during his second term in the Senate, had distanced himself from the Prendergast scandals and was known for his fairness and integrity. He earned nationwide praise for chairing the Special Committee Investigating National Defense, which exposed graft in the defense industry. That November, Roosevelt easily defeated the Republican Thomas E. Dewey and Truman was carried into the White House as vice president, perhaps the highest position the farm-boy from Missouri could ever have hoped to aspire to.

But within only a few months, on April 12, 1945, Franklin Roosevelt suddenly died of a cerebral hemorrhage and Harry Truman became president of the most powerful country in the world, locked in the most deadly struggle the world had ever known. He had served 82 days as vice president and had little knowledge of international affairs. He told reporters: "When they told me [about Roosevelt's death], I felt like the moon, the stars, and all the planets had fallen on me."

Truman was faced with numerous challenges over the next few years. With the war over, defense production was no longer driving the economy, and America experienced inflation, severe housing shortages, and wage strikes. At the same time, the Cold War began. Russia attempted to build its own atomic bomb, and aggressively tried to extend its control in Europe by blockading Berlin, a situation Truman resolved by airlifting supplies to the beleaguered city. The Berlin Airlift was one of Truman's few foreign-policy triumphs, but the American people, tired of the stress of foreign entanglements and inflation in the post-war world, were not convinced Truman was the charismatic leader they needed. By the election year of 1948 his performance on the domestic front was seen as so dismal that "To err is Truman" became a common saying. Although he made an astounding comeback against Thomas E. Dewey to win a full second term as president, his popularity continued to decline.

Nevertheless, without having the required experience, Truman made several seminal and historic decisions: the first use of the atomic bomb in August, 1945, sparing Emperor Hirohito in Japan, establishing NATO, supporting the Marshall Plan to help rebuild post-war Europe, overseeing the Korean War, and firing General MacArthur.

THE COMPARISON OF CLEMENT ATTLEE
WITH HARRY S. TRUMAN

Clement Attlee and Harry Truman both took power unexpectedly and in the shadow of giants: in Attlee's case, Churchill; in Truman's, Franklin Roosevelt. Following these great leaders at the end and towards the end of the Second World War, they inherited something of a poisoned chalice.

Attlee and Truman met Stalin at Potsdam in July, 1945, but both were inexperienced in flexing global power. Neither had expected to become leader of their country, and while Attlee had been Churchill's understudy for five years, Truman had had barely two hours of conversation with Franklin Roosevelt before ascending to the presidency.

Both men came from relatively modest backgrounds, and each served in local politics, Attlee as mayor of Stepney, and Truman in Missouri. They didn't make a grand entry onto the world's stage, but by force of character they were able to change things both at home and abroad. Both were scrupulously honest and died without amassing great wealth.

In Shakespearean terms, they were two men "who were not born great, but had greatness thrust upon them." There is no doubt that in the critical post-war period, they made important decisions that allowed the Western world to stand firm against Stalinist aggression during the early years of the Cold War. These were historic and lasting legacies.

CHAPTER 22

Louis Mountbatten of Burma and Douglas MacArthur

—◆—

Louis Mountbatten of Burma

Right, now I understand people think you're the Forgotten Army on the Forgotten Front. I've come here to tell you you're quite wrong. You're not the Forgotten Army on the Forgotten Front. No, make no mistake about it. Nobody's ever heard of you.   —On taking over as Supreme Allied Commander

SE Asia in late 1943

NO MAN HAD SUCH A GLAMOROUS AND CONSEQUENTIAL LIFE in the twentieth century as Louis Mountbatten, last Viceroy of India, Supreme Commander in South East Asia in World War II, and First Lord of Admiralty.

Mountbatten was born Prince Louis of Battenberg in Frogmore House, Berkshire, on June 25, 1900, the youngest of the four children of Prince Louis Alexander of Battenberg and Princess Victoria, the daughter of Louis IV of Hesse. He was a great-grandson of Queen Victoria (who held him at his baptism). As a child he was known as Prince Louis or as Dickie.

His father was a naval man, First Lord of the Admiralty, so Louis enrolled in the Royal Naval College at Oxborne in 1913. "All my term pity me," he wrote, "because I have without the least exaggeration been asked over 100 times my name, whether I was a prince; our Cook's name (the only thing I refuse) etc. I get pointed at, have my cap knocked off . . . However, I am now so used to this I don't

Louis Mountbatten of Burma   Douglas MacArthur

mind it much." Louis gained a reputation for being industrious, enthusiastic, and funny. He was, however, deeply affected when his father – the First Sea Lord – was hounded from office because of his German ancestry. He was determined to restore the family name, which was changed from Battenberg to Mountbatten.

In 1914, Louis moved on to Dartmouth, and did his final course at the Royal Naval College at Devonport, where he graduated first in class of 72. In 1916, he was assigned as midshipman to the *Lion*, the flagship of Admiral Sir David Beatty.

In 1917, Prince Louis was transferred to the HMS *Queen Elizabeth*, the flagship of the fleet. He read in the papers that his father and other members of the royal family had abandoned their German titles, and his family had taken the name Mountbatten, so he now became Lord Louis Mountbatten.

Towards the end of 1919 he was dispatched to Cambridge to gain further education. In 1920, he accompanied the Prince of Wales on a tour of Australia and Southeast Asia on the *Renown*. In 1921–2, he was invited on another royal tour, this time of India and Japan. During this tour, he became engaged to Edwina, daughter of Wilfrid William Ashley; her maternal grandfather was the wealthy Sir Ernest Cassel. When he died in 1921, she inherited £2.3 million and a number of houses.

They were happily married in 1922, but Mountbatten soon began getting a reputation as a playboy. He enjoyed fast cars, speedboats, and polo. Nevertheless, he was well liked by those who served under him. When he joined the HMS *Revenge* in 1923, he found himself in charge of about 160 men, and awarded prizes to encourage readiness and efficiency.

In 1925, Mountbatten rose to the top of his signals course, signals being his chosen specialty. From 1927 to 1933, he held a number of signaling posts. His love of gadgets and gizmos was obvious to all around him.

In 1934, Mountbatten was appointed commander of the HMS *Daring*, a new destroyer. However, after only eight months, he took command of the HMS *Wishart*, an older destroyer, which he was determined to make the most efficient ship in the fleet. He trained his men ceaselessly in rowing so that they could take the trophy at the annual navy regatta, and developed a new stroke that allowed rowers to increase their strokes per minute by one quarter. But his sailors were able to relax when Mountbatten's friend Noël Coward came on board to share a martini.

Mountbatten sought to ensure that every entertainment and diversion were provided to his men to keep up their morale, and this included ensuring Coward's latest movies were shown. He launched the Royal Naval Film Corporation in order to pursue the issue for the whole navy.

Near the outbreak of the war, in 1939, Mountbatten became captain of the destroyer *Kelly*, which had been constructed with some of his own ideas (especially concerning bridge layout). He was joined by the *Kingston* and became captain of the Fifth Destroyer Flotilla.

Mountbatten's wartime experience as a destroyer captain was not entirely happy, and he gained a reputation for lacking "sea sense." His ship almost capsized when it turned abreast of a wave in heavy seas at full speed, and one sailor was lost. She collided with a mine at the head of the Tyne, and during a snowstorm in March, 1940, she collided with the *Gurkha*.

Soon thereafter, the *Kelly* was torpedoed by a German U-boat, but managed to make it back to port – under fire – with a gaping hole in her side after more than 90 hours in tow. Mountbatten had abandoned his mission – to harass German mining vessels – in order to pursue a U-boat, and at night had lost visual contact with other forces, signaled, and was rewarded with a torpedo. Nevertheless, the return of the *Kelly* under such circumstances came to Churchill's attention, and he suggested a DSO. The Admiralty brass – who felt Mountbatten would not have had to demonstrate such heroics had he not made such poor decisions – prevented that. This worked to Mountbatten's favor, because in Churchill's mind, he became a gallant young officer kept down by the idiot admirals that were giving Churchill so much trouble.

In the spring of 1941, the *Kelly* was dispatched to the Mediterranean, where it was sunk by dive bombers. More than half the crew perished, and Mountbatten escaped only by swimming from under the ship as it capsized. The Germans shot at him and other survivors with machine guns while they were in the water. Eventually they were picked up by the *Kipling*. All this became the basis for Noël Coward's propaganda film *In Which We Serve*, which further enhanced Mountbatten's glamorous, public image.

In October, 1941, Mountbatten was appointed commander of the aircraft carrier *Illustrious*, which had been damaged and sent to the United States for repairs. He flew there and established good connections, including President Roosevelt.

In 1942, in a phenomenally fast promotion, Mountbatten became overall chief of combined operations, with the acting rank of vice admiral, lieutenant general and air marshal, and *de facto* Chiefs of Staff membership. Churchill instructed Mountbatten to focus on offensive operations, which meant, first, raiding the European coast to raise morale and harass the Germans, and second, preparing for a full invasion.

General Ismay recalled:

> Mountbatten was by all odds the most colourful on the British Chiefs of Staff level. He was charming, tactful, a conscious gallant knight in shining armor, handsome, bemedaled, with a tremendous amount of self-assurance. Because of his youthfulness, which was emphasized by his appearance, it was obvious that the older officers did not defer readily to his views. They were careful, however, to give him a semblance of courteous attention. After all, he was a cousin of the King and, no doubt about it, a great favourite of the Prime Minister.

In August 1943, Mountbatten was appointed supreme commander designate, Southeast Asia. His first job was to restore morale and motivate the British armed forces. As chief of combined operations, he had already established a reputation for working at a furious pace and he continued to do so in India, visiting units and touring facilities rapidly. In Delhi he tried to cut through some of the complacency that had developed in the fat years of the Raj.

In 1945, Mountbatten received the formal surrender of the Japanese at Singapore, and was soon made a Viscount. He was now responsible for roughly 1.5 million square miles, 128 million people, 750,000 Japanese soldiers, and 125,000 allied prisoners of war, spread over South Vietnam, the Netherlands East Indies, Burma, and Malaya. He was charged with rescuing the prisoners, disarming the Japanese, and restoring the various territories to their colonial owners.

By the time Mountbatten left Southeast Asia as supreme Allied commander after the war, he had acquired a reputation for being committed to decolonization. This made him the perfect man for a Labour government seeking to end the empire in India, and he was invited to become the last viceroy in 1946. His initial mission was to deliver a united India – but he immediately discovered that this would be impossible. The historian Michael Edwardes painted the following picture of him:

> Two main factors had contributed to Mountbatten's success as Supreme Allied Commander in South-East Asia – his choice of subordinates, and his very lively sense of the uses of personal publicity. He had, of course, other qualities too, including immense charm. "Charm" is often an empty word, but not in Mountbatten's case. With him, it managed to be simultaneously egalitarian and superior. Once, during the war Mountbatten arrived at a town in Burma a few hours after its capture. Everybody was very tired and rather grubby, but Mountbatten himself looked fresh and purposeful. Yet the impression he gave was not that he had just arrived from a comfortable base headquarters but that, somehow, he had managed to slough off the sweat and dirt to which everyone else had succumbed. He brushed aside the officers and the general 'bull' of a commander's parade, told the soldiers to break ranks, and began to confide his thoughts and hopes to them. It was a masterly performance, and at least one sceptical soldier – the author of this book – went away convinced

that great events lay in the hollow of Mountbatten's hands and that there was no need to worry about their outcome. Wartime troops had been mellowed by the Mountbatten propaganda and personality, and in 1947 the time had come for Indian leaders to receive the same treatment.

Mountbatten got on well with Nehru and Gandhi, but never worked his magic on Jinnah, the leader of the Muslim League. Nevertheless, by May, 1947, Mountbatten had a plan under which there would be two predominant states, and in which the provinces of India could choose whether to retain their independence or join one of the larger states.

Mountbatten was taken aback at the level of violence that accompanied partition. In June, 1948, with order more or less restored, Mountbatten – who had been made an earl the previous year – left India. Some believed that the creation of Pakistan would go down as one of the strategic blunders of the century.

Mountbatten returned to the rank of rear admiral, and took control of the 1st Cruiser Squadron in the Mediterranean, under Admiral Sir Arthur Power. Power was impressed by how easily he moved from a position of supreme command to one of subordination, and Mountbatten once again worked to bring his squadron up to a high level of efficiency. The command allowed him to return to playing polo and skin diving, and in this sense constituted something of a holiday. He was feted wherever his squadron went in the Mediterranean.

In 1949, Mountbatten became vice admiral, and in 1950 entered the Admiralty as Fourth Sea Lord, in charge of supplies and transport. While he had hoped for Second (Personnel), supplies and transport were more Mountbatten's line, and he was able to draw on his extensive work on technical and supply questions.

In 1952, Mountbatten took control of the Mediterranean fleet, and was promoted to admiral. In January, 1953, he was appointed supreme allied commander of the new NATO Mediterranean command.

In 1954, Mountbatten was appointed First Sea Lord. The same position his father had occupied in 1914, and from which he had been so unjustly ejected. So justice, and history, were eventually righted. As was often the case in his career, the leadership of the Admiralty resented him, but they had to concede that he was one of the best people to carry the fight for the Royal Navy against the other services in Whitehall.

Mountbatten's great coup as First Sea Lord was winning over Admiral Rickover, the genius who turned nuclear submarines into true spearheads of the 1960s Western navies. This paved the way for British acquisition of American technology for their own nuclear submarines and, eventually, for Polaris. Mountbatten also convinced Whitehall that the Royal Navy was the natural mobile missile-launching platform of the post-war era.

One of the major trials facing Mountbatten was the Suez Crisis in 1956. Mountbatten thought that Eden could seize the canal and Port Said within three days with Royal Marine commandos. Eden – who preferred something more along the lines of Normandy to unseat Nasser – deprecated the idea. At every stage in the planning process, Mountbatten distanced himself from the debacle that Eden created: he believed it necessary to bring Arab nationalism to their side, and that any military force be agile.

Mountbatten was made Chief of the Defense Staff in 1959 and sought to implement organizational changes that would support the future conduct of joint operations, rather than the internecine warfare of the service chiefs. "To this task," Michael Howard claimed, "he brought outstanding qualifications. Apart from outstanding personal qualities of energy and ingenuity, he had behind him a professional career of unique distinction. He was moreover – to put it mildly – very well connected. His association with the Crown was not negligible in any matter concerning the Armed Forces. He enjoyed the close friendship of the prime minister and by more junior politicians he was held in a respect bordering on awe. And the wealth and patrician background which had been disadvantages he had had to live down at an earlier stage in his professional career were now tactical assets which he knew very well how to use.

In July 1965, Mountbatten finally retired. He had only agreed to stay on as Chief of the Defense Staff after his wife's death, (in

1960,) until 1964, but then stayed on one more year. He was asked to lead an investigation of prison security in 1966, and completed a report in two months, most of whose recommendations were implemented.

In retirement, Mountbatten was associated with hundreds of organizations, mostly in a formal way, though in some substantively. He played a godfather role to the Prince of Wales, whom he advised to sow his wild oats, then to marry a pure girl from a good family.

In 1979, the Irish Republican Army blew up Mountbatten's fishing boat in County Sligo, killing the old man and his grandson, as well as an Irish boy. Mountbatten was given a public funeral in Westminster Abbey and buried in Romsey Abbey.

———

Douglas MacArthur

Today the guns are silent. A great tragedy has ended. A great victory has been won ... We have known the bitterness of defeat and the exultation of triumph, and from both we have learned there can be no turning back. We must go forward to preserve in peace what we won in war ... If the historian of the future should deem my service worthy of some slight reference, it would be my hope that he mention me not as a commander engaged in campaigns or battles, even though victorious to American arms, but rather as one whose sacred duty it became, once the guns were silenced, to carry to the land of our vanquished foe the solace of hope and faith of Christian morals.

—Radio broadcast on the battleship USS *Missouri*
after the surrender of Japan, officially ending
World War Two, 2 September 1945

My major advisors are just two – George Washington and Abraham Lincoln: one founded the United States; the other saved it.

ORN IN LITTLE ROCK, ARKANSAS, IN 1880, DOUGLAS MACARTHUR had the blessing and the curse of being the son of a great American hero. His father, Arthur MacArthur, Jr., had, as an eighteen-year-old lieutenant, led his Wisconsin regiment up Seminary Ridge at the Battle of Gettysburg, and won America's highest military honor, the Congressional Medal of Honor. Arthur MacArthur remained in the army after the Civil War and Douglas, the youngest of three brothers, said that his first memory was the sound of a bugle.

From the beginning, Douglas was the chosen one in his family. He entered West Point military academy in 1898, at the age of 18, accompanied by his mother Pinky, who took a suite of rooms near the campus to make sure he had everything he needed. He finished first in his class of 94, and was named the cadet that best embodied the military ideal. After graduating in 1903, he was posted to the Philippines, where his father had been sent during the Spanish-American War.

MacArthur's connections proved invaluable, as he became an aide-de-camp to President Theodore Roosevelt in 1906 and was sent to Vera Cruz, Mexico, in 1914, when the United States became embroiled in an armed dispute with the new government of Mexico. In his first combat, MacArthur demonstrated daring when he raced behind Mexican lines to steal three boxcars that the United States army needed to transport men and supplies.

MacArthur was brave, but also flamboyant, vain, and not completely trustworthy. He spent some months after Vera Cruz angling for a Medal of Honor (he did not get one) and probably exaggerating his exploits. The thirty-four-year-old major had also begun wearing an ostentatious cravat around his neck and smoking a pipe – becoming, as one historian has written, "a peacock among pigeons." If he did not quite speak in the royal "we," he certainly acted as if his opinion were the only one that mattered. In this he appeared to take after his father – Arthur MacArthur's longtime aide reportedly said: "Arthur MacArthur was the most flamboyantly egotistical man I had ever seen – until I met his son."

Unlike his father, whose career had essentially stalled after the Civil War, Douglas MacArthur continued to ascend. Service in the First World War would see him win an astonishing seven Silver Stars for bravery.

During the War, MacArthur developed a caricature of himself, which would become increasingly colorful in the years to come. Regardless of where he was, he wore a smashed cap (instead of a steel helmet), either a plum-colored satin necktie or a four-foot muffler knitted by his mother, a turtleneck sweater, immaculate riding breeches, and cavalry boots with a mirror finish. His cigarette holder jutted from his mouth at a jaunty angle and he carried a riding crop. This attire failed to follow rules and regulations, as did his refusal to carry a weapon or gas mask.

Colonel MacArthur, as he became, delegated authority for operations, intelligence, and administration to subordinates, which freed him to cross no-man's land with his assault troops. Appreciating the way he shared their discomforts and dangers, joining them in the trenches and on the battlefield, his soldiers idolized him. He encouraged them to call him "Buddy" but the Doughboys soon began calling him "the fighting Dude." They credited him with a sixth sense that allowed him a charmed life. His legend had begun.

After the War, he continued to rise through the peacetime army, becoming superintendent of West Point. At the end of his time at West Point, in 1922, MacArthur finally abandoned bachelorhood and married Louise Cromwell Brooks. After a few years, tensions ended the marriage – Louise demanded he attend endless rounds of social events that meant nothing to him. In 1927, MacArthur was ordered back to Manila. Louise refused to go with him and they finalized a divorce in 1929.

In 1930 MacArthur became Chief of Staff. He and his mother moved into the traditional home of the Chief of Staff, Fort Myer's Number One quarters. MacArthur's mother was his confidante. He rode home to eat lunch with her every day, and preferred spending evenings with her to attending the social events constantly occurring in the capital, paying his Eurasian mistress, Isabel, hush money to keep her out of the public (and his mother's) eye.

In 1934, at the end of MacArthur's term as Chief of Staff, President Roosevelt appointed him as military adviser to the newly elected Philippine president and MacArthur's old friend, Manuel Quezon. MacArthur and his ailing eighty-four-year-old mother headed for Manila. On the voyage, he met a petite Tennessee native named Jean Faircloth, eighteen years his junior. His mother passed away a month after arriving in Manila in 1935, and MacArthur married Jean in 1937. He called her his "finest soldier," and she devoted herself to providing him ceaseless moral and emotional support. In 1938, MacArthur and Jean had a son, Arthur MacArthur IV. Though old enough to be Arthur's grandfather, the fifty-eight-year-old MacArthur was a devoted father and spoiled his son.

When the Second World War began, Douglas MacArthur had officially retired from the army after bickering with the Roosevelt administration over his hawkish views on Japan and Nazi Germany's military build-up. By 1941, he had accepted an offer from Manuel Quezon, still President of the Philippines, to help him create a Philippine army. When Japanese planes bombed Pearl Harbor and the Philippines in December, 1941, drawing America into the War, Roosevelt, who had recalled him to the United States army the previous July, made him commander of the US forces in the Far East. As the Japanese invaded the Philippines, MacArthur was made a four-star general.

Like the rest of the American military, MacArthur was caught off guard by the Japanese attacks. He was forced to abandon his army to the Japanese in the Philippines and fled to Australia. Despite the fact that President Roosevelt awarded him the Congressional Medal of Honor, the defeat smarted and he announced to the Philippine people and the world: "I shall return."

In an extraordinary rebuilding and organizational feat, he helped launch the counteroffensive against the Japanese in 1942, a strategy based on cutting off and isolating major Japanese island bases in the Pacific, while ferociously attacking others as the Americans "island-hopped" their way north to within striking distance of Japan. As the invasion of Japan was being planned – an invasion that was predicted to cost millions of casualties, both Japanese and American – the United States dropped an atomic bomb on each of the cities of Hiroshima and Nagasaki in August 1945. Douglas MacArthur accepted the official surrender of Japan on September 2nd, acting as surrogate for President Harry S. Truman, the man who had ordered the bombs dropped.

Douglas MacArthur excelled as Supreme Commander for the Allied Powers (SCAP) in Japan. "SCAP was in effect an absolute monarch. Never before in the history of the US had such enormous power been placed in the hands of a single individual." While many were calling for the execution, or at least abdication, of Emperor Hirohito, MacArthur refused, knowing that the Japanese needed this figurehead in their lives as a link to the past. Sparing Hirohito was a masterly move. While MacArthur did prosecute numerous Japanese as war criminals, he also helped rebuild the nation as a constitutional democracy, extended the vote to women, allowed the formation of labor unions, liberalized school curriculums, and encouraged free enterprise by dismantling huge, state-run monopolies.

As always with MacArthur, there were contradictions. He himself lived like a lord in the so-called Big House, drove everywhere in his Cadillac V-12 sedan with fender flags flying (one American flag, and the other with the five silver stars denoting his rank) and a license plate that simply read "1." He made few attempts to actually meet the ordinary Japanese people he was helping, and several hundred of them lined up daily outside the Dai Ichi building where he worked, simply to get a look at him. In the meantime, the general's press officers were busy bombarding the public back home with press releases about what a great job MacArthur was doing.

In 1945, after the surrender of Japan, America and the Soviet Union had divided the Korean peninsula (formerly controlled by Japan) at the 38th parallel. Two separate countries were created:

South Korea, closely allied with the United States, and North Korea, strongly aided by the Soviets and Chinese Communists under Mao Zedong. On June 25th, 1950, the North Korean People's army swept out of the mountains and down through the valleys of South Korea, driving the ill-prepared Republic of Korea (ROK) armies before them. The United Nations called on its members to support South Korea (sixteen nations agreed, although the United States provided over 90 per cent of troops and funds) and appointed MacArthur as overall commander. Nevertheless, within two months the North Koreans were advancing on the port city of Pusan. UN forces established a perimeter around Pusan and held it in fierce fighting, but the situation was dire.

In what many historians feel is his finest hour, the seventy-year-old MacArthur immediately sensed that the way out of the situation was not a massive frontal attack against the North Koreans at Pusan, which would cost thousands of lives, but instead an attack on the enemy's rear. The same strategy that he had successfully undertaken against the Japanese in 1943 and '44. In a dramatic presentation to the Joint Chiefs of Staff, he convinced them (and therefore Truman) that a landing could be made at Inchon, 150 miles northwest of Pusan. The North Koreans would be caught between the two UN forces and destroyed. Despite the difficulties of the operation, MacArthur made an amphibious assault on Inchon on September 15th and caught the North Koreans by surprise. Outflanked, they retreated and the UN forces broke out of the Pusan perimeter. Joining MacArthur's invasion force, they were in Pyongyang, the North Korean capital, by October 20th.

China felt threatened by MacArthur and his troops. Thousands of Chinese troops began crossing into Korea and MacArthur ordered a withdrawal, though he believed he could defeat the Chinese if he had the unrestricted ability to wage war. He could not bear to end his military career with a checkmate and viewed Truman's capitulation as a loss of the will to win. He submitted a "military appraisal" that was basically an ultimatum to the enemy, claiming that the UN forces would win if they waged an all-out war. The statement was an unacceptable foray into politics and Truman and his administration agreed that MacArthur had to go. MacArthur's recall was hastily administered because of a rumor that he was about to quit. Truman wanted to ensure he was fired, and as a result, publicly humiliated after 52 years of military service.

On his return to the US, MacArthur was greeted by crowds of supporters. For the remainder of his life, he lived in New York, appearing at various events, giving addresses, and serving a ceremonial function. He died in 1964 at 84.

THE COMPARISON OF LOUIS MOUNTBATTEN WITH DOUGLAS MACARTHUR

Douglas MacArthur came from a high-society military family. Vain, haughty, egotistical, ambitious, he used his social and political connections to advance his career. Nevertheless, he was also patriotic, brave, Christian, high-minded, and he understood Asia. Never a prominent public figure in his own country, his great successes were in the Philippines and Japan. Although he held the highest office open to a serving soldier – Chief of Staff – he never stood as a candidate for political office, let alone the presidency. It may be argued, however, that, when he held absolute authority over the Japanese during his time as Supreme Commander for the Allied Powers (SCAP), he achieved more than he could have done as US president. The success of the Japanese economy and the stability of Japanese society during the 40 years after MacArthur's "rule" is testimony to his wisdom in preserving the Emperor's role, in introducing democratic systems to the Japanese and in reorganizing the economy after the devastation of the Pacific war.

Louis Mountbatten came from a naval and aristocratic background and attracted if anything even more envy than MacArthur because of his royal connections and swift ascent up the ranks of the Royal Navy. Like MacArthur, he too enjoyed the limelight, handled the press well, and, during the war, became, as MacArthur had, a glamorous and successful commander. However, his career followed a different trajectory; he achieved his position, as Proconsul, or Viceroy, of India in 1946, at a younger age (he was 46 while MacArthur was 65) and for a far shorter duration (6 months as opposed to 6 years).

If we are to judge the achievements of Mountbatten and MacArthur in terms of the subsequent histories of Japan and India we can't say that Mountbatten was as successful. Partition was disastrous in terms of human lives and in the ensuing history of the sub-continent. But what about Mountbatten's career after India? Like MacArthur, he rose to the top of his profession and by 1955 became First Lord of the Admiralty. He had considerable influence in Britain up to the time of his death in 1979, not least in his continuing influence on the Royal Family: the Prince of Wales looked to him as a mentor and guide in the extraordinarily difficult task of being a prince in a media-dominated world.

MacArthur, on the other hand, was discredited by his "failure" in Korea and his subsequent dismissal by Truman. Even his triumphant return to Washington in 1950 to address the joint houses of Congress, and his idealization by the American people, could not take away the sting of this final humiliation. MacArthur had the vision to see that a war fought with limited objectives would never defeat communism. Once the Chinese had entered the Korean War it was logical, as he saw it, to push them back into their home territory and to involve nationalist Taiwan with allied forces. The later example of the Vietnam War seems to prove his point.

Between these two men, MacArthur appears to have left a deeper and more lasting legacy – in the Philippines and in Japan and even on American military history. Mountbatten's mark on India was fleeting, and divisive.

CHAPTER 23

Harold Macmillan and John F. Kennedy

Harold Macmillan

I was determined that no British government should be brought down by the action of two tarts.

—on the Profumo scandal

At home, you always have to be a politician; when you're abroad, you almost feel yourself a statesman.

AS AN OXFORD UNDERGRADUATE IN THE EARLY 1970S, I WAS privileged to attend a small dinner party at the London home of the great English novelist, C.P. Snow, the guest of honor being the former Prime Minister Harold Macmillan. Three of us young students were former Eton scholars, as Macmillan himself had been before the First World War, in which he fought. He talked to us in a confidential, but magisterial, tone about the world of the 1970s (as the Vietnam War was winding down), with his clipped patrician accent, keen eyes, heavy eyebrows, and a rather trained use of a cane.

"There are three great restaurants in the world, boys . . ." – this caught our attention – "the prairies of North America, the steppes of Russia, and the rice paddies of Southeast Asia – that is what all the wars will be fought about in the future . . ." Looking back, I cannot believe that he overlooked the importance of oil in global conflict. Soon afterwards in 1973, the Arab-Israeli War broke out, and in 1979 the Chinese invaded Vietnam and the Soviets invaded Afghanistan, with the subsequent growth of Mujahedeen, jihadis, and Al-Qaeda.

Macmillan also told me stories about my great-grandfather, whom he had known well as a young MP in the 1930s. Lloyd George had given him hints on speaking in the House of Commons: "Vary

Harold Macmillan

John F. Kennedy

the pitch, and realize the value of a pause . . . You can only make one telling point that the House will remember – as a minister, perhaps two points, not more."

Macmillan used to say he came from a family of Scottish crofters. In fact, they were a very prosperous family that had founded the publishing house Macmillan. He was a scholar at Oxford as well as Eton. He was commissioned in the King's Royal Rifle Corp in 1914 and transferred to the Grenadier Guards, in which he became a captain. He was wounded at the Battle of Loos of 1915 and at the Somme in 1916, and was out of action for the rest of the war. He went to Canada as ADC to the Governor General, the 9th Duke of Devonshire, and married his daughter, Lady Dorothy Cavendish, in 1929. It was not an entirely happy marriage, and his wife was unfaithful to him. He kept a stiff upper lip and maintained a taciturn silence on the subject.

Macmillan was elected as a Conservative MP for Stockton in 1924. It was a working-class constituency where, after his experience in the trenches in the First World War, he became deeply interested in the problem of unemployment, especially among returning soldiers. After 1935 he began to turn yet more of his attention to foreign affairs and to defense, and joined Churchill and the group opposing the Baldwin and Chamberlain governments in the late 1930s. As a result, he gained office in 1940 when he was 46 years old as Parliamentary Secretary to the Minister of Supply, until 1942, when he went to the Colonial Office. At the end of 1942, Churchill appointed him British government representative in the Mediterranean, and he became a member of the Cabinet. Macmillan held this office for 2½ years, working closely with the Americans under Eisenhower. It was a position of great importance and power. This was the period when he said "We are the Greeks in this American Empire." He was political adviser to the Supreme Allied Commander, Eisenhower, and acting President of the Allied Commission in Italy. His duties came to an end in May, 1945, and he returned to the United Kingdom. He lost his seat in the 1945 election but was only out of Parliament briefly, returning as a Conservative candidate for Bromley.

In 1951 Churchill returned to power and offered Macmillan Minister of Housing. "It is a gamble," said Churchill. "It will make or mar your political career, but every humble home will bless your name if you succeed." Macmillan accepted and became the darling of the Conservative Party Conference when he built over a million houses in three years. He was Minister of Defense in 1954 and, when Eden took over as Prime Minister the following year, Macmillan became Foreign Secretary and then Chancellor of the Exchequer later in the year.

After the Suez Crisis, when Anthony Eden resigned because of ill health at the beginning of 1957, Macmillan competed with R.A. Butler to become prime minister. An overwhelming majority of cabinet ministers supported Macmillan, and the Queen asked him to form a government. Not many people expected his government to last long, but it lasted for six years. Like Melbourne in 1834, he thought that, even if it only lasted three months, it would be worthwhile to have been Prime Minister of England. His American mother had always spurred his ambition hold the office, but he had always been confident of his ability. When he took office, his party was in disarray and Britain's time as an imperial power was at an end. He needed to restore the confidence of the people.

Macmillan went to Bermuda in 1957 to meet Eisenhower. Like Churchill, he got on very well with the American leaders, especially Eisenhower and Dulles. Macmillan and Eisenhower were already old friends from the war and instituted a system of constant communication that lasted throughout Eisenhower's presidency and continued under Kennedy. "Our relations with America were so good," wrote Macmillan, "that our influence could, during my term of office, be exerted to the full." However, Macmillan resisted any commitment in Indochina.

He reduced the size of the British army from nearly 700,000 to half that size in five years and relied on nuclear weapons as Britain's main means of defense. In 1957, with US agreement, the first British hydrogen bomb was detonated. Macmillan went to Russia in 1959 to meet Khrushchev to try and reduce the tension in the relationship between the east and the west and act as a go-between between the United States and the USSR.

Macmillan restored British confidence and was re-elected in 1959 with a substantial majority. The Suez Canal reopened, and in 1960 he traveled in Africa and spoke in Cape Town: "The wind of change is blowing through the continent. Whether we like it or not, this growth of national consciousness is a political fact. We must all accept it as a fact." However, neither South Africa nor Rhodesia (now Zimbabwe) was willing to accept black majority rule.

Macmillan saw that the world was changing. Economically Britain was doing well. "Let's be frank about it," he said, "most of our people have never had it so good. Go around the country and you will see a state of prosperity such as we have never had in my lifetime or, indeed, in the history of this country. Is it too good to be true? But there is the problem of rising prices. This is the problem of our time." Again, Macmillan had put his finger on the issue that was to dominate the 1960s and 1970s. He was nicknamed Supermac. Unflappable, he was calm in crises. "Quiet calm deliberation disentangles every knot," he quoted from *The Gondoliers*. Underneath, however, he suffered from great anxiety and worried about his decisions.

In 1963 he was faced not only with ill health, but with the crisis in Britain's application to join the European community, which was rejected by de Gaulle. Finally, the Profumo Scandal had a dramatic effect on confidence. In October, he resigned as prime minister. He was succeeded by Sir Alec Douglas-Home, who, born in 1903, was ten years his junior.

—

John F. Kennedy

I think this is the most extraordinary collection of talent, of human knowledge, that has ever been gathered together at the White House - with the possible exception of when Thomas Jefferson dined alone.   —[Remark made at a 1962 White House dinner honoring Nobel Laureates]

THE NEAREST THING TO A ROYAL FAMILY THAT WE ENCOUNTER IN America in this historical survey is probably the Kennedy family. They were, in fact, from humble origins. All four of JFK's grandparents were children of Irish immigrants; but (possibly except for the Roosevelts) the Kennedys became the nearest thing to a royal family that the American people have seen in the last century. In the 1960s the White House was known as Camelot because of the glamour attached to Jack and, even more, to Jackie Kennedy, and their young family in his three-year presidency. When Kennedy visited Ireland, he was received as a visiting prince, the most powerful man in the world acknowledging his roots in a country that was in 1963 – before it became part of the European Union – still poor, backward, and cut off from the world.

John F. Kennedy was born in 1917. He was named after his maternal grandfather, John "Honey Fitz" Fitzgerald, who made history as a congressman and was the first Irish American Catholic Mayor of Boston, the New England port city in which WASP (White Anglo-Saxon Protestant) elitism had secured all senior political posts since the Pilgrims landed in 1620. When Fitz had been growing up in the 1860s, a common sign on hiring boards was: No Irish Need Apply.

JFK's father, in contrast to the humorous and popular Fitzgerald, was a serious and cynical man. Son of an East Boston bar owner, Joe Kennedy was clever and ruthlessly ambitious; he became the youngest bank president in America, a wartime shipyard manager, stock market operator, millionaire movie producer and, after 1933, chairman of the SEC (Securities Exchange Commission). In return for his support of FDR, Joe Kennedy asked to be made US Ambassador at the court of St. James in 1938. He was a passionate isolationist and opposed any American involvement in Europe's troubles. By 1940, as Britain stood alone against Hitler, Ambassador Kennedy became one of Churchill's bitterest foes, as was his eldest son, Joe Kennedy, Jr.

Joe Kennedy, Jr. was killed in action in 1944, so his younger brother, Jack, whom no one had expected to succeed, took on his father's expectations. Jack had suffered reoccurring illnesses, and spent much of his childhood in the hospital sick room or sanitarium. He was, however, blessed with magnetic charm, and with his tousled hair, wide cheeks, perfect teeth, and mischievous blue eyes, could smile his way out of any trouble. Furthermore, he had a quick, sharp mind and a fascination with world politics. While at Harvard, he interned at the US Embassies in London and Paris, traveled through Russia and Germany during 1939, and wrote a thesis on the British failure to rearm in response to Hitler's aggression, published as a book, *Why England Slept*, in the summer of 1940. The twenty-three-year-old JFK took issue with his father. "If England is defeated, America is going to be alone and estranged in a hostile world," he warned Joe. "There will be a general turning of people's opinions. They will say, 'Why were we so stupid not to have given Britain all possible aid.'" This had an effect on his father, who withdrew his planned opposition to the Lend Lease Bill.

By then JFK, despite his health issues, had managed to enlist in the Navy. When his torpedo boat was rammed and sunk by a Japanese destroyer in the Solomon Islands, Kennedy brought the nine surviving crew members back to safety after four days and five nights behind Japanese lines, and became a minor national hero. In 1946 he ran for the vacant Congressional seat in Massachusetts and, to everyone's amazement, proved a born campaigner and won. Elected three times as Congressman for Massachusetts, he ran for the Senate in 1952 and managed to dislodge the distinguished incumbent Republican

Henry Cabot Lodge, Jr. He was supported by veterans, immigrants, community groups and college professors, who warmed to his liberal Truman-like notion of government – firm on defense and international alliances and compassionate on domestic issues from veterans' housing, education, the minimum wage, and social security. He married the glamorous Jacqueline Bouvier, a New England White Anglo-Saxon French Catholic (rather than a WASP), and unsuccessfully ran for vice president in 1956. However, he made a brilliant speech that included a history of the Democratic Party, gaining national recognition at the age of only 39. He stood again for election to the Senate in 1958, and won by the largest majority in Massachusetts's history. He became the presidential candidate in August, 1960, offering his beaten rival, Lyndon Johnson, the vice presidency, though he never believed Johnson would surrender his powerful position as Senate Majority Leader to accept it. To Kennedy's surprise, Johnson did accept, and in a thrilling campaign that autumn the race for the presidency looked too close to call. However, in the first TV debate ever, Kennedy appeared much more attractive than Richard Nixon, and managed to win by a tiny number of votes in Illinois.

In his inaugural speech in January, 1961, Kennedy said:

> Let the word go forth from this time and place to friend and foe alike that the torch is being passed to a new generation of Americans born in this century, tempered by war, disciplined by a hard and bitter peace, proud of our ancient heritage, and unwilling to witness or permit the slow undoing of those human rights to which this nation has always been committed, and to which we are committed today, at home and around the world. Let every nation know whether it wishes us well or ill that we shall pay any price, bear any burden, meet any hardship, support any friend, oppose any foe in order to assure the survival and the success of liberty.

It was magnificent oratory, but it was also a dangerously ambitious commitment which was to result in the Vietnam War. Within weeks of his inauguration, Kennedy began working to achieve these high ideals with the establishment of the Peace Corps, the volunteer program to send young Americans abroad to aid Third World countries. Youth was a key issue of the 1960s and Kennedy was a symbol of that youthful energy and idealism. This was balanced by the April, 1961, debacle of the Bay of Pigs invasion of Cuba, which was a catastrophe for the Kennedy administration. Despite Admiral Burke, the Chief of the US Navy Staff, entreating Kennedy to use the Navy or the Air Force to ensure its success, the president refused, saying, "I don't want the United States involved in this," and held by that decision. He accepted failure; at his live press conference the following week, the President said, "There is an old saying that victory has 100 fathers, and defeat is an orphan. I am the responsible officer of this government." Viewers and reporters were amazed and impressed by his admission of responsibility, and his popularity rating jumped 10 points.

During that same spring, there was a further shock to the West when Yuri Gagarin was rocketed into space and made the first orbit of the earth, a propaganda victory for the Soviet Union. Kennedy's response was dramatic. He made a pledge to put a man on the moon within the decade. Soon after, he flew to Vienna to meet Khrushchev. The meeting was, as he afterwards admitted, "one of the roughest things in my life." He wasn't prepared for Khrushchev's brutality. Khrushchev dismissed any nuclear disarmament, proposed to recognize East Germany and reject third-party occupation rights in Berlin, and insisted Russia would continue to support Communist movements worldwide. Kennedy appeared to Khrushchev inexperienced and immature. He spoke of him as the boy, the president who doesn't have the backbone to stand up to a serious challenge. The Russians thought that the president was scared.

Macmillan, whom Kennedy visited in London on his way back to America, noted in his diary that "the president was still in shock" and that, for Kennedy, the Vienna summit had been like meeting Napoleon for the first time. Kennedy told the *Times*, "I talked about how a nuclear exchange could kill 70 million people in 10 minutes, and he just looked at me as if to say, 'so what'." Khrushchev had been amazed by apparent American pusillanimity over Cuba and had fully expected Castro to be overwhelmed by a full-scale American invasion. "I don't understand Kennedy," he told his son, Sergei. "What's wrong with him? Can he really be that indecisive? Perhaps he lacks determination." The result of all this was that it tipped the scales in the now icy Cold War. Khrushchev was an opportunist; on August 13th, 1961, he ordered the erection of the Berlin Wall, which went unopposed.

By September, 1962, the civil-rights crisis in Mississippi was heating up, and Kennedy had to send in 3,000 soldiers to guard African-American students. Immediately after this, he had to confront the greatest crisis of his presidency with the revelation that the Soviets were shipping nuclear missiles to Cuba. This development brought the world closer to a nuclear exchange than at any other time in the 50 years of the Cold War.

Kennedy realized they were dealing with a madman. On October 22nd, after six days of considering his options, Kennedy appeared on television and addressed the world, outlining the threat 90 miles off the coast of Florida. The president called on Khrushchev to halt and eliminate the clandestine and reckless threat to world peace and to stabilize relations between the two superpowers by withdrawing the nuclear missiles from the western hemisphere. He announced a naval blockade around Cuba.

Two days later, six Russian vessels reached the 500-mile exclusion perimeter. Then they stopped. As Secretary of State Dean Rusk said, "We're eyeball to eyeball, and I think the other fellow just blinked." It was true. Khrushchev had gambled, and failed. He was soon to be out of power as a result of his dangerous escapades. In the greatest international crisis since the Second World War, Kennedy had shown firmness and statesmanship, overruling the hawks in the Pentagon and ensuring the peaceful resolution of the crisis.

In the spring of 1963, Kennedy had to face his next challenge, that of Civil Rights. He made his position clear:

> This is not even a legal or legislative issue alone. We are confronted primarily with a moral issue. It is as old as the Scriptures and is as clear as the American Constitution . . . If an American, because his skin is dark . . . cannot enjoy the full and free life which all of us want, then who among us would be content to have the color of his skin changed and stand in his place? Who among us would then be content with the councils of patience and delay? . . . We face, therefore, a moral crisis as a country and a people. It cannot be met by repressive police action. It cannot be left to increased demonstrations in the streets . . . It is time to act in the Congress . . . and . . . in . . . our daily lives.

With these words the president announced that he would be introducing a comprehensive Civil Rights bill into Congress. He was well aware of the political risks of losing the South as a Democratic power base. In August, 1963, Martin Luther King led his famous march on Washington. After the march was over, Kennedy invited King to a private meeting in the White House and congratulated the preacher in person. "It's going to be a crusade then," said King, "and I think nobody could lead this crusade but you, Mr. President." Taking a deep breath, Kennedy vowed that he would.

The other issue that was beginning to rear its head was Vietnam, where the president had committed 16,000 military advisors to prop up the corrupt and ineffective government of South Vietnam. He appointed the former senator, Cabot Lodge, as Ambassador to Saigon. But Lodge was a fiercely anti-Communist Republican and Kennedy realized that he had made a mistake. When a coup occurred in South Vietnam on November 1st, 1963, President Diem and his brother were taken prisoner and swiftly assassinated. Kennedy was shocked and upset. Jackie recalled that he burst into tears. Like Julius Caesar, he saw it not only as a mistake but an omen. "I should not have given my consent to [the coup] without a roundtable conference . . . I was shocked by the death of Diem and Nhu. I'd met Diem . . . many years ago. He was an extraordinary character. He'd held his country together, maintained its independence under very adverse conditions." The way he was killed made it particularly abhorrent. Only two weeks later, Kennedy himself was assassinated by Lee Harvey Oswald.

THE COMPARISON OF HAROLD MACMILLAN WITH JOHN F. KENNEDY

In 1944, while Churchill's pro-consul in the Mediterranean and North Africa, Macmillan quipped: "We are the Greeks . . . in this American Empire." It was his – only half joking – contention that it was Britain's historical duty to guide the power of the United States as the ancient Greeks had the Romans. When he became Prime Minister in 1957, he continued to play this role (conceived from his Eton and Oxford grounding in the classics) of organizing high-level conferences between America and Russia and of supporting US policy internationally. Macmillan later said, "I was a sort of son to Ike [Eisenhower], and it was the other way round with Kennedy." With his family links to the young American president of 1960 (his wife's nephew had married a sister of Kennedy's), he forged a strong and avuncular relationship with Kennedy and eased the way for the US to take over many of Britain's imperial responsibilities in the Middle East and the Far East.

Kennedy was, at the age of 46, only just finding his own voice and independent vision when he was cut down by an assassin in Dallas. Macmillan had succumbed to poor health and resigned only the month before, at 69. He felt he had been hounded out of office by a backbench minority, saying, "Some few will be content with the success they have had in the assassination of their leader." Both were gifted statesmen and great speakers, but there is a sense of unfulfilled destiny in both their careers.

The 1960s were an era of rapid social and economic change in both Britain and America. The major transatlantic trend was the conclusion of the shift of imperial power from the UK to the US. The UK was undergoing economic crisis, a shrinking of its influence in the Persian Gulf and the Far East. The end of Empire had come slowly but steadily after 1945, with the independence of India in 1947, the debacle at Suez in 1956, the granting of independence to all of Britain's remaining African colonies and Caribbean islands in the 1960s, and this process was almost complete by 1966. In the meantime, the American empire was expanding. It had large bases in Germany, Italy, Turkey, Korea, Japan, Guam and in many other parts of the world, and gradually filled the vacuum left by the departing British.

The baby boomers, the first generation born after the war, were coming to maturity, serving in Vietnam, experiencing the explosion of TV and media, and the advent of the pill, which liberated sexual habits and mores; there was a transformation in the old system of class distinctions and deference in Britain and, to some extent, in the United States too. The old class system loosened and a new ruling class of celebrity arrived on the scene – the Beatles and the Rolling Stones replaced the film stars of the wartime generation. Kennedy's youth, good looks and charm were part of this social revolution. Macmillan – older, upper class and more old-fashioned – was seen as part of the establishment that needed overthrowing, but, in fact, he embodied change in his own life and opinions (for example, foreshadowing the end of Apartheid in South Africa by almost 30 years in his "Winds of Change" speech, as it was with Kennedy and Civil Rights legislation in Congress).

Edward Heath

Richard Nixon

CHAPTER 24

Edward Heath and Richard Nixon

Edward Heath

I have no interest in sailing around the world. Not that there is any lack of requests for me to do so.

E DWARD HEATH WAS SUCCESSFUL IN FOREIGN POLICY; IN TAKING Britain into the European Union in 1972; and in opening up relations with China after visiting there in 1974 and 1975. He remained an honored guest in China on his frequent visits thereafter.

Heath was born in Broadstairs, Kent. His father was a carpenter and builder; his mother was a maid. He eventually become the first working-class leader of Britain's Conservative party. A talented musician, he won a scholarship to Oxford in 1935.

Heath became President of the Oxford University Conservative Association but was a supporter of the Republicans in Spain and went there during the civil war. There were plenty of Conservatives who supported Franco, so this revealed a liberal and populist side. He traveled widely in Europe during his time at Oxford and was at the Nuremberg Rally in 1937 where he met some of the Nazi leaders. He opposed the appeasers and later described Himmler as "the most evil man I have ever met." He was on a debating tour of the United States in the winter of 1939–40, but was called up and joined the Royal Artillery in 1941 as a second lieutenant. He appears not to have seen very much action, but he participated in the Normandy landings as an adjutant, and when the Second World War ended, he left as a major. After the war, he joined the civil service and was involved in the aviation industry, planning new airports. He then worked in London for a merchant bank for two years, and became a Member of Parliament in 1950.

From the beginning, Heath was an enthusiastic supporter of European economic union; his maiden speech in the House of Commons appealed to the then Labour government to participate in the Schuman Plan (a forerunner of the EU). Winston Churchill appointed him as an opposition Whip, and he remained in the Whip's office for almost five years, before Macmillan appointed him Minister of Labour and a cabinet minister in 1957. Macmillan asked him to lead negotiations to get Britain into the common market in 1960, and there was great disappointment when this application was vetoed by President de Gaulle in 1963.

The Conservatives were defeated in the general election of 1964. In opposition, Heath was unexpectedly elected as leader of the Tory Party in 1965. He was the youngest leader of the party at that time.

In 1970, again unexpectedly, Heath won the general election with a healthy working majority of 42 and formed a Conservative government including Alec Douglas-Home, the former prime minister, as foreign secretary, and Margaret Thatcher as Minister for Education and Science. It was a difficult time in Britain, and inflation was rising. Unemployment was increasing and Heath encouraged his rather inexperienced chancellor, Anthony Barber, to inflate the money supply. Although unemployment fell, by 1974 Britain was in a slump again and industrial relations became a major issue. The three-day working week started at the beginning of 1974, and Heath called an election as a test of "just who governs Britain?" (Inflation reached 25% in Britain that year.)

When Heath lost the election, he had few supporters and there was a clear movement in the Conservative party to try and find new leadership. To everyone's amazement, the Conservative party elected a woman to lead them in 1975. Margaret Thatcher defeated Edward Heath for the leadership by 130 votes to 119. Although she had promised to give him a seat in the shadow cabinet, he refused it and went into a deep sulk for the next 20 years. She later offered him posts such as ambassador in Washington and secretary-general of

NATO, but he turned them down too. In 1992, in addition to being the oldest MP, he became Father of the House (longest-serving MP). He continued in Parliament until 2001, when he was 85 years old. He died in 2005, aged 89.

Richard Nixon

When the president does it, that means that it's not illegal.

"NIXON WAS A GREAT MAN, WITH VISION," BUT HE HAD A tragic flaw, as I discovered in conversation with a member of his family. The biographer and the family must see him differently. He had great strategic insight into world politics, and he altered the balance of power in the 1970s; but he also suffered from paranoid suspicion of his political opponents, which led him to the unscrupulous tactics exhibited in his earliest run for office in 1948 in California and continued until the notorious "Watergate" break-in during the 1972 presidential campaign. He remains the only president to have resigned.

Richard Nixon was born in January, 1913, the second son of a devoted Quaker mother and her uneducated but irascible Irish American husband, Frank Nixon, who praised Nixon in Yorba Linda, California. Like Herbert Hoover and William Penn, he was a Quaker by upbringing. He attended Whittier College and Duke University School of Law.

He came from a very poor background: "We were poor, but the glory of it was we didn't know it." But, as his biographer Conrad Black said, "His family life could not have been a barrel of laughs." Two of his brothers died young. The Nixon family ranch failed in 1922; Frank Nixon then ran a gas station but was still always short of money.

Nixon was gifted and hardworking. He was just under six feet tall and had wavy dark hair, an extruded nose, and a deep voice.

Ambitious, he was admitted to the Bar in 1937 when he was 24 and practiced as an attorney. In 1940, he married Pat Ryan. They had two daughters, Tricia and Julie, and were happily married for over 50 years.

During the Second World War, Nixon served in Washington; eventually, although a Quaker, he didn't claim exemption from the drat, but instead applied to join the Navy. He served in the South Pacific, although he saw no real action.

Nixon was elected to the House of Representatives in 1946. His Senate race in 1950, against Representative Helen Douglas in California, revealed a mean and vicious streak in his character. He distributed a "Pink Sheet," which suggested that his opponent voted as a communist. He himself was financed by Republicans and oilmen. His opponent coined the epithet, "Tricky Dick," but his stance against communism carried the day, and he became the youngest senator at the age of 37. Nixon's campaign was effective, but smear tactics would be the hallmark of his political strategy from then onwards.

Once he had established himself as a prominent anti-communist, he was selected by Eisenhower to be his vice president in 1952. He was only 39, and there was a major crisis about his political fund, which had been maintained primarily by Californian backers. Nixon went on television only weeks before the election to make the so-called "Checkers Speech," which was heard by almost 60 million Americans. Listing his assets and liabilities, he declared, "Well, that's about it, that's what we have and that's what we owe. It isn't very much, but Pat and I have the satisfaction that every dime is honestly ours. I shouldn't say this, but Pat doesn't have a mink coat, but she does have a respectable Republican cloth coat, and I always tell her that she would look good in anything." However, he confessed to one last gift: "A man in Texas heard that our two young daughters would like to have a dog. It was a little cocker spaniel in a crate, and our little six-year-old named it Checkers, and you know the kids loved the dog; and I just want to say this right now that regardless of what they say about it, we are going to keep it." This was somewhat akin to Roosevelt's dog, Fala, and touched an emotional cord. The senator then made a plea for the little man in American politics, saying that his Democratic opponent, Adlai Stevenson, was a rich man. The vast positive public response made it impossible for Eisenhower to dump Nixon. Eisenhower never trusted him but put up with him – and so would America.

During the eight years of the Eisenhower presidency, Eisenhower barely allowed Nixon entry to the White House, although Nixon took on many of the more active roles, particularly foreign trips; Eisenhower was almost 70 and suffered from heart problems. There was some question as to whether Nixon would again be the running mate in 1956, but he managed to hold on. Among his overseas trips, he went to the Far East, to South America – where he was the object of demonstrations – and to Moscow in 1959, where he engaged in the "Kitchen Debate" with Khrushchev. So he undoubtedly had foreign policy experience and knowledge of the global power balance.

In 1960 Nixon launched his first campaign to be president of the United States. He chose Senator Henry Cabot Lodge as his running mate. He expected a close race but was confident of defeating John F. Kennedy. However, in the first ever television debate held between presidential candidates, Nixon appeared unshaven and pale. Although his points were well made, he lost on looks and likability to the photogenic young Democrat. Although there were charges of vote fraud, particularly in Illinois, which Kennedy won by a small margin, Nixon didn't contest the election and accepted his defeat. He returned to California, challenging the governor, Pat Brown, in 1962. He was again defeated and believed that was the end of his political career: "You won't have Nixon to kick around anymore, gentlemen, this is my last press conference." He became a senior partner in a New York law firm, and although he didn't run for office in 1964, he continued to keep himself ready, and had broad support among the Republican Party.

With the crisis of the Vietnam War in 1968 and the chaos on the Democratic side after Robert Kennedy's assassination, Nixon ran for president against Vice President Hubert Humphrey, who was an unconvincing candidate. There is a well-attested story that Nixon undermined President Johnson's Vietnam peace talks before the vote on November 5, 1968, when he promised that he would win peace in Vietnam and did not want to see this happen before he was elected.

When Nixon took office in January, 1969, he promised to be a peacemaker, and he initially appeared to be one during his visit to China in 1972 with Henry Kissinger, his National Security Advisor and future Secretary of State, who had prepared the way. Forty years later, it is clear that this visit was immensely favorable to China, while the gains for the United States were less apparent. The Chinese helped end the Vietnam War, but didn't sacrifice any of their national self-interest. Nevertheless, it was a historic breakthrough and changed the balance of power, isolating the Soviet Union. Within seventeen years, communism would collapse in Russia and Eastern Europe – whether as a result of the opening to China is another question. In the meantime, Nixon made a U-turn with regard to the Vietnam War and increased the bombing of North Vietnam, Cambodia, and Laos. He began to negotiate peace with North Vietnam at the same time and eventually started withdrawing American troops. Nevertheless, his invasion of Cambodia in 1970 was a mistake that opened the door to Pol Pot and the Khmer Rouge and the genocide they committed. Eventually, in 1973, the Vietnam War ended, but that didn't stop the North Vietnamese from taking Saigon in 1975.

The arrogance of American power was very clear in the foreign policy of Nixon and Kissinger, who were determined to combat communism everywhere, including in countries such as Chile, where they intervened to overthrow President Salvador Allende. In 1971 Pakistan broke in two. Nixon had a close relationship with the military dictator of Pakistan, General Yahya Khan, although he was committing barbaric acts of genocide in East Pakistan, which was to become Bangladesh. This was perhaps another example of Nixon's realpolitik, where he cared little for human rights and everything for his ultimate objective of using Pakistan as a conduit to improve relations with China.

Then, in 1972, appalling revelations that gradually began to trickle out about Nixon's presidential campaign: he had ordered the burgling of the Democratic party headquarters in the Watergate complex on the Potomac River in Washington. The story was broken by Bernstein and Woodward, young reporters for the Washington Post, whose informant "Deep Throat" (later revealed to be associate director of the FBI) eventually linked the guilty men all the way up to the president. Then in 1973 Vice President Spiro Agnew was convicted of bribery, and Nixon chose Gerald Ford to replace him. The following month, Nixon, answering questions from the press, said, "People have got to know whether or not their president is a crook. Well, I'm not a crook. I've earned everything I got." He probably believed this, but, by the summer of 1974, tapes had revealed him to be guilty of a cover-up, and he was under threat of impeachment. So on August 9, 1974, he resigned the presidency. He never admitted any wrongdoing, and a month later, Ford granted him a full, free, and absolute pardon, which completely destroyed Ford's political future.

Nixon expressed deep regret and, in subsequent years, somewhat rehabilitated his reputation and began to be seen in public again. When speaking at the Oxford Union in 1978, he said, "Some people say I didn't handle [Watergate] properly and they're right. I screwed up. *Mea culpa*. But let's get on to my achievements. You'll be here in the year 2000 and we'll see how I am regarded then."

He died in 1994 at the age of 81. His funeral was attended by President Clinton as well as four other former presidents. History would show that, despite his flaws, he was one of the most far-sighted chief executives in American history, but not everyone liked him. The tapes had revealed him as anti-Semitic, profane, ruthless, and cynical in his approach to governing. His behavior as president damaged the office for at least 10 years, until Reagan restored respect to it.

THE COMPARISON OF EDWARD HEATH
WITH RICHARD NIXON

Edward Heath and Richard Nixon were almost exact contemporaries and held the top job at the same time: Heath was Prime Minister from 1970 to 1974, and Nixon was president from 1969 to 1974.

They met on two or three occasions, but they didn't form a close relationship. Heath proposed that they proceed on a first-name basis, a proposal that was greeted with stony silence by Nixon. In fact, Conrad Black reported that Nixon found Heath so unsympathetic that Heath made Nixon like Harold Wilson.

Mao Tse-tung told Heath that he thought Nixon was a man who knew what he stood for as well as what he wanted and had the strength of mind to get it. (Mao, on the other hand, was suspicious of Kissinger, Nixon's secretary of state: "Just a funny little man; he is stuttering all over with nerves every time he comes to see me." This, at any rate, was the account given by Heath, whom Black had called a misanthropic raconteur.)

Both Nixon and Heath were socially awkward and difficult, who suffered from this failing in the political world. Both were mistrusted, maligned and lost office in circumstances of failure and disgrace. Both subsequently tried to rehabilitate themselves – Nixon perhaps more successfully than Heath, whose reputation has been overshadowed by the brilliance of his successor, Margaret Thatcher.

They both achieved their greatest success in foreign policy. The comparison must, however, give Nixon the advantage of having achieved considerable breakthroughs: ending the war in Vietnam, opening up relations with China, and other major initiatives. Heath's only real legacy is Britain's membership in the Common Market, or what is now the European Union.

Both Nixon and Heath had to face the domestic challenge of militarism and it's unarguable that Nixon's decision in August,

1971, to take the United States dollar off the Gold Exchange standard was to result in a decade of rising prices and deprecating currencies. (However, the gold price rose from $35 in 1971 to $800 in 1980 and eventually to $1900 in 2010, which is about 60 times its original value.) This was perhaps one of the most maligned decisions of Nixon's presidency; or perhaps it was just part of history's unrelenting cycle.

Margaret Thatcher

Ronald Reagan

CHAPTER 25

Margaret Thatcher and Ronald Reagan

Margaret Thatcher

In politics if you want anything said, ask a man. If you want anything done, ask a woman.

No one would remember the Good Samaritan if he'd only had good intentions. He had money as well.

MARGARET THATCHER IS THE ONLY CHARACTER WHOM I WAS able to interview personally and with whom I had an acquaintance. She was a good listener and humble enough to believe she could learn from others.

I had two encounters with Margaret Thatcher. On the first occasion, I had prepared a number of questions for her about her youth, her entry into politics, and her beliefs. She fixed me with her steely blue eyes, however, and, for half an hour, interrogated me about my knowledge of China and Hong Kong, which she was about to visit. This was perhaps five years after her leaving office. This capacity of hers to listen, to learn, and to be interested in other people impressed me deeply. On the second occasion, I attended a small dinner with her, perhaps ten or twelve years ago in London, when she was nearly eighty years old. Our host had warned us that her memory might be failing, but I didn't observe this to be the case. Over dinner, I presented her with my book *David and Winston*, saying, "This is the story about the two great prime ministers of the 20th century, and I would like to present it to you, Lady Thatcher, because you are the third great prime minister." Flattered, she replied, "You shouldn't have said that, but I'm glad you did," with a twinkle in her eye. After dinner we sat together having coffee, and I asked her, "Lady Thatcher, did you ever doubt the outcome of the Falklands War?" There was a long silence, and I feared that her mind was wandering, but she came out with a lapidary response, "You have to have courage." Those were her last words to me, and it defined for me not only the bedrock of her character but that of many of the men and women depicted in this book. (As Churchill said, courage is the quality on which all else depends.)

Courage was a defining characteristic of Margaret Thatcher. As she said at the 1980 Conservative Party conference, "The Lady's not for turning." She was willing to stick to her convictions even when, in 1981, 364 of the leading economists in Britain signed a letter to *The Times* saying that her economic policies were completely mistaken and were going to lead the country into a slump. She defied the miners in their long strike and violent demonstrations and, against all the odds, took on the Argentine forces in the Falkland Islands 8,000 miles from Britain in an extraordinarily short war, which as much as anything restored Britain's sense of identity and determination to stand against the enemies of democracy. Taking a leaf out of Churchill's book, she stood for the principles of freedom, self-determination, and courage in the face of what was essentially a fascist military dictatorship in Argentina who were seeking a diversion from its economic problems by making what it thought was an easy conquest of the Falkland Islands, which had been occupied by British settlers since 1830. The islands only had about 500 inhabitants, but it was possible that there was oil and gas resources in the surrounding waters.

Thatcher undertook the campaign against the advice of her cabinet and of the Americans, who very much doubted that it was a winnable one. On the back of her extraordinary military victory, in 1983, she was reelected with a large majority. She then started her campaigns of privatization of those great industries like British Petroleum, British Gas, and British Rail that had been nationalized forty years before by Attlee's Labour government after the war. She single-handedly restored Britain's economic vibrancy and self-confidence after the long decades of decline. It was Margaret Thatcher who said that there was no need to "manage the decline." On the contrary; it was possible to restore Britain's confidence and greatness, to start growing again, and to encourage the entrepreneurial energy and the spirit of the country. She cut taxes, deregulated, and denationalized, and after the Falklands War, a powerful message reached the new leader of Russia, Mikhail Gorbachev: that Britain was again a nation to be reckoned with and would not submit to Soviet pressure any longer. Thatcher also played a very important role in encouraging President Reagan's hardline stance against the communists and his belief in free enterprise instead of big government.

Margaret Roberts, as she then was, was born in 1925 and lived in a flat above her father's grocery store in Grantham, Lincolnshire. Her father was a strict Methodist, and she was brought up in an austere culture of saving, charity, and Christian virtues, which she retained throughout her life. Beneath her sometimes strident exterior was a warm, caring person who was always liked and respected by those who worked for her.

As a woman, she had to overcome enormous odds to climb the slippery slope to 10 Downing Street. It began when she went to Oxford on a scholarship to read chemistry. She was an accomplished chemist and took an honors degree in 1947 before going to work in industry. She was always a staunch conservative and, by the age of 25, had been selected for the Conservative Party Central Office List. She was adopted as a Conservative candidate for Dartford in Essex. Although she lost, she met Denis Thatcher, a successful, wealthy businessman and divorcee. He had made money in Burmah Oil and was able to fund Margaret's political career and her studies for the Bar. They were married in 1951 and had twins in 1953, Carol and Mark. In 1959 she was finally elected to the safe Conservative seat of Finchley in North London. Because the Conservative Party saw the need to promote women, she quickly climbed the ladder to the front bench, first as a Parliamentary Undersecretary and, after 1964, to the Shadow Cabinet Treasury team. In 1967 she was selected to go to the

United States on a six-week exchange program mainly focused on economic issues. There, she met many leading personalities, and she was soon appointed as the Shadow Cabinet as spokesman on fuel and power.

After the 1970 Conservative victory under Edward Heath, she became Secretary of State for Education. Her spending cuts made her highly visible, and she became known as "Margaret Thatcher Milk Snatcher." She learned about the difficulties of doing what she thought was the right thing and receiving poor publicity for it. She was, however, always pragmatic in her policies; for example, she accepted changes in education that pushed the British school system towards comprehensive schools.

After the Conservatives were unexpectedly defeated in 1974, there was a leadership contest because of Heath's increasing unpopularity. Nobody expected Margaret Thatcher to win, but she had a well-organized campaign led by Airey Neave, a Second World War hero who was subsequently blown up by the IRA as he drove out of the House of Commons car park. Thatcher won the contest and became party leader in February, 1975. Willie Whitelaw was the runner-up and became her second-in-command and loyal supporter. Edward Heath could never reconcile himself to this defeat or Thatcher's leadership and became a thorn in her side despite attempts to include him in the Conservative leadership.

Thatcher's economic policies were now influenced by the right-wing thinking of Friedrich von Hayek and Arthur Seldon, and later by Sir Keith Joseph. In 1976 her outspokenness in condemning the Soviets for trying to secure world domination led them to christen her the "Iron Lady," a title which she reveled in.

In the 1970s Britain's economy was in dire straits under Labour Prime Minister Jim Callaghan, culminating in the "winter of discontent" in 1978. The Conservatives came up with the campaign slogan "Labour isn't working" and, in May, 1979, history was made when Margaret Thatcher became the first female British prime minister. Despite her stridency, by sheer strength of character and conviction, she had conveyed to the British people that she would mean a fresh start for the country. An extremely frugal person, she insisted on cash accounting in all government departments and also refused to take a salary as prime minister because her husband was already a wealthy man. But it set an example. However, her first two years as prime minister were very difficult; the recession of 1980–1 was deep and lasting, and unemployment was at a high of over three million. However, after 1982 the economy recovered rapidly, and with it, Thatcher's popularity.

Thatcher was divisive. She was widely hated: by the working class, especially the miners; by Oxford University, which refused to give her an honorary fellowship; by the IRA, who tried to assassinate her in 1984 at the Brighton Hotel during the Conservative Party Conference – five people were killed, and by sheer providence or good luck, she escaped because she was working on her speech, which she gave the next day.

After her victory in the Falklands, she was riding high, and in September of that year, 1982, traveled to China and met with Deng Xiaoping to discuss the future of Hong Kong after 1997. She said, "We don't negotiate with people who don't stand by their treaties," referring to the ninety-nine-year lease that only covered the new territories of Hong Kong, not the island itself and the Kowloon Peninsula, which had been ceded in perpetuity. However, Deng was adamant that China was going to take back the whole territory in 1997, and there was nothing Thatcher could do about it; during the 45 negotiating sessions with Chinese officials that followed, despite Governor of Hong Kong Chris Patten's attempts, China didn't concede an inch, and Britain was powerless to maintain any form of democracy after the handover.

But Margaret Thatcher was pragmatic when faced with an immovable power such as China. However, when it came to Europe, she was deeply suspicious and declared, "We have not successfully rolled back the frontiers of the state in Britain only to see them reimposed at a European level with a European super state exercising a new dominance from Brussels." Though her cabinet was in favor, she was firmly opposed to the pound going into the exchange-rate mechanism (the precursor of the Euro). This resulted in the resignation of Geoffrey Howe, who had been Deputy Prime Minister, and who gave a wounding speech in the House of Commons. Soon after, the anger about the poll tax, or community charge, blew up, and Thatcher's popularity plummeted. After a record eleven years as prime minister, in November, 1990, she was put under pressure by a Conservative party leadership contest; she felt betrayed by her colleagues and decided that she had to retire, leaving Downing Street in tears. She was replaced by her chancellor, John Major, who managed to lead the Conservatives to victory in 1992. That year, at the age of 66, Thatcher retired from the House of Commons and was granted a peerage. She died in 2013 at the age of 87, and was given a state funeral at Saint Paul's Cathedral – the first such since Winston Churchill's funeral in 1965 – which was attended by the Queen and the Royal Family, an indication of the high regard in which she was held.

Margaret Thatcher is Britain's only female prime minister, yet she hated feminism and did not wish to be considered simply as the first female prime minister. She would rather have been considered the first scientist prime minister. Nevertheless, at a fiftieth-anniversary dinner of Britain's leading economic think tank, there was a series of speeches by men before hers, and when called to speak, she said, "As the tenth speaker and the only woman, I have this to say, 'the cock may crow, but it's the hen who lays the egg.'" She was feminine and attractive and always beautifully turned out, but being a woman was a great challenge for her in the deeply male and conservative House of Commons.

She influenced George H. W. Bush when she said, "This is no time to go wobbly, George," after Saddam Hussein invaded Kuwait in 1991. She was the only British leader since Churchill to have a perceptible influence on world events, both directly and through her high standing in Washington.

Ronald Reagan

I will not make age an issue in this campaign. I am not going to exploit, for political purposes, my opponent's youth and inexperience.

[of Walter Mondale in the 1984 presidential campaign]

I used to say that politics was the second-oldest profession. I have come to know that it bears a gross similarity to the first.

What I'd really like to do is go down in history as the president who made Americans believe in themselves again.

I have always stated that the nearest thing to eternal life we'll ever see on this earth is a government program.

Whoever would understand in his heart the meaning of America will find it in the life of Abraham Lincoln.

RONALD REAGAN DEMONSTRATED THAT A SINGLE INDIVIDUAL CAN change the tone of a nation. He achieved this through his sunny optimism and strong convictions about economic and political freedom. As well as the direction of the American economy, which had been mired in low growth, high inflation, and unemployment in the 1970s, Reagan's presidency from 1981 to 1989 changed history – it led to the fall of Communism.

Reagan came to power at the age of seventy and served until the age of seventy-eight, so he was already an old man with deeply formed convictions. The historian Paul Johnson said, "Reagan was a man at ease with himself." *Bien dans sa peau* (comfortable in his skin), as the French would say. He was both confident and serious about the business of government. "Successful government," as Johnson says, "depends less on intelligence and knowledge than on simplicity – that is, the ability to narrow aims to three or four important tasks which are possible, reasonable, and can be communicated." Reagan was ignorant of much of the political process and history, as well as intellectually lazy, but he had clear ideas about what was important: he wanted smaller government, strong defense, and to reveal the weakness of communism.

Reagan had been an actor for the first half of his life – an unusual background for a successful president. He was known as "the great communicator," and himself said, "There have been times in this office when I wondered how you could do the job if you hadn't been an actor." He has been compared to Lincoln in his simple and humorous approach to communicating ideas to the voters. "The big decisions are simple," he used to say. "That doesn't mean they're easy." Like Lincoln, he used jokes to defuse the seriousness of situations. After the attempted assassination in 1981 in which the bullet narrowly missed his heart, he said to the team of doctors as he was wheeled into surgery, "I hope you're all Republicans." When his wife Nancy was allowed to come to his bedside, he said, "Honey, I forgot to duck." In his debate with Jimmy Carter in 1980, he destroyed him with the one quiet remark: "There you go again." One of his weak points was economics, but he had a clear idea that government does not solve problems, it subsidizes them. "I'm not worried about the deficit," he used to say. "It's big enough to take care of itself."

As a young man, Reagan had struggled from a poor background in the Midwest and made a breakthrough as a radio announcer in Iowa, broadcasting football games. He was paid $10 a game; one of his strengths was his marvelous voice. Handsome, charming, well-mannered and able to act out any leading role without great depth, he went to Hollywood and made a number of B movies.

After 1950, Reagan's film career began to decline, and he went to work for General Electric, making a series of weekly television dramas, touring GE plants, sometimes giving up to 14 speeches a day. His salary at the time was equivalent to $1 million a year. In 1940 he married Jane Wyman, an actress. They had two children, but divorced in 1948. He is, curiously, the only American president to have been divorced. (Until now.) He remarried in 1952 to Nancy Davis and was happily married to her for the rest of his life; they also had two children.

Reagan only became a Republican when he was about 50, having been a Democrat all his life. By this time he had espoused the conservative values of General Electric and the wealthy Californian conservatives who supported him when he ran for governor in 1966. Reagan was in Sacramento at the time of the student protests at Berkeley and the height of the hippie movement in the mid-1960s. He promised to send the welfare bums back to work and clean up the mess. He froze government hiring and hiked taxes.

Reagan's first attempt at running for president – in 1976 – narrowly failed. Gerry Ford was re-nominated but he was defeated by Jimmy Carter. By 1980 the country was ready for another change; Reagan swept to a landslide victory, and they also recaptured the senate.

It was, above all, in foreign policy that Reagan's impact on the world was felt. He spoke in the British Parliament in 1982 saying, "The forward march of freedom and democracy will leave Marxism Leninism on the ash heap of history." He predicted that communism would collapse, saying, "It was another sad, bizarre chapter in human history whose last pages, even now, are being written." He memorably called the Soviet Union "the evil empire." Ironically, one of his most effective projects was the "Star Wars," a fantasy, space-based system to protect the United States against attack by strategic nuclear missiles. The Russian economy was already collapsing under the strain of competing with American defense spending – and so began the end of the Cold War as the reduction of nuclear arsenals became increasingly desirable to both sides.

It was, in fact, only ten months after Reagan left office in November, 1989, that the Berlin Wall was torn down, fulfilling his call in 1987: "Mr. Gorbachev, tear down this wall." Two years later, the Soviet Union itself collapsed, largely as a result of Reagan's policies in the previous decade.

After leaving office, Reagan suffered from dementia, or Alzheimer's disease, the gradual loss of memory. He bravely spoke about it in 1994 at the age of 83. He lived for another ten years and died in 2004.

Backed by the power of the American defense establishment, Ronald Reagan was perhaps the man – with help from Mikhail Gorbachev and other key figures such as Pope John Paul II and Lech Walesa, as well Margaret Thatcher – most responsible for ending the Cold War and bringing about the end of Soviet communism.

THE COMPARISON OF MARGARET THATCHER WITH RONALD REAGAN

Margaret Thatcher and Ronald Reagan marched together for eight years in the same direction with the same ideological convictions. Together they changed history.

Both of them had a few strongly held core beliefs. Thatcher was more intellectual. She had degrees in both chemistry and law. She had studied political economists like Hayek, Popper, and Friedman. She was clear-thinking and methodical. Reagan had hardly read any economics, but it didn't seem to matter. He was a better communicator. Thatcher's voice could be combative. Reagan, on the other hand, had the smooth delivery and confident, smiling appearance of the actor he had once been.

Like Thatcher, Reagan introduced many radically new policies to free up the economy and reduce inflation. He was able to boost economic growth through cutting taxes. In this, Thatcher had influenced him. Both were robust in building up defense against the Soviet Union and deploying cruise missiles in Europe in 1982, despite widespread protests in Britain.

Thatcher was divisive. You either loved her or hated her. Reagan was popular. He inspired affection and was an extraordinarily difficult man to dislike, as even his opponents found.

Both of them were perhaps lucky in their careers: Margaret Thatcher, in the Falklands War; Ronald Reagan, in surviving assassination and in presiding over a period marked by economic expansion and the end of communism.

Acknowledgments

—

AMONG THE MANY FRIENDS WITH WHOM I HAVE DISCUSSED THIS BOOK (or who have assisted me in many ways) over the past 40 years, I would like to recognize: Carl Fischer, Peter Mather, Curtin Winsor, Daniel Alegria, Philip Snow, Margaret MacMillan, Philip Mansel, Martin Taylor, Alexander Lloyd George, Hugo de Klee, Peter Mayer, Donna Lloyd George, Julia Lloyd George, Parker Ladd, Barton Starr, Elizabeth Klink, Andrew Baker, Elizabeth Schwall, Kim Waterfield, and Pam O'Neill.

But I am, of course, solely responsible for the views expressed, and for any historical errors or solecisms that may have crept into the text.

Appendices

—

1. UK Sites: Homes, museums, and libraries
2. US Sites: Homes, museums, and libraries

Appendix 1. UK Sites: Homes, museums, and libraries

1 Duke of Wellington
Apsley House and Museum
149 Piccadilly, Hyde Park Corner
London W1J 7NT, UK
44 20 7499 5676

2 William Penn
Three Rivers Museum
Basing House
46 High St. Rickmansworth
Hertfordshire WD3 1HP, UK
44 19 2372 7333

3 William Pitt, Earl of Chatham
Portraits
British Museum
Great Russell St., London WC1B 3DG, UK
44 20 7323 8299

4 William Pitt the Younger
Portraits and Artifacts
Museum of London
150 London Wall, London EC2Y 5HN, UK
44 20 7001 9844

5 Edmund Burke *On US map*
Burke Museum
4331 Memorial Way NE
Seattle, WA 98195, USA
(206) 616-3962

6 Lord Mansfield
Mansfield Museum
Leeming St., Mansfield
Nottinghamshire NG18 1NG, UK
44 20 16 2346 3088

7 Viscount Melbourne
Portrait
Government Collection, Queen's Yard
179a Tottenham Court Rd.
London W1T 7PA, UK
44 20 7580 9120
7b *Also* National Gallery, Trafalgar Square
London WC2N 5DN, UK
44 20 7747 2885

8 George Canning
Portrait
British Museum
Great Russell St., London WC1B 3DG, UK
44 20 7323 8299

9 William Wilberforce
Wilberforce House
23-25 High St., Hull, Yorkshire HU1 1NQ, UK
44 14 8230 0300

10 Spencer Perceval
Portrait
British Museum
Great Russell St., London WC1B 3DG, UK
44 20 7323 8299
10b *Also* The National Portrait Gallery
St. Martin's Pl., London WC2H 0HE
44 20 7306 0055

11 Charles James Fox
Portraits
Chertsey Museum
The Cedars, 33 Windsor St., Chertsey
Surrey KT16 8AT, UK
44 19 3256 5764

11b *Also* Athelstan Museum
Malmesbury, Wiltshire SN16 9BZ, UK
44 16 6682 9258

12 Sir Robert Peel
The Peel Collection and Police Museum
Middle Hall
Middleton, Tamworth
Warwickshire B78 2AE, UK
44 1827 283095

13 Duke of Marlborough
Exhibit
National Army Museum
Royal Hospital Rd., Chelsea
London SW3 4HT, UK
44 20 7730 0717

14 Joseph Chamberlain
Birmingham Museum and Art Gallery
Chamberlain Square
Birmingham B3 3DH, UK
44 12 1348 8032

15 William Gladstone
Gladstone's Library
Church Lane, Hawarden
Flintshire CH5 3DF, UK
44 12 4453 2350

16 Benjamin Disraeli
Benjamin Disraeli's House and Gardens
Hughenden Manor
High Wycombe
Buckinghamshire HP14 4LA, UK
44 14 9475 5573

17 David Lloyd George
Lloyd George Museum
Llanystumdwy, Criccieth
Gwynedd LL52 0SH, UK
44 17 6652 2071

18 Winston Churchill
Blenheim Palace
Woodstock
Oxfordshire OX20 1PP, UK
44 19 9381 0530

18b *Also* Chartwell House
Mapleton Rd., Westerham
Kent TN16 1PS, UK
44 17 3286 8381

19 Lord Mountbatten
Monument
Broadlands Museum
Stalham Straithe
Norfolk NR12 9DA, UK
44 16 9258 1681

20 Edward Heath
Arundells
59 Cathedral Close
Salisbury
Wiltshire SP1 2EN, UK
44 17 2232 6546

21 Margaret Thatcher
Childhood home
North Parade
Grantham,
Lincolnshire NG31 8AN, UK

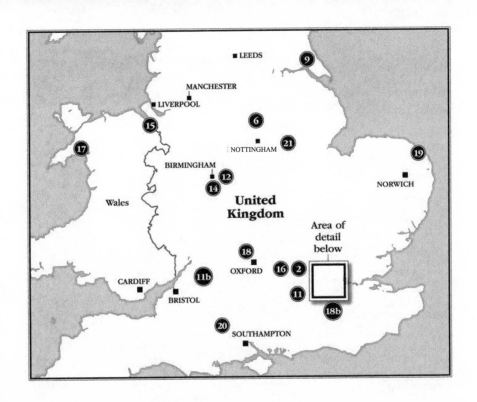

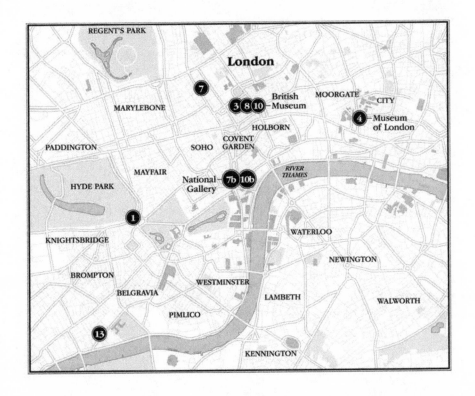

Appendix 2. US Sites: Homes, museums, and libraries

1 George Washington
George Washington's Mount Vernon
3200 Mount Vernon Hwy.
Mt. Vernon, VA 22121
(703) 780-2000

2 Brigham Young
Winter Home and Office
200 North and Main, St. George, UT 84770
(435) 627-4525

3 Benjamin Franklin
Benjamin Franklin Museum
317 Chestnut St., Philadelphia, PA 19106
(215) 694-3773

4 Alexander Hamilton
Hamilton Grange National Memorial
414 W 141st St., New York, NY 10031
(646) 548-2310

5 Thomas Paine
Thomas Paine Cottage
20 Sicard Ave., New Rochelle, NY 10804
(914) 633-1776

6 John Marshall
John Marshall House
818 E Marshall St., Richmond, VA 23219
(804) 648-7998

7 James Madison
James Madison Museum
129 Caroline St., Orange, VA 22960
(540) 672-1776

8 James Monroe
Museum and Memorial Library
908 Charles St., Fredericksburg, VA 22401
(540) 654-1043

9 John Quincy Adams
Adams National Historical Park
1250 Hancock St., Quincy, MA 02169
(617) 770-1175

10 James Garfield
James A. Garfield National Historic Site
8095 Mentor Ave., Mentor, OH 44060
(440) 255-8722

11 Aaron Burr
The Burr Homestead
739 Old Post Rd., Fairfield, CT 06824
(203) 259-1598

12 Andrew Jackson
Andrew Jackson's Hermitage
4580 Rachel's Lane
Hermitage, TN 37076
(615) 889-2941

13 General Robert E. Lee
General Lee's Headquarter's Museum
401 Buford Ave.
Gettysburg, PA 17325
(717) 334-3141

14 Theodore Roosevelt
Theodore Roosevelt Birthplace
National Historic Site
28 East 20th St., New York, NY 10003
(212) 260-1616

15 Woodrow Wilson
Woodrow Wilson Presidential Library
and Museum
20 N Coalter St., Staunton, VA 24401
(540) 885-0897

16 Thomas Jefferson
Thomas Jefferson's Monticello
931 Thomas Jefferson Pkwy.
Charlottesville, VA 22902
(434) 984-9800

17 Franklin Roosevelt
Franklin D. Roosevelt Presidential Library
and Museum
4079 Albany Post Rd., Hyde Park, NY 12538
(845) 486-7770

18 Herbert Hoover
Herbert Hoover Presidential Library
and Museum
210 Parkside Drive, West Branch, IA 52358
(319) 643-5301

19 James Buchanan
James Buchanan's Wheatland Home
1120 Marietta Ave., Lancaster, PA 17603
(717) 392-4633

20 Abraham Lincoln
Abraham Lincoln Presidential Library
and Museum
112 N 6th St., Springfield, IL 62701
(217) 558-8844

21 Harry Truman
Harry S. Truman Presidential Library
and Museum
500 W. U.S. Highway 24, Independence, MO 64050
(816) 268-8200

22 Douglas MacArthur
MacArthur Memorial and Museum
198 Bank St., Norfolk, VA 23510
(757) 441-2965

23 John F. Kennedy
John F. Kennedy Presidential Library
and Museum
Columbia Point, Boston, MA 02125
(617) 514-1600

24 Richard Nixon
Richard Nixon Library and Birthplace
18001 Yorba Linda Blvd., Yorba Linda, CA 92886
(714) 993-5075

25 Ronald Reagan
Ronald Reagan Presidential Library
40 Presidential Drive, Simi Valley, CA 93065
(805) 522-2977

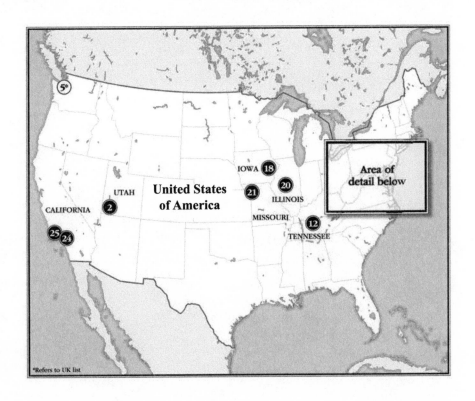

IOWA **18**

United States of America

20

UTAH

CALIFORNIA

2

21

ILLINOIS

MISSOURI

12

TENNESSEE

5*

Area of
detail below

25 **24**

*Refers to UK list

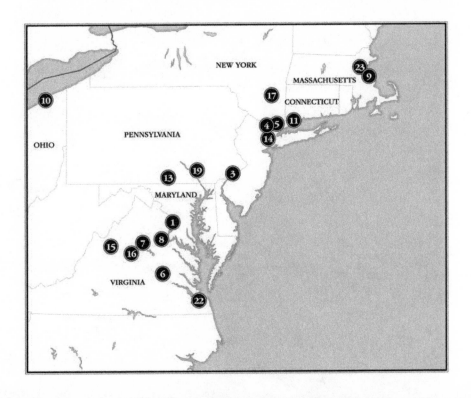

NEW YORK

23
9

MASSACHUSETTS

17
CONNECTICUT

10

PENNSYLVANIA

4 **5** **11**
14

OHIO

13 **19** **3**

MARYLAND

1

15
16 **7** **8**

6

VIRGINIA

22

Suggested Reading

ADAMS, JOHN QUINCY
Kaplan, Fred, *John Quincy Adams: American Visionary*
Thomas, Louisa, *Louisa: The Extraordinary Life of Mrs. Adams*
Unger, Harlow Giles, *John Quincy Adams*

ATTLEE, CLEMENT
Harris, Kenneth, *Attlee*
Jenkins, Roy, *Mr. Attlee: An Interim Biography*

BALDWIN, STANLEY
Jenkins, Roy, *Baldwin*

BUCHANAN, JAMES
Baker, Jean H. *James Buchanan: The American Presidents Series:
    The 15th President, 1857*

BURKE, EDMUND
Norman, Jesse, *Edmund Burke: Philosopher, Politician, Prophet*

BURR, AARON
Isenberg, Nancy, *Fallen Founder: The Life of Aaron Burr*
Parmet, Herbert S. and Marie B. Hecht, *Aaron Burr: A Portrait of an
    Ambitious Man*
Vidal, Gore, *Burr: A Novel*

CANNING, GEORGE
Dixon, Peter, *George Canning: Politician and Statesman*

CHAMBERLAIN, JOSEPH
Powell, J. Enoch, *Joseph Chamberlain*

CHURCHILL, WINSTON
Gilbert, Martin, *Churchill: A Life*
Jenkins, Roy, *Churchill: A Biography*
Keegan, John, *Churchill: A Life*
Manchester, William and Reid, Paul, *The Last Lion, Winston Spencer*
   Churchill: Defender of the Realm, 1940-1965

DISRAELI, BENJAMIN
Blake, Robert, *Disraeli*
Weintraub, Stanley, *Disraeli: A Biography*

FOX, CHARLES JAMES
Mitchell, Leslie G., *Charles James Fox*

FRANKLIN, BENJAMIN
Clark, Ronald, W., *Benjamin Franklin: A Biography*
Isaacson, Walter, *Benjamin Franklin: An American Life*
Morgan, Edmund S., *Benjamin Franklin*
Van Doren, Carl, *Benjamin Franklin*

GARFIELD, JAMES
Peskin, Allan, *Garfield: A Biography*

GLADSTONE, WILLIAM
Biagini, Eugenio, *Gladstone*
Jenkins, Roy, *Gladstone: A Biography*
Magnus, Philip, *Gladstone: A Biography*
Matthew, H.C.G., *Gladstone: 1809-1874*
Morley, John, *The Life of William Ewart Gladstone*

HAMILTON, ALEXANDER
Brookhiser, Richard, *Alexander Hamilton, American*
Miller, John C., *Alexander Hamilton: Portrait in Paradox*
Randall, Willard Sterne, *Alexander Hamilton: A Life*

HEATH, EDWARD
Ziegler, Philip, *Edward Heath: The Authorised Biography*

HOOVER, HERBERT
Burner, David, *Herbert Hoover: A Public Life*

JACKSON, ANDREW
Marquis, J., *The Life of Andrew Jackson*
Meacham, Jon, *American Lion: Andrew Jackson in the White House*

JEFFERSON, THOMAS
Bernstein, R. B., *Thomas Jefferson*
Cunningham, Noble E., *In Pursuit of Reason: The Life of Thomas Jefferson*
Meacham, Jon, *Thomas Jefferson: The Art of Power*
Onus, Peter, *"Most Blessed of the Patriarchs": Thomas Jefferson and the Empire of the Imagination*
Randall, Willard Sterne, *Thomas Jefferson: A Life*

KENNEDY, JOHN F.
Dallek, Robert, *An Unfinished Life: John F. Kennedy, 1917-1963*

LEE, ROBERT E.
Freeman, Douglas S., *R.E. Lee: A Biography*

LINCOLN, ABRAHAM
Sandburg, Carl, *Abraham Lincoln: The Prairie Years and the War Years*

LLOYD GEORGE, DAVID
Grigg, John, *Lloyd George: War Leader 1916-1918*

MACARTHUR, DOUGLAS
Manchester, William, *American Caesar: Douglas MacArthur 1880-1964*

MACMILLAN, HAROLD

Thorpe, D.R., *Supermac: The Life of Harold Macmillan*

MADISON, JAMES

Brookhiser, Richard, *James Madison*

LORD MANSFIELD

Heward, Edmund, *Lord Mansfield: A Biography of William Murray, 1st Earl of Mansfield, 1705-93, Lord Chief Justice for 32 Years*

DUKE OF MARLBOROUGH

Holmes, Richard, *Marlborough: England's Fragile Genius*
Winston Churchill, *Marlborough*

MARSHALL, JOHN

Smith, Jean Edward, *John Marshall: Definer of a Nation*

VISCOUNT MELBOURNE

Ziegler, Philip, *Melbourne: A Biography of William Lamb*

MONROE, JAMES

Hart, Gary, *James Monroe (The American Presidents Series)*

LORD MOUNTBATTEN

Hough, Richard, *Mountbatten*
Ziegler, Philip, *Mountbatten*

NIXON, RICHARD

Black, Conrad, *Richard M. Nixon: A Life in Full*

PAINE, THOMAS

Hawke, David Freeman, *Paine*
Nelson, Craig, *Thomas Paine: Enlightenment, Revolution, and the Birth of Modern Nations*

PEEL, ROBERT
Hurd, Douglas, *Robert Peel*

PENN, WILLIAM
Peare, Catherine O., *William Penn: A Biography*

PERCEVAL, SPENCER
Linklater, Andro, *Why Spencer Perceval Had To Die: The Assassination of a British Prime Minister*

PITT, WILLIAM (THE ELDER)
Brown, Peter Douglas, *William Pitt, Earl of Chatham*
Plumb, J.H., *Chatham*

PITT, WILLIAM (THE YOUNGER)
Hague, William, *William Pitt the Younger*

REAGAN, RONALD
Reeves, Richard, *President Reagan: The Triumph of Imagination*

ROOSEVELT, FRANKLIN
Black, Conrad, *Franklin Delano Roosevelt: Champion of Freedom*
Morgan, Ted, *FDR*

ROOSEVELT, TEDDY
Kearns Goodwin, Doris, *The Bully Pulpit: Theodore Roosevelt, William Howard Taft, and the Golden Age of Journalism*
McCullough, David, *Mornings on Horseback: The Story of an Extraordinary Family, a Vanished Way of Life and the Unique Child Who Became Theodore Roosevelt*
Morris, Edmund, *Colonel Roosevelt*
Morris, Edmund, *Theodore Rex*

THATCHER, MARGARET
Moore, Charles, *Margaret Thatcher: From Grantham to the Falklands vols I and II*

TRUMAN, HARRY S.

Dallek, Robert, *Harry S. Truman (The American Presidents Series)*

WASHINGTON, GEORGE

Flexner, James, *George Washington*

Flexner, James, *Washington: The Indispensable Man*

Freeeman, Douglas Southall, *Washington*

DUKE OF WELLINGTON

Hibbert, Christopher, *Wellington: A Personal History*

Longford, Elizabeth, *Wellington: Pillar of State*

WILBERFORCE, WILLIAM

Furneaux, Robin, *William Wilberforce*

Hague, William, *William Wilberforce: The Life of the Great Anti-Slave Trade Campaigner*

WILSON, WOODROW

Brands, H.W., *Woodrow Wilson*

Heckscher, August, *Woodrow Wilson*

YOUNG, BRIGHAM

Turner, J.G., *Brigham Young: Pioneer Prophet*

GENERAL READING SUGGESTIONS

Bryce, Lord James, *The American Commonwealth*

Hamilton, Nigel, *American Caesars*

Paul Johnson, *Heroes*

About the Author

Robert Lloyd George is the author of several books, including *David & Winston*, a comparative look at David Lloyd George and Winston Churchill, also published by The Overlook Press. He has also written extensively on Asia and the development of capital markets. In *The East West Pendulum*, he looks at China's history in reaction to the west and predicted China's extraordinary rise to economic and political prominence. He divides his time among the UK, Asia, and the United States.